# THE MYSTERIOUS SCIENCE
# OF THE LAW

The Awesome Majesty of English Law

# THE MYSTERIOUS
# SCIENCE OF THE LAW

An Essay on Blackstone's *COMMENTARIES*
Showing how Blackstone, Employing Eight-
eenth-century Ideas of Science, Religion,
History, Aesthetics, and Philosophy, made
of the Law at once a Conservative and a
Mysterious Science

By DANIEL J. BOORSTIN

With a new Foreword

THE UNIVERSITY OF CHICAGO PRESS
CHICAGO AND LONDON

*To*
*My Mother and Father*

The University of Chicago Press, Chicago 60637
The University of Chicago Press, Ltd., London
Copyright 1941 by the President and Fellows of Harvard College
Copyright © renewed 1969 by Daniel Boorstin
Foreword © 1996 by Daniel J. Boorstin
All rights reserved. Originally published 1941
University of Chicago Press Edition 1996
Printed in the United States of America
02 01 00 99 98 97 96    6 5 4 3 2 1

ISBN 0-226-06498-0 (pbk.)

Library of Congress Cataloging-in-Publication Data

Boorstin, Daniel J. (Daniel Joseph), 1914–
    The mysterious science of the law : an essay on Blackstone's Commen-
taries showing how Blackstone, employing eighteenth-century ideas of
science, religion, history, aesthetics, and philosophy, made of the law at
once a conservative and a mysterious science / by Daniel J. Boorstin ;
with a new foreword.
        p.   cm.
    Originally published: Cambridge, Mass. : Harvard University Press,
1941.
    Includes bibliographical references and index.
    1. Jurisprudence—Great Britain.   2. Law—Philosophy. 3. Black-
stone, William, Sir, 1723–1780.   Commentaries.
KD640.Z9B66   1996
340'.1—dc20                                                    96-2210
                                                                   CIP

∞ The paper used in this publication meets the minimum requirements of
the American National Standard for Information Sciences—Permanence
of Paper for Printed Library Materials, ANSI Z39.48-1984.

# CONTENTS

# ILLUSTRATIONS

This is an artist's impression of the impeachment of Warren Hastings delivered at the Bar of the House of Lords by the Commons of Great Britain in Parliament assembled, on February 13, 1788. Although actually depicting an event after Blackstone's death, the scene shows the panoply and splendour of English law in Blackstone's day, and illustrates some of the impressive qualities which enabled the *Commentaries* to make the study of English law a mysterious science. The trial of Hastings for corruption and cruelty while first governor-general of British India extended at intervals from 1788 to 1795. The trial lasted altogether 145 days, and in the course of it evidence of corruption and cruelty on a vast scale was presented to the House. Hastings was finally acquitted. This trial symbolized the eighteenth-century growth of the British Empire, the new methods of imperialism, and the expansion of English commerce to the ends of the earth (see Chapter IX). The engraving reproduced here hangs in Langdell Hall, Harvard Law School.

The scientific accuracy of this conception of Noah's Ark, showing the precise form of construction, as well as the methods of feeding the animals and cleaning the stalls, is an excellent example of the manifold uses of science to support belief. The women in the Ark are, of course, wearing eighteenth-century dress. This engraving is taken from the *Universal History* (2d edition, London, 1747), I, 219. Blackstone relied heavily on this work for the materials of the science of human nature (see Chapter II).

This table, translating the Scriptural measures into English feet and inches, illustrates the precision with which the eighteenth-century social scientist made his comparisons of the experiences and methods of different ages and peoples in his quest for the uniform laws of human nature. Scientific accuracy was of

melancholy reflection upon vanished glories. A feeling of the grandeur of a dead civilization was occasioned by the sublime disorder of the rough stones and the overwhelming obscurity of the past from which it was pretended that they survived. In contrast to the "sublime," which was represented by the ruin, one can see through the arch a neo-classical pavilion, the perfect symmetry and neatness of which observed the canons of "beauty." From the Victoria and Albert Museum, reprinted in B. Sprague Allen's *Tides in English Taste*, II, 170 (figure 73).

Rowlandson in this drawing shows punishment as a public entertainment, attracting a great crowd at Charing Cross in London; the pillory exemplifies the humanity of English law and Blackstone's notion of the appropriateness of English punishments. The *Commentaries* classified this as among the punishments "that consist principally in their ignominy, though most of them are mixed with some degree of corporal pain: and these are inflicted chiefly for such crimes as either arise from indigence, or render even opulence disgraceful. Such as whipping, hard labour in the house of corrrection, or otherwise, the pillory, the stocks, and the ducking-stool," IV, 377. Like Hogarth, Thomas Rowlandson (1756–1827) became well-known for his caricatures; he also illustrated the works of Smollett, Goldsmith, and Sterne. From R. Ackermann's *Microcosm of London* (London, 1833), II, 226.

This is Hogarth's impression of an election entertainment given by a county candidate for Parliament; it illustrates the importance of requiring a property qualification for voting and for holding office in order that Liberty as the expression of the individual's free will might be fully realized. As Blackstone explained, "The true reason of requiring any qualification, with regard to property, in voters, is to exclude such persons as are in so mean a situation that they are esteemed to have no will of their own. If these persons had votes, they would be tempted to dispose of them under some undue influence or other. This would give a great, an artful, or a wealthy man a larger share in elections than is consistent with general liberty," I, 171. Note the word "Liberty" inscribed on the banners displayed outside the window and within the room. This engraving is the first in Hogarth's series, "The Election," and is found in the 1833 edition of his works (referred to above), I, 117.

This engraving by Hogarth is the eighth in his series, "Industry and Idleness." The dozen plates in the series tell the story of the contrasting careers of the idle apprentice and the industrious apprentice. The idle apprentice wastes his life among prostitutes and criminals, and is finally executed at Tyburn. Meanwhile the industrious apprentice leads an exemplary life, marries his master's daughter, becomes a successful merchant, and finally Lord Mayor of London. It was through his career in commerce that the industrious apprentice reached the happy state depicted in the dinner which he, now Sheriff of London, gives in the Guildhall. The Sheriff's annual banquet in the Guildhall, at the public expense, was for many years a symbol of the extravagant wealth and prosperity of London commerce. From the 1833 edition of Hogarth's works (referred to above), I, 99.

# FOREWORD

"A TOWN that can't support one lawyer," goes a proverb of the expanding American West, "can always support two." The history of American law and lawyers in the half-century since my book was published has amply confirmed the wisdom of this observation. If lawyers have had a peculiarly pervasive influence in American life, one explanation is Blackstone's cogent and conveniently readable survey of the English common law. He provided an elegant and eloquent do-it-yourself guide to becoming a lawyer. Though created for the sophisticated audience of Oxford University, England, it was providentially suited to the needs of ambitious young Americans seeking to make a living from the law on this side of the ocean without the aid of ancient monopolies. According to Edmund Burke, by 1790 it had sold nearly as many copies in the American colonies as in England. Even without Blackstone, the Americans surely would have fought their Revolution and doubtless would have preserved English institutions in America. But the convenient appearance of the *Commentaries* within the decade before the Declaration of Independence made it much easier for Americans to see what they were preserving, and made it feasible to perpetuate those institutions in remote villages without trained lawyers or law libraries. From Blackstone we can learn even more about what the American colonists were defending than we can by reading the violent tracts of Thomas Paine.

In England access to the legal profession had been controlled by the Inns of Court, old privileged societies with venerable headquarters in London. Before the 1750s only the civil (or Roman) and canon law were taught in the universities. Knowledge of English law, though ironically known as "the common law" and revered as a tradition from the "Time whereof the memory of man runneth not to the contrary," had remained an arcane preserve. It was not for the university student, nor the literate layman, nor the unauthorized youth seeking to make his way in the world.

Then, in 1753, William Blackstone, an energetic thirty-year-old Fellow of All Souls College, Oxford, who had become a barrister of the Middle Temple, offered the first lectures on English law ever given in a university. He had practised as a barrister with only moderate success, but was a man of broad interests—having, among other things, written a treatise on architecture—and the master of a graceful English style. When the Vinerian professorship of common law was founded at Oxford in 1758, Blackstone was elected the first holder. His lectures, repeated annually, became the basis of his *Commentaries*, published in four volumes (1756–69).

A man of affairs, Blackstone was known in the university community for having managed the completion of a new library and for initiating reforms in the administration and typography of the university press, which would publish his *Commentaries*. His feeling for what interested people set him apart from the legal pedants. He served for nine years as a member of Parliament (even as he was writing the *Commentaries*) and sat as a judge of the Common Pleas. Though not an avid politician, with clear Tory inclinations he opposed the repeal of the Stamp Act (1766) and favored the expulsion of the reformer John Wilkes from the House of Commons.

Blackstone probably would not have been sorry to know that his book would help create an American legal profession. For, as Tocqueville later observed (in his *Democracy in America*, 1835), "the legal profession tempers the tyranny of the majority in the United States." But there were no Inns of Court in the United States. The first American law school, founded by Tapping Reeve at Litchfield, Connecticut, in 1784, closed its doors in 1833. It was a half-century after the Revolution before many American law schools were established at universities, and by the time of the Civil War most still required only one year's work. Though Harvard Law School dates back to 1817, its first law professorship was not founded until 1829. The numerous American states, the diversity of jurisdictions, and the geographic spread of the nation complicated the tasks of legal education. Luckily Americans had inherited Blackstone's survey, which became a kind of American democratic equivalent of the Inns of Court. While Blackstone's lectures had been directed to the privileged gentlemen of Oxford, in America they would help ambitious and industrious young Americans—countless young Abe Lincolns—learn to speak the language of law and so dare to put up their shingle as country lawyers. And no family credentials were required.

Blackstone's work—as explained and elaborated by numerous American editors—became the bible of American legal institutions. The qualities which fitted it for its role were not merely its literary grace, its sprightliness, and its readability, although without these the book might never have done its job. The underlying assumption of the book was that intelligent laymen ought to, and could, understand their laws. "In no country perhaps in the world is the law so general a study," Burke observed in his speech on conciliation with America. "All who read, and most do read, endeavor to obtain some smattering in that science." As Burke and many since have noted, a people who know their traditional rights will not let themselves be put upon. Blackstone did more than any other writer in the English-speaking world to break down the lawyers' monopoly of legal knowledge.

The conservative attitude which pervaded his book was especially congenial to America. Although Blackstone's explicit Toryism offended some Americans like Jefferson, they shared his distrust of new-fangled plans and grand social theories. In this respect the time of appearance of the *Commentaries* was crucial. His account of the British constitution and the common law was so comprehensive, so compendious, and so at-

tractive that Americans were hardly tempted to make preten-
tious and dogmatic codifications of their own. The English
tradition lived on and became the Anglo-American legal tradition; the American Bar Association still occasionally meets in
London. Thus, Blackstone's conservatism proved more vital
than he could have imagined, and eventually produced an
American renaissance of the common law.

As American legal education and the apparatus of the profession developed—with the multiplication of law schools for
separate jurisdictions, with the so-called "case-method" of instruction at Harvard in 1871, with the "key-number" scheme
for classifying precedents, and finally with the new electronic
systems of finding relevant earlier cases—the student and legal practitioner entered an expanding wilderness of particulars. And so they were drawn ever further from the literary
exposition of the principles of the common law, of which
Blackstone's work remained the classic example. All these advances give Blackstone's *Commentaries* an unprecedented new
role in the self-education of lawyers, reminding them and
other literate citizens of the uncanny coherence and appealing
rationale of our ancient system of common law.

Daniel J. Boorstin

# PREFACE

THIS BOOK is addressed to the lawyer, to the student of history, and to people generally concerned with the problem of method in the social sciences. For the lawyer, it is designed to suggest how he, in common with the rest of the community, employs the ideas and assumptions of his day about the whole of human experience; for the student of history it is meant to give evidence that the lawyer's work, whether or not the lawyer is aware of it, is in the main stream of the history of thought; for the student of method in the social sciences, it is meant to contribute to an understanding of the place of reason and rationalization in the study of institutions. For all these readers this book attempts to indicate how the ostensibly impartial processes of reason are employed by the student of society to support whatever social values he accepts.

I have taken as a microcosm for this problem a classic — perhaps the most important single book — in the history of the common law. By making a detailed study of Sir William Blackstone's *Commentaries on the Laws of England*, I have approached the general problem of the function of reason which faces the student of institutions in every age. For this work employed the assumptions prevalent in its day about science, religion, philosophy, history, art, and reason, to give the legal system and the values embodied in it an appearance of rationality and acceptability. Because a principal task of the lawyer in all periods is to find a rationale for institutions, the study of the law provides a convenient laboratory in which to study the use of reason in the explanation of social phenomena.

To deal adequately with the process of rationalization of

any age one should, of course, have an encyclopaedic
knowledge of the life and thought of that age. Lacking
that knowledge, I have thought it better to attempt this
task with the materials at my command, and with the expectation of just criticism from learned specialists, than to
impose an inappropriate and perhaps misleading limitation
on the problem which I am considering. In several of the
following chapters, therefore, I hope that the relationships
I have pointed out between legal thought and thought
about things other than law, and my description of the
use of these ideas in the process of rationalization, will be
suggestive rather than simply expository. I have hoped
at least to suggest the all-inclusiveness of the intellectual
vocabulary of the lawyer, the implications of his uses of
these ideas, and something of the intricacy of the workings
of the human mind in turning logic to its moral purposes.

Because of the different interests of the readers to whom
this book is directed, I have tried to use an arrangement
which would serve the purposes of all without encumber-
ing the pages with what might seem to any of the readers
to be digressive or uninteresting. Therefore, and because
most of the materials in the notes will concern only the
scholar or the specialist, I have collected the notes and
references at the end of the volume, where they are numbered consecutively by chapters. A glossary of legal terms,
which follows the notes, may help the person unlearned in
the law to understand the significance of the illustrations
given. No bibliography is appended, because full references for the books used are to be found in the notes, and
a "complete" bibliography would be unnecessary even if
I were qualified to provide it.

To avoid distracting quaintness, the eighteenth-century
spelling has not been retained in quotations from the
*Commentaries*. I have adopted the text of the popular
American edition by Thomas M. Cooley (Chicago, 1871).
Cooley, like most other editors of Blackstone, followed,

although not with perfect accuracy, the text and pagination of the ninth English edition. The last edition published in Blackstone's lifetime (1723–1780) was the eighth; Richard Burn produced the ninth edition in 1783. Burn claimed that all changes from the eighth edition were based on manuscript corrections which Blackstone himself had made. Although there is doubt whether the stylistic emendations from the previous edition were entirely Blackstone's, this is never a crucial consideration for the purpose of the present study. The substance of the *Commentaries* was given in lectures at the University of Oxford beginning in 1753; the four volumes of the work were first published, successively, in 1765, 1766, 1768, and 1769. The best discussion of the various editions is to be found in the Preface to Volume I of William G. Hammond's edition of the *Commentaries* (San Francisco, 1890); a more recent bibliography, by Miss Catherine Spicer Eller, is found in the *Yale Law Library Publications*, Number 6 (June, 1938). References to the *Commentaries* in my notes are indicated without other identification simply by Roman and Arabic numerals denoting respectively volume and page.

I wish to give acknowledgement to the Cambridge University Press for permission to quote from Gierke's *Natural Law and the Theory of Society* in Chapter II.

Publication of this work has been supported by the Harvard Law School Publication Fund, and I should like to thank Professor Erwin N. Griswold and the other members of the Publication Committee for their generous interest.

For valuable criticism and suggestions in the early stages of this book, I am indebted to Professors Walton H. Hamilton and Myres S. McDougal of the Yale Law School, where as a Sterling Fellow I submitted a primitive version of this work for the degree of Doctor of the Science of Law. I am further indebted to Professors Zechariah

Chafee Jr. and Lon L. Fuller, who have shown special interest in the project, and Professors Sheldon Glueck and Sidney Post Simpson, all of the Harvard Law School; to Professor Mark Howe of the University of Buffalo Law School; and to my colleagues in the department of History and Literature in Harvard College, Professors David Owen, F. O. Matthiessen, and Perry Miller. For the benefit of his vast knowledge of the eighteenth century and for incisive and helpful criticism, I am grateful to Professor Knox Chandler of Vanderbilt University. Mr. Paul Dobin and Mr. Bennett Frankel have given valuable suggestions and assistance. For their patience and care in preparing the manuscript I am grateful to Mrs. H. M. Irwin, Mrs. Meyer Abrams, Mrs. Donald McGranahan, and Miss Catherine Grassl. The encouragement of Miss Ruth Frankel has been of the greatest help. For much friendly criticism and advice, I wish to thank Dr. Meyer Abrams of the department of English in Harvard College. Finally, I wish to thank Dr. Hugh Cunningham of the department of History and Literature in Harvard College, who has helped at every stage of the writing and has done more than anyone else to improve the ideas and language of this book.

D. J. B.

Harvard Law School,
Cambridge, Massachusetts
February 6, 1941

# THE MYSTERIOUS SCIENCE
## OF THE LAW

So convenient a thing it is to be a reasonable creature, since it enables one to find or make a reason for every thing one has a mind to do.

BENJAMIN FRANKLIN

# INTRODUCTION

IF A LAWYER TODAY were to encompass the whole of our legal system in a single book, and if that book were to become the principal document by which our law was translated to another continent, he would be doing for twentieth-century America what Sir William Blackstone did for eighteenth-century England. In the fourteen centuries since Justinian's *Institutes*, Blackstone's *Commentaries* are the most important attempt in western civilization to reduce to short and rational form the complex legal institutions of an entire society. And Justinian's role in the reception of the civil law in western Europe was Blackstone's in the reception of the common law in America.

Since the first volume of Blackstone's *Commentaries on the Laws of England* appeared in 1765, this work has thus filled a place unique in the history of law in the English-speaking world. It is the first important and the most influential systematic statement of the principles of the common law. For generations of English lawyers, it has been both the foremost coherent statement of the subject of their study, and the citadel of their legal tradition. To lawyers on this side of the Atlantic, it has been even more important. In the first century of American independence, the *Commentaries* were not merely an approach to the study of law; for most lawyers they constituted all there was of the law. The influence of Blackstone's ideas on the framers of the Federal Constitution is well known. And many an early American lawyer might have said, with Chancellor Kent, that "he owed his reputation to the fact that, when studying law . . . he had but one book, Blackstone's *Commentaries*, but that one book he mastered." [1] For generations of American lawyers from Kent to Lincoln, the *Commentaries* were at once law school and law library. In view of the scarcity of lawbooks during the earliest years of the Republic, and the limitations of life on the frontier, it is not surprising that Blackstone's convenient work became the bible of American lawyers.

From the very beginning of the organized study of law in this country, the *Commentaries* held a central place. When Judge Tapping Reeve lectured to the first law school in America at Litchfield, Connecticut, he gave his students the substance of Blackstone. Now reposing in the Yale Law Library, are sets of his students' lecture notes, yellowed with age and worn from much use. These notes were carried west to Ohio to comprise the law library of the frontier practitioner. In this way Blackstone's work, copied in the handwriting of the American law student, was diffused throughout the West, and was to help provide a foundation of legal ideas for the American hinterland.

In the more sophisticated days since case books and law schools have come to take the place of the *Commentaries* and the law office, in the education of the American lawyer, the significance of Blackstone's position in American legal history has been easily forgotten. Buried beneath mountains of lawbooks, he shares obscurity with most of the other classics of the common law tradition. But even if Blackstone's *Commentaries* have become for almost every American lawyer an unread (though still highly readable) classic, the very phrases which the lawyer uses every day attest the pervasive influence of Blackstone in America.

Despite this expanding influence of the *Commentaries* on the law of this country, and despite its universal significance as an attempt to reduce the institutions of a society to a rational system, Blackstone's work, like every human document, was the product of a particular time and a particular place. Although it was the embodiment of the English legal tradition, this treatise had been written specifically for the squirearchy, merchants, and law students of eighteenth-century England. It had been written under the influence of the temporary assumptions and ways of thought of the author's own time.

Our purpose in this book will be to see how Blackstone employed these ways of thinking to make the complex legal institutions of eighteenth-century England appear to be a coherent and rational system. We will, therefore, be concerned with the intellectual history of the eighteenth century; and any study of this period is attended with very special difficulties. Until recently, such an attempt has been like trying to distinguish the color red through red-colored spectacles. For most of intellectual history, including the history of the eighteenth century, has been written in the eighteenth century's own terms. Under the influence of rationalist notions, the historian of ideas has been in quest of consistency for every period in the past, and has considered his task to be to piece the fragmentary remains into a "philosophy." Intellectual history has tended to be considered the History of Reason, and by a just irony the history of the eighteenth century has been oversimplified into the History of the Age of Reason.

But this rationalist fallacy of attempting to discover a reasoned coherence in the philosophy of any age, and indeed our very interest in intellectual history, are themselves mere phenomena of history. In the course of the last hundred years, and under the influence of the ideas of Comte, Darwin, Marx, Freud, and Veblen, we have come to minimize the importance of "reason" in determining the course of history. According to these ideas, "reason" ceases to be the power holding in check the dark forces of superstition, self-interest, and unreason, and instead rational systems become themselves the expression of dark and uncontrollable forces. In the vocabulary of intellectual history "reason" has been gradually displaced by "rationalization."

Consequently, when we examine Blackstone's attempt to reduce to rational order the legal institutions of his day, we are inclined to be less impressed by the solvent powers of reason, and the rational harmony of his "philosophy"; we are inclined to focus our attention on the extent to which Blackstone's statements were influenced not by the desire to discover what he did not know, but by the desire to prove what he already believed. As Swift wrote, "Reason itself is true and just, but the reason of every particular man is weak and wavering, perpetually swayed and turned by his interests, his passions, and his vices." We are struck by the dissonance between the impartial pretensions of reason and the imperative demands of belief, between the social necessity of going through the accepted methods of logical demonstration, and the equal urgency of using those methods to the end of demonstrating the desirability of certain preconceived social values.

Without suggesting that there is anything diabolical or unfair in any man's using his rational faculty to demonstrate the validity of the moral and social values which he accepts, we will attempt to see how Blackstone made an apparently rational structure of the law of eighteenth-century England. We will attempt to see how he used the prevailing ideas and assumptions of his day so as to prevent questioning of the existing social arrangements, and to demonstrate the acceptability of the society in which he believed. Much of the ensuing discussion will be devoted to detailed inquiry into the meaning of "reason" in Blackstone's England. Still, it may be desirable here to suggest in a general way the kind of concepts with which we are dealing. Where "reason" is contrasted with "faith" or "belief," we use "reason" to refer to that technique of talking about society by which one asked questions and sought, or supplied, a logical demonstration or "rational" argument in reply. We shall use "faith" or "belief" to refer to the attitude by which one expressed acceptance of

values in existing social arrangements, and by which one
indicated that the acceptance need not or could not be
supported by logical demonstration. "Reason" inquired;
"faith" accepted. "Reason" set the stage for argument;
"faith" created the atmosphere of affirmation and unquestioning acceptance. Dr. Johnson defined "Reason"
as "The power by which man deduces one proposition
from another, or proceeds from premises to consequences;
the rational faculty; discursive power." In the rational
mood one asked, "Why?"; in the mood of faith one
affirmed, "I believe."

It is important to make clear at the outset that we are
not concerned with Blackstone's motives. That is a task
for the psychologist or the biographer. We are not suggesting that there was anything perverse about Blackstone's pressing the method of reason only to a certain
point, and in his balancing against it the affirmation of
faith in such a way as to persuade his reader of certain
things. We are not suggesting that Blackstone's use of the
prevailing ways of thought to bring his reader to a certain
conclusion was always, or even often, conscious. Like the
modern social scientist, Blackstone was faced with a
society which accepted many contradictory ways of thinking. And we are interested in seeing how the numerous,
and apparently inconsistent assumptions of eighteenth-
century England were woven into a document in such a
way as to give the document, and the institutions which it
purported to describe, some kind of coherence and unity.

For the purposes of our analysis we have broken down
the *Commentaries* into the elements with which Blackstone, and indeed every social scientist, must deal. First
there is "Nature," or the materials of experience. Then
ratiocination, or the process of "Reason." And, finally,
"Values" or the moral beliefs which the writer accepts.

So long as we are dealing with "Nature" and "Reason,"
we shall discern apparent inconsistencies and internal

tensions in Blackstone's ideas. Beginning with our initial chapter in which we discuss Blackstone's concept of method, we shall see the assumptions of eighteenth-century England enlisted in our author's attempt to show a rational inquisitiveness without inspiring his reader with unhealthful doubts. Discords in Blackstone's assumptions, as we shall see, were not the product of dullness or stupidity; they were rather the normal response of a living man to the desire to be "rational" without calling into doubt the very values from which he began. And at the heart of the *Commentaries* was a core of "Values" moral and social, which he felt had to be defended. In Blackstone's scheme of values, which we will finally discuss, we shall not find the same kind of inconsistencies and internal tensions found in the realms of "Nature" and "Reason." Rather we shall find a hierarchical system in which some values are subordinated to others. It was this scheme of values that gave the *Commentaries* a unity. These central beliefs harmonized the contradictory ways of thinking which were at hand in Blackstone's day, and enabled him to make of the *Commentaries* a persuasive "rational" exposition of the laws of England.

As we examine the texture of Blackstone's reasoning we may apply to him Dostoyevsky's parable:

The Apostle Thomas said that he would not believe till he saw, but when he did see he said, "My Lord and my God!" Was it the miracle forced him to believe? Most likely not, but he believed solely because he desired to believe and possibly he fully believed in his secret heart even when he said, "I do not believe till I see." [2]

# I. NATURE

# CHAPTER ONE

# THE LAW:

## SCIENCE *and* MYSTERY

### I. THE ADMIRING SCIENCE

WHEN BLACKSTONE began to write his *Commentaries,* the world of ideas was disturbed by a mid-eighteenth-century version of the fundamentalist controversy. Science and religion seemed to many men to be in conflict, and this conflict presented a problem which no thinker could ignore. Toward the end of the seventeenth century, the physical science of Newton and the scientific philosophy of Locke had revealed vast powers in man's critical faculties. And as these new scientific techniques were developed, new problems every day arose for the religionist and the theologian. As the growth of science produced a problem for the proponents of the old faith in religion, similarly the application of the new scientific technique to social studies was to create a new problem for the proponents of old faiths in society. A thoughtful conservative like Blackstone could not fail to use what he considered to be the best scientific method, and yet he was obliged to apply it in such a way as to prevent its use against accepted beliefs and existing institutions. To see how the conflict between science and religion, between the new ways of thinking and the old, was reflected in Blackstone's attitude to the nature of legal studies, will be our concern in this chapter.

That the most ambitious rationalization of English law which had yet been undertaken, should have been written in the eighteenth century, is itself impressive evidence of the power that the new scientific technique held over men's imaginations. Blackstone was, in a sense, doing for the English legal system what Newton had done for the physical world, and what Locke had done for the world of the mind. Although Blackstone's purpose was perhaps less ambitious than that of the physical scientists and the scientific philosophers, his work held greater dangers. Systems of physics and philosophy might have implications for the philosopher and the theologian, but a system of legal thought had immediate implications for the squire, the merchant, and indeed for every member of society. In working out his theory of social science, and his approach to the study of law, Blackstone was therefore expressing an attitude toward the everyday practices of his society. It was important for him to start with a theory which would not let the new science get out of hand. If he did not insist on a boundary where science must stop its cold and abstract criticism, and where men must repose on their faith in existing social arrangements, the new science might provide a means for criticizing the law.

Indeed, we shall see that Blackstone, like many of the religious opponents of the new science, was careful to use a theory which would not question the main outlines of the society which he found about him. He was not alone in this. In the eighteenth century, many of the most profound and most influential students of society approached their study with the conviction that institutions were fundamentally beyond human criticism. They tried to close the way to revolutionary thought by limiting the field for the operation of man's reason. Many of these men who wrote about institutions set for themselves a double purpose: to understand and to admire. And they used "admire" in the primary sense which Dr. Johnson gave it in his *Dictionary*, "To regard with wonder: generally in a good sense." Some might have said with

Montesquieu, writing in 1748 in the Preface to *The Spirit of Laws*,[1] "If this work meets with success I shall owe it chiefly to the grandeur and majesty of the subject." Few profound social philosophers of the Enlightenment were satisfied to consider their work as merely a display of the critical powers of human reason.

Knowledge and awe were not by nature irreconcilable, but to draw the line where desire for one would extinguish concern for the other was not easy. And the inner conflict of the theory of social studies in the eighteenth century was the conflict of these two aims. Writing in 1791, Edmund Burke eloquently summed up the two purposes which many students of society in the hundred years before him had been trying to harmonize. When we examine the writers and artists of the past, he wrote, we ought "to study them until we know how and what we ought to admire; and if we cannot arrive at this combination of admiration with knowledge, rather to believe that we are dull, than that the rest of the world has been imposed on. It is as good a rule, at least, with regard to this admired constitution. We ought to understand it according to our measure; and to venerate where we are not able presently to comprehend. . . . Let us improve it with zeal, but with fear. Let us follow our ancestors, men not without a rational, though without an exclusive, confidence in themselves."[2]

Yet the very cause of inner conflict in the theory of social science in eighteenth-century England was that men had been given good reasons for confidence in themselves. In the light of the discoveries of Newton and Locke, there no longer seemed a great disproportion between the complexity of the world and man's feeble understanding. The public interest in the works and names of these men, and the place which they soon were given in the popular imagination, showed the growing attraction of the conception of "science." Like Darwin in the nineteenth century, New-

ton and Locke became symbols — and highly popular
symbols — of the new science. Even before his death in
1727, Newton had become a national hero, and in the half-
century after his grand funeral, his fame was everywhere.
Within the century, his *Principia* was to be reprinted at
least eighteen times, and to be presented to laymen in
countless popular books. Men went about the country
delivering lectures like Benjamin Martin's "Plain and
Familiar Introduction to the Newtonian Philosophy in Six
Lectures. . . . Designed for the use of such Gentlemen and
Ladies as would acquire a competent Knowledge of this
Science without Mathematical Learning." [3]  Alexander
Pope was making articulate a widespread admiration
when he proposed for Newton's epitaph:

> Nature and Nature's laws lay hid in Night:
> God said, *Let* NEWTON *be!* and all was Light.[4]

Later in the century, Dr. Johnson expressed the general
enthusiasm when he declared that "if Newton had flour-
ished in ancient Greece, he would have been worshipped
as a Divinity." [5]

While Newton had been showing how man could
methodize the physical world, Locke had demonstrated
man's ability to understand himself. The ideas in his
*Essay Concerning Human Understanding*, first published
in 1690, were to have great vogue in the years from 1725
to 1765.[6] In 1734, Queen Caroline, decorating her grotto
at Richmond, ordered, among others, the busts of Newton
and Locke. Mark Akenside's effusive "Hymn to Science"
spoke the public mind when it declared:

> Next, to thy nobler search resign'd,
> The busy, restless, Human Mind
>   Through every maze pursue;
> Detect Perception where it lies,
> Catch the Ideas as they rise,
>   And all their changes view.[7]

By 1760 there had been thirteen English editions of the *Essay*. And in that very year Laurence Sterne, showing in *Tristram Shandy* that Locke's doctrine could be the basis of a new form of fiction, brought philosophy down to the level of the layman.

As the layman's enthusiasm for the method of science was growing, philosophers were pushing forward, developing its latent possibilities, and applying the method to new fields. By 1739, Hume, acknowledging his debt to Newton, had produced in his *Treatise* a new "science of human nature."

Man's new power, a source of self-confidence, was also to be a source of doubt. Even during Locke's lifetime it had become apparent that, however much the new knowledge might have strengthened man's belief in himself, this very knowledge might disintegrate his other beliefs. Until late in the seventeenth century, the work of Descartes and of Spinoza was yet to be done in England. In 1695, Locke, writing his *Reasonableness of Christianity*, hopefully declared that reason was a strong support of religion. But in the very next year, John Toland's *Christianity not Mysterious* carried the argument a dangerous step further: he said that there was "nothing in the Gospel contrary to reason or above it." From praising Christianity because it was rational, men came to doubt Christianity wherever it could not be proved rational. And deism was one attempt to solve the growing conflict between science and religion. But the method of the new science had so insinuated itself, even into theological minds, that by 1736 Bishop Butler was trying to refute deism by the very arguments of natural religion. In another twenty years Hume was publishing his *Natural History of Religion* and, before the end of the eighteenth century, Gibbon was to show dramatically how the new science could be used to sow doubts of the virtues of primitive Christianity. No one could say to what diabolical uses the new method of reason might not be put by irreverent souls.

Yet some of the same voices that had shown man the power of reason had also attempted to define its limits. Locke's *Essay Concerning Human Understanding* had dwelt at length on the problem of the "Extent of Human Knowledge," concluding that "we must, in many things, content ourselves with faith and probability." [8] "It is past controversy, that we have in us something that thinks; our very doubts about what it is confirm the certainty of its being, though we must content ourselves in the ignorance of what kind of being it is: and it is in vain to go about to be sceptical in this, as it is unreasonable in most other cases to be positive against the being of anything, because we cannot comprehend its nature. For I would fain know, what substance exists, that has not something in it which manifestly baffles our understandings." [9] And many writers in the early eighteenth century also suspected than man by limiting his knowledge to experience, had doomed himself to doubt. In the Second Epistle of the "Essay on Man" Pope wrote in 1734:

> Know then thyself, presume not God to scan,
> The proper study of Mankind is Man.
> Placed on this isthmus of a middle state,
> A being darkly wise, and rudely great:
> With too much knowledge for the Sceptic side,
> With too much weakness for the Stoic's pride,
> He hangs between; in doubt to act, or rest;
> In doubt to deem himself a God, or Beast;
> In doubt his Mind or Body to prefer;
> Born but to die, and reas'ning but to err;
> Alike in ignorance, his reason such,
> Whether he thinks too little, or too much.[10]

The power which first had seemed to give man security, might actually take from him the only belief that could give him rest.

Men who had not yet worked out a philosophy which would reconcile religion and science, needed to hold tight

SCIENCE ENLISTED IN AID OF RELIGION

to any faith which seemed to limit the destructive power of reason. Edward Young's *Night Thoughts*, extremely popular as they came out after 1742, exhorted the reader, and the young Lorenzo, to return to faith:

> I quite mistook my road.
> Born in an age more curious than devout;
> More fond to fix the place of heaven, or hell,
> Than studious this to shun, or that secure.
> 'Tis not the curious, but the pious path,
> That leads me to my point: Lorenzo! know,
> Who worship God, shall find him.   Humble Love,
> And not proud Reason, keeps the door of heaven;
> Love finds admission where proud Science fails.[11]

Many of the popular interpreters of Newton were careful to make clear their conviction that proud Science had not driven out, and could not drive out a religious Love. The new science, they insisted, must be the servant and not the master of religion. An example of this is found in Colin Maclaurin's popular *Account of Sir Isaac Newton's Philosophical Discoveries*, first published in 1748. At the very outset of his work, he declared:

But natural philosophy is subservient to purposes of a higher kind, and is chiefly to be valued as it lays a sure foundation for natural religion and moral philosophy; by leading us, in a satisfactory manner, to the knowledge of the Author and Governor of the universe. To study nature is to search into his workmanship: every new discovery opens to us a new part of his scheme. And while we still meet, in our enquiries, with hints of greater things yet undiscovered, the mind is kept in a pleasing expectation of making a further progress; acquiring at the same time higher conceptions of that great Being, whose works are so various and hard to be comprehended.[12]

The problem which here faced the physical scientist was, in different form, also to confront the social scientist. A student of society like Blackstone was faced with the problem of using scientific notions for the purpose of fruitful inquiry, without allowing them to call into question fundamental conservative beliefs. He had to have a social science, and particularly a science of law, that could be used to admire, but not to destroy. Long before Blackstone's day, the subversive possibilities of the new science had been recognized, when, in 1667 Sprat's *History of the Royal Society* had defended science from the imputation that it was inevitably a radical study. Sprat's argument, popular in the eighteenth century, so clearly described the kind of danger which Blackstone must have seen in a Science of Law, that it is worth quoting at length:

> I will now proceed to the weightiest, and most solemn Part of my whole Undertaking; to make a Defence of the Royal Society, and this new Experimental Learning, in Respect of the Christian Faith. I am not ignorant, in what a slippery Place I now stand; and what a tender Matter I am enter'd upon. . . . I do here, in the beginning, most sincerely declare, that if this Design should in the least diminish the Reverence that is due to the Doctrine of Jesus Christ, it were so far from deserving Protection, that it ought to be abhorr'd by all the Politic and Prudent, as well as by the devout Part of Christendom. And this, I profess, I think they were bound to do, not only from a just Dread of the Being, the Worship, the Omnipotence, the Love of God, all which are to be held in the highest Veneration, but also out of a Regard to the Peace and Prosperity of Men. . . . Whoever shall impiously attempt to subvert the Authority of the Divine Power, on false Pretences to better Knowledge, he will unsettle the strongest Foundations of our Hopes: he will make a terrible Confusion in all the Offices and Opinions of Men: he will destroy the most prevailing Argument to Virtue: he will remove all Human Actions, from their firmest Center. . . .
>
> 'Tis true, his [the experimenter's] Employment is about material Things. But this is so far from drawing him to oppose invisible Beings, that it rather puts his Thoughts into an excellent good Capacity to believe them. In every Work of Nature that he handles, he knows that there is not only a gross Sub-

stance, which presents itself to all Mens Eyes; but an infinite Subtilty of Parts, which come not into the sharpest Sense.[13]

As Sprat had shown that reverence for God and for man's settled beliefs need not be upset by the new physical science, so Blackstone, applying the scientific method to the study of law, would have to show that his method would not upset settled institutions. Blackstone, even more than Sprat, was standing in a "slippery Place." And if a Science of Law was not to make men "impiously attempt to subvert the Authority of the Divine Power, on false Pretences to better Knowledge," if it was not to lead men to question the divinely-sanctioned existing order of society, the Science of Law would surely have to be an admiring science.

Soon after Blackstone's death, the French Revolution was to show where men might go when they were led by "proud Reason" alone. Burke, in his trenchant *Reflections on the Revolution in France*, then saw the problem as Blackstone might have seen it. "Nothing is left which engages the affections on the part of the commonwealth. On the principles of this mechanic philosophy, our institutions can never be embodied . . . in persons; so as to create in us love, veneration, admiration, or attachment. But that sort of reason which banishes the affections is incapable of filling their place. These public affections, combined with manners, are required sometimes as correctives, always as aids to law." [14]  It is not surprising that, less than fifty years before the French Revolution, an intelligent conservative like Blackstone should have refused to apply a narrowly rational social science.   Still, when Blackstone came to rationalize English law in the years after 1753,[15] the vocabulary of his day, as we have seen, required that he should somehow present the study of law as a science.

## 2. THE QUEST FOR LEGAL PRINCIPLES

In his Introductory Lecture to the *Commentaries*, Blackstone described the "science of law" which he conceived had been "committed to his charge, to be cultivated, methodized and explained." [16]  Again and again in the course of his work he recurred to the theme that his subject was a proper exercise for man's reason.  He urged the prospective lawyer "to lay the foundation of his future labours in a solid scientifical method," and reminded him that "law is to be considered not only as matter of practice, but also as a rational science." [17]  To say that legal institutions could be rationalized and reduced to discoverable first principles was simply another way of saying, in eighteenth-century terms, that rational man was not wasting his time in studying the law.

Blackstone began by taking for granted that since the law was worth studying, it must be capable of being rationalized and reduced to principles.  And he passed quite imperceptibly to a very different assumption, that because the laws of England ought to be studied, these laws themselves contained such principles.  He had taken up "the task of examining the great outlines of the English law, and tracing them up to their principles." [18]  The discussion of every section of the law became the exposition of "rational principles."  The law of slavery was merely an elaboration on the theme that "the law of England acts upon general and extensive principles." [19]  In describing the action of ejectment, he sought "to delineate, with some degree of minuteness, its history, the manner of its process, and the principles whereon it is grounded." [20]  Everywhere in English law "principles" were waiting to be found.

But not in all departments of the law were principles discovered with equal ease.  And, since Blackstone's primary interest was in these principles, he focussed the reader's attention on the departments of the law where the principles were most readily found. He explained, therefore, that he would not "perplex" his readers by discussing the proceeding in real actions, "which are frequently mere positive establishments, the *forma et figura judicii*, and conduce very little to illustrate the reason and fundamental grounds of the law. Wherever I apprehend they may at all conduce to this end, I shall endeavour to hint at them incidentally." [21] The study of property law was "a little perplexed and intricate," therefore it was his "endeavour, principally, to select such parts of it as were of the most general use, where the principles were the most simple, the reasons of them the most obvious, and the practice the least embarrassed." [22] Since he was interested in the "elements and first principles" which were the components of a "general map of the law," [23] he could provide merely a general discussion of the nicety of creating and securing a contingent remainder; then the student "will in some measure see the general reasons, upon which this nicety is founded. It were endless to attempt to enter upon the particular subtleties and refinements, into which this doctrine, by the variety of cases which have occurred in the course of many centuries, has been spun out and subdivided: neither are they consonant to the design of these elementary disquisitions." [24]

Blackstone allowed the assumption of a rationale in legal institutions to include the very vocabulary which the lawyer used. "Terms of art there will unavoidably be in all sciences; the easy conception and thorough comprehension of which must depend upon the frequent and familiar use; and the more subdivided any branch of science is, the more terms must be used to express the nature of these subdivisions, and mark out with sufficient precision the ideas they are meant to convey." [25] The student must have confidence, then, that a term of art has a precise and discoverable meaning. "The truth is, what is generally denominated law-Latin is in reality a mere technical language, calculated for eternal duration, and easy to be apprehended both in present and future times; and on those accounts best suited to preserve those memorials which are intended for perpetual rules of action. . . . And my academical readers will excuse me for suggesting, that the terms of the law are not more numerous, more uncouth, or more difficult to be explained by a teacher, than those of logic, physics, and the whole circle of Aristotle's philosophy, nay even of the politer arts of architecture and its kindred studies, or the science of rhetoric itself." [26] Behind every legal term, as behind every rule of law, there lurked a rational principle which the student must try to discover.

Any data that could not be distilled into "principles" could be disregarded for they were by definition no part of a "science of law." The provisions of martial law, used "for the raising of armies, and the due regulation and discipline of the soldiery . . . are to be looked upon only as temporary excrescences bred out of the distemper of the state, and not as any part of the permanent and perpetual laws of the kingdom. For martial law, which is built upon no settled principles, but is entirely arbitrary in its decisions, is, as Sir Matthew Hale observes, in truth and reality no law, but something indulged rather than allowed as a law." [27] This method of selection was important also in helping the student of the Science of Law determine which decided cases were proper materials for his study. Though "it is an established rule to abide by former precedents. . . . Yet this rule admits of exception, where the former determination is most evidently contrary to reason; much more if it be clearly contrary to the divine law. But even in such cases the subsequent judges do not pretend to make a new law, but to vindicate the old one from misrepresentation. For if it be found that the former decision is manifestly absurd or unjust, it is declared, not that such a sentence was *bad law*, but that it was *not law*." [28]

We have seen that Blackstone presupposed that anything which was not intelligible according to reason could not be law. But he actually went much further, and by a convenient inversion of logic said, in effect, that what was customarily thought of as law must by definition have an intelligible reason. The maxim, "*cessante ratione, cessat et ipsa lex*," was here very useful.[29] "If a ferry is erected on a river, so near another ancient ferry as to draw away its custom, it is a nuisance to the owner of the old one. . . . But . . . it is no nuisance to erect a mill so near mine, as to draw away the custom, unless the miller also intercepts the water." This was because "where the reason ceases, the law also ceases with it." [30] Blackstone coördinated by this maxim the miscellaneous exceptions to the rule that *autrefoits attaint* was a good special plea in bar.[31] He assumed that wherever there was an exception to a rule the diligent student was sure to find a good reason. In this way the maxim was itself used as authority for its converse, and the Science of Law proceeded on the unexpressed assumption that "where the law ceases, the reason also ceases with it."

In this quest for the rational principles of the law, Blackstone was satisfying the eighteenth-century desire to methodize and make a "science" of the data of experience. The charm of the Science of Law was great: it was witness to the power of man's reason, to the beauty of English institutions, and, ultimately, to the Intelligence of God.

But if there was appeal in the concept of the Science of Law, there were also risks. In theology "reasonableness" had first been a measure of the excellence of Christianity, but by the middle of the eighteenth century had already become the test of its truth; legal thought might have a similar development. The reasonableness of the legal system might at first be merely a way of showing that man could discover the infinite wisdom of the great Creator of all legal systems.[32] Yet if man ever should come to feel that he understood all the criteria of law, what would prevent him from concluding that his own reason was the sole test of legal institutions?

Moreover, a mere Science of Law would be incomplete, because it alone could never reveal in institutions that "infinite Subtilty of Parts, which come not into the sharpest Sense." Without something more than science, man might fail to have the awe for the marvelous institutional arrangements of God, which was accessible only to the man of faith. If man's reason were to be the sole judge of the validity of English laws, there was no assurance that men would retain regard for the laws which they found around them.[33] If everything about the law should have been intelligible, someone might have said of English law what Voltaire was writing about the French legal system. "In short," he said, "to what side soever we turn our eyes, we are presented with a confused scene of contradictions, uncertainty, hardships and arbitrary power. In the present age, we seem universally aiming at perfection; let us not therefore neglect to perfect the laws, on which our lives and fortunes depend."[34]

If "proud Science" were to sit in judgment on law, the stability of the legal system might be no more. Man might become arbiter in place of God. As Voltaire himself wrote:

Every prophane legislator who dared to feign that the Divinity had dictated to him his laws, was a palpable blasphemer, and a traitor; a blasphemer, because he calumniated the gods; a traitor, because he subjected his country to his own opinions. . . . If I had met with one of those great quacks in a public square, I should have called out to him, Stop, do not compromise thus with the Divinity; thou wouldest cheat me, if thou makest him come down to teach us what we all knew; thou wouldest avail thyself of my agreeing to eternal truths, to draw from me my consent to thy usurpation; I will impeach thee to the people as a tyrant who blasphemeth.[35]

If the fundamentals of law came to be defined as "what we all knew," the study of society might cease to be an admiring science. The quest for legal principles might become a perilous inquisition into the foundations of society.

### 3. THE MYSTERIOUS CLARITY OF LAW

Naturally, Blackstone, who saw the law as the bulwark of existing society, could not be satisfied with a theory which pointed the way to dangerous inquiry. The Science of Law was not enough. There must also be a Mystery of Law, a decent veil to protect ultimate values from the devouring gaze of Reason. As Burke, high priest of the Mystery of Law and the century's most eloquent conservative, was later to express it, men must be wary of "extravagant and presumptuous speculations," and must instead seek "the passport of Heaven to human place and honour." [36] In a lucid passage he showed the way of thinking that had, "in this enlightened age," made Blackstone complement the Science by the Mystery of Law. Significantly using the metaphors of a commercial society, he wrote:

We are afraid to put men to live and trade each on his own private stock of reason; because we suspect that this stock in each man is small, and that the individuals would do better to avail themselves of the general bank and capital of nations and of ages. Many of our men of speculation, instead of exploding general prejudices, employ their sagacity to discover the latent wisdom which prevails in them. If they find what they seek, and they seldom fail, they think it more wise to continue the prejudice, with the reason involved, than to cast away the coat of prejudice and to leave nothing but the naked reason; because prejudice, with its reason, has a motive to give action to that reason, and an affection which will give it permanence. Prejudice is of ready application in an emergency; it previously engages the mind in a steady course of wisdom and virtue, and does not leave the man hesitating in the moment of decision, sceptical, puzzled, and unresolved. Prejudice renders a man's virtue his habit; and not a series of unconnected acts. Through just prejudice, his duty becomes a part of his nature.[37]

Therefore there were limits beyond which man should not let his reason wander.

Throughout the *Commentaries* Blackstone insisted on these limits. He warned, in his discussion of the Revolution of 1688, "But care must be taken not to carry this inquiry farther, than merely for instruction or amusement. . . . I therefore rather choose to consider this great political measure, upon the solid footing of authority, than to reason in its favour from its justice, moderation, and expediency: because that might imply a right of dissenting or revolting from it, in case we should think it unjust, oppressive, or inexpedient. . . . It is now become our duty at this distance of time to acquiesce in their [our ancestors'] determination; being born under that establishment which was built upon this foundation, and obliged by every tie, religious as well as civil, to maintain it." [38] The royal dignity was important because, "the mass of mankind will be apt to grow insolent and refractory, if taught to consider their prince as a man of no greater perfection than themselves." [39] But even the scholar of the law must approach his subject with awe, and with the certainty that there would be much that he could not understand. Since, "upon these two foundations, the law of nature and the law of revelation, depend all human laws . . . with regard to such points as are not indifferent, human laws are only declaratory of, and act in subordination to, the former." [40] Although the law of nature which was "dictated by God himself" was ideally discoverable by reason, man must realize that since the fall of Adam "his reason is corrupt, and his understanding full of ignorance and error." [41] Because of the disproportion between the faculties of the Creator and those of the created, man should not expect to be able to comprehend rationally the full perfection of God's laws.

Now this unfathomable perfection of the laws of God was attributed by the *Commentaries* to the laws of eighteenth-century England. Although the law of society was only "a kind of secondary law of nature," a kind of humanly imperfect copy of the law of nature,[42] Blackstone approached it with a great distrust of his own faculties. While the reasons for particular rules might seem unclear, man had only to defy these rules to discover that there were reasons for them which passed his understanding. "And it hath been an ancient observation in the laws of England, that whenever a standing rule of law, of which the reason perhaps could not be remembered or discerned, hath been wantonly broken in upon by statutes or new resolutions, the wisdom of the rule hath in the end appeared from the inconveniences that have followed the innovation." [43] To be sure, the conception of a Science of Law required that no precedent "contrary to reason" should be considered law. "And hence it is that our lawyers are with justice so copious in their encomiums on the reason of the common law; that they tell us, that the law is the perfection of reason, that it always intends to conform thereto, and that what is not reason is not law." [44] Yet man should not presume that he could always determine whether a decision had been grounded on reason. "Not that the particular reason of every rule in the law can at this distance of time be always precisely assigned; but it is sufficient that there be nothing in the rule flatly contradictory to reason, and then the law will presume it to be well founded." [45]

It was only sensible, therefore, that man should be wary of criticizing where he could not comprehend. If the reader accepted Blackstone's assumption that "the wisdom of our ancient law determined nothing in vain," then he could understand "how difficult and hazardous a thing it is, even in matters of public utility, to depart from the rules of the common law; which are so nicely constructed and so artificially connected together, that the least breach in any one of them disorders for a time the texture of the whole." [46] For example, the student must humbly admire the institution of benefit of clergy, which showed how "the wisdom of the English legislature . . . in the course of a long and laborious process, extracted by a noble alchemy rich medicines out of poisonous ingredients." [47]

But the fact that there had to be a Mystery of Law did not mean, according to Blackstone, that the law was itself uncertain or confused. Instead, he found in the law a mysterious clarity. "But is not (it will be asked) the multitude of law-suits, which we daily see and experience, an argument against the clearness and certainty of the law itself? By no means: for among the various disputes and controversies which are daily to be met with in the course of legal proceedings, it is obvious to observe how very few arise from obscurity in the rules or maxims of law. . . . The law rarely hesitates in declaring its own meaning; but the judges are frequently puzzled to find out the meaning of others." [48] The essences distilled by the "noble alchemy" of the law possessed a purity and perfection that were immeasurable. That man could sometimes not discover the rationale of a law was evidence not of any vagueness in the rationale itself but of the crudeness of man's instrument of analysis.

One of the first efforts of the student of law should be, then, to avoid preoccupation with the confusions and perversions which had been the work of men, and instead to devote himself to the search for the pure essences which were properly the substance of his study. [49] The mistakes of lawyers and judges could not pollute the quintessential perfection of law. Thus, statutes since the time of Charles II had helped reveal the theoretical perfection of the law by "cutting off . . . a vast number of excrescences, that in the process of time had sprung out of the practical part of it." [50] "And in proportion as the decisions of courts of judicature are multiplied, the law will be loaded with decrees, that may sometimes (though rarely) interfere with each other: either because succeeding judges may not be apprized of the prior adjudication; or because they may think differently from their predecessors; or because the same arguments did not occur formerly as at present; or, in fine, because of the natural imbecility and imperfection that attends all human proceedings." [51] Judges, whether of law or equity, should not direct their attention to the imperfect human practice, but to "the true sense of the law in question"; they could not "enlarge, diminish, or alter that sense in a single tittle." [52] The powerful and mysterious clarity of law thus shone through all the imperfections of men.

For many of his judgments Blackstone depended on his intuitions of the "genius of the common law," and the "spirit of our constitution." [53] The Revolution of 1688 "however it might in some respects go beyond the letter of our ancient laws . . . was agreeable to the spirit of our constitution, and the rights of human nature." [54] Although in trials of contempts the defendant could be made to answer upon oath to a criminal charge, "this method . . . is not agreeable to the genius of the common law in any other instance," and this explained why the defendant was required to answer upon oath in no other instance. [55] The abolition of the canonical doctrine of purgation in the court of chancery showed how "the genius of the English law having broken through the bondage imposed on it by its clerical chancellors . . . asserted the doctrines of judicial as well as civil liberty." [56] Genii and spirits were natural paraphernalia of the Mystery of Law.

The notion of the mysterious clarity of law, however strange it may seem nowadays,[57] was not strange or paradoxical in Blackstone's day. That the law should consist of principles which were really clear, but of which man could never perfectly discern the clarity, was natural if the study of law was to be an admiring science. In an age when the conflict between science and religion was showing itself sharply in the physical sciences, it was inevitable that the social sciences, and particularly the study of the law, should reflect the dissonance of ideas. The lawyer in an age of science would surely feel the desire to use a "scientific" technique. Yet he might have good cause to fear lest the method of reason be used to call in doubt the fundamental values of society. The method which Blackstone adopted showed the discord between the demands of science and the demands of religion, between the call for logical demonstration, and the urgency of faithful and conservative affirmation. The apparent resolution of this conflict in the *Commentaries* was achieved by developing a concept that was to allow the desire to understand and the desire to admire to exist side by side. In a short dialogue in his *Philosophical Dictionary*,[58] Voltaire gives a clue to the kind of reconciliation that was to be made:

A. Have you no laws in your country?

B. Yes; some good, and others bad.

A. Where could you have taken the idea of them, but from the notions of natural law which every well-constructed mind has within itself? They must have been derived from these or nothing.

B. You are right; there is a natural law, but it is still more natural to many people to forget or neglect it.

A. It is natural also to be one-eyed, humpbacked, lame, deformed, and sickly; but we prefer persons well-made and healthy.

B. Why are there so many one-eyed and deformed minds?

A. Hush! Consult however the article OMNIPOTENCE.

# CHAPTER TWO

# THE USE OF
# HISTORY

## I. THE SCIENCE OF HUMAN NATURE

THE CONFLICT between Blackstone's Science of Law and
his Mystery of Law was never to be entirely resolved.
For this was nothing less than the conflict between man's
desire to understand all and his fear that he might discover too much. Yet eighteenth-century England was
able to find a partial solution of the difficulty by appealing
to experience. Since Locke had destroyed all innate ideas
and made experience the primary source of ideas, the student of society, like the philosopher, could abandon the
*a priori* path for the path of experience. In practice this
meant that the eighteenth-century mind came to make
every social science, as Blackstone made the study of law,
simply a branch of the study of history. The accumulation of all experience, history became the whole study of
man, and the entire practical aspect of philosophy. In
1735, Bolingbroke summed up this notion when he said
that history was "philosophy teaching by examples." [1]
By "philosophy" was meant not the abstruse distinctions
of metaphysics, but the practical "science of human
nature." "Nature has done her part. She has opened this
study to every man who can read and think: and what
she has made the most agreeable, reason can make the
most useful, application of our minds." [2] "By comparing,
in this study, the experience of other men and other ages

with our own, we improve both: we analyse, as it were, philosophy. We reduce all the abstract speculations of ethics, and all the general rules of human policy, to their first principles." [3]

This conception of a science of human nature, the confluence of the streams of Locke and Newton, was no mere notion of popular science. It had the dignity which came from the devotion of some of the most rigorous minds. Hume, in 1739, called his *Treatise* an attempt to write another *Principia* by applying the Newtonian method to philosophy.[4] But how was this to be done? Here he answered with the voice of Locke. "And as the science of man is the only solid foundation for the other sciences, so the only solid foundation we can give to this science itself must be laid on experience and observation."[5] That he thought history the final and proper source of this experience and observation, Hume was to dramatize by finally turning from philosophy to the study of the past. But he was clear in defining the data and method of this science:

Mankind are so much the same in all times and places, that history informs us of nothing new or strange in this particular. Its chief use is only to discover the constant and universal principles of human nature, by shewing men in all varieties of circumstances and situations, and furnishing us with materials from which we may form our observations, and become acquainted with the regular springs of human actions and behaviour. These records of wars, intrigues, factions, and revolutions, are so many collections of experiments by which the politician or moral philosopher fixes the principles of his science; in the same manner as the physician or natural philosopher becomes acquainted with the nature of plants, minerals, and other forms concerning them. Nor are the earth, water, and other elements, examined by Aristotle or Hippocrates, more like to those, which at present lie under our observation, than the men described by Polybius and Tacitus, are to those who now govern the world.[6]

Such a description of the nature of history would have been accepted also by Robertson and Gibbon, who, with Hume, were the great trio of British historians of the period. While Hume had sought his materials in England, Robertson was going to Scotland, ancient India, and distant America, and Gibbon was to explore the ruins of Rome. Yet they all would have agreed that they were discussing the same problem; they were students of the same science and historical record was their laboratory notebook.[7]

Nor was the historian alone in this laboratory. Many other thinkers who sought to justify or explain their work liked to think they were fellow-students of this universal science. Adam Smith first attained prominence through his *Theory of Moral Sentiments*, published in 1759, which sought in human sympathy an explanation of the cohesion of society; in 1776 his *Wealth of Nations* drew many examples from Africa, Greece, and Rome, and inquired into such problems as the social bases of religion.[8] For Burke, also, the study of past and present was the attempt to understand the general laws of human behaviour.[9]

Artists joined the enterprise, and their contribution lay in portraits and in the "nobler branches" of historical painting. As Sir Joshua Reynolds said in his "Discourse" in 1771, "A History Painter paints man in general; a Portrait Painter, a particular man, and consequently a defective model."[10] Yet even these defective models, since they were models of human nature, were given much attention in the eighteenth century, and Reynolds himself, like Gainsborough and Romney, sought the qualities of human nature through the art of portraiture. The "nobler branch" was cultivated by Benjamin West who was in 1772 appointed historical painter to the king, and became so popular that he later succeeded Reynolds as president of the Royal Academy.

The new art of the novel was quickly adapted to the

purposes of the science of human nature. Henry Fielding, in *Joseph Andrews* in 1742, actually applied the method of this science to an analysis of the lawyer as a species:

I question not but several of my readers will know the lawyer in the stage-coach the moment they hear his voice. . . . I declare here once for all, I describe not men, but manners; not an individual, but a species. Perhaps it will be answered, Are not the characters then taken from life? To which I answer in the affirmative; nay, I believe I might aver, that I have writ little more than I have seen. The lawyer is not only alive, but hath been so these four thousand years; and I hope G – – will indulge his life as many yet to come. He hath not indeed confined himself to one profession, one religion, or one country; but when the first mean selfish creature appeared on the human stage, who made self the centre of the whole creation, would give himself no pain, incur no danger, advance no money, to assist or preserve his fellow-creatures; then was our lawyer born.[11]

Fielding continued this kind of study and, in the "bill of fare" to *Tom Jones*, in 1749, explained that "the provision then which we have here made is no other than *Human Nature*."[12] Historians, philosophers, artists, and novelists seemed to be obeying the poetical command of Dr. Johnson:

> Let Observation with extensive view,
> Survey mankind from China to Peru.[13]

Everybody seemed to be collaborating on a universal encyclopaedia of the science of man.

## 2.  LEGAL HISTORY IN SEARCH OF LAW IN GENERAL

In this imaginary encyclopaedia, it is not hard to define the chapters which were Blackstone's. That his study of the law was just another voyage in the quest for "man in general" is clear from the moment one picks up a copy of the *Commentaries*. In the first place, what Blackstone was writing was not an "Abridgement," an "Institutes," or simply a "Treatise." [14] He was writing a "Commentary," and "The Laws of England" were merely his text. From that text Blackstone was deriving generalizations about the nature of man, just as Hogarth had found them in "The Harlot's Progress," or as Gibbon was to derive them from the history of Rome. Indeed, he might not inappropriately have described his study, in the manner in which Adam Smith was later to define his own, as "An Inquiry into the Nature and Causes of the Laws of Nations, Illustrated from the Laws of England." For this main enterprise the particular laws of England were little more than examples. True, one should have "an accurate knowledge of our own municipal constitutions," but the center of interest was to be in "their original, reason, and history." And even more important than these in Blackstone's treatment of the law were "the general spirit of laws and principles of universal jurisprudence." [15] The laws of England were for Blackstone a body for studying the anatomy of laws in general.

This understanding of laws in general was to be sought in the *Commentaries* by studying the English law historically, an approach which before the eighteenth century had not been seriously undertaken. Now the awakening historical consciousness of the Enlightenment was beginning to show itself in legal scholarship. Although the first half of the seventeenth century had been, in Maitland's words, "the heroic age of English legal scholarship," [16] abounding in treatises and institutes of the law, historical works had been rare. With the exception of Bacon's unfinished *Reading on the Statute of Uses*, and Selden's *History of Tithes*, both works of limited scope, there had been no English legal history worthy of the name. Then in the late seventeenth and in the eighteenth century, came a sudden flowering; in this development, Blackstone was to have a crucial place. Sir Matthew Hale's *History of the Common Law of England* was first published in 1713. Though imperfect and fragmentary, it was the first essay at a history of the law as a whole.[17] So when Blackstone accepted the arrangement of Hale's *Analysis of the Civil Part of the Law* as "the most natural and scientifical of any, as well as the most comprehensive," he was adopting the technique of the most historically-minded of earlier English lawyers.[18] Hale, the first English legal historian, had most shaped Blackstone's general conception, and the *Commentaries* themselves were in turn the inspiration for John Reeves' *History of English Law.*[19] This work, published in 1783–84, was, next to Blackstone's, the most important work in legal history that the century produced. In the tradition of legal history then, as well as in the tradition of legal treatises, the *Commentaries* must be given a prominent place.[20]

But at the time when Blackstone was writing, these traditions were one; in law as elsewhere, history was the data of the science of human nature. The treatment of every subject in the *Commentaries* begins with an historical exposition. As he explains in the chapter on the feudal system, though "we may have occasion to search pretty highly into the antiquities of our English jurisprudence, yet surely no industrious student will imagine his time misemployed, when he is led to consider that the obsolete doctrines of our laws are frequently the foundation upon which what remains is erected; and that it is impracticable to comprehend many rules of the modern law, in a scholar-like, scientifical manner, without having recourse to the ancient. Nor will these researches be altogether void of rational entertainment as well as use: as in viewing the majestic ruins of Rome or Athens, of Balbec or Palmyra, it administers both pleasure and instruction to compare them with the draughts of the same edifices, in their pristine proportion and splendour." [21]

The development of the existing rules of law is given in detail: the history of ambassadors' rights, the story of the surveyors of the highways, the background of titles of nobility.[22] A full chapter is devoted to the feudal system, to make clearer the rules of land law, which are described according to their chronological changes.[23] Every crime is explained in the stages of its growth. "In the year 1650, when the ruling power found it for their interest to put on the semblance of a very extraordinary strictness and purity of morals, not only incest and wilful adultery were made capital crimes; but also the repeated act of keeping a brothel, or committing fornication, were (upon a second conviction) made felony without benefit of clergy. But at the restoration, when men, from an abhorrence of the hypocrisy of the late times, fell into a contrary extreme of licentiousness, it was not thought proper to renew a law of such unfashionable rigour. And these offences have been ever since left to the feeble coercion of the spiritual court, according to the rules of the canon law." [24] Blackstone shows himself most at home and most successful as an expositor in those branches of the law where he can give himself up to these historical problems. He is clearest and most effective in expounding the land law; weakest and most fragmentary in treating the law of commerce.[25]

That a rule is obsolete makes it to Blackstone none the less an example of the kind of laws man is capable of making; it is part of the Science of Man. "I have been unavoidably led to touch upon such obsolete and abstruse learning, as lies intermixed with, and alone can explain the reason of, those parts of the law which are now more generally in use. For, without contemplating the whole fabric together, it is impossible to form any clear idea of the meaning and connection of those disjointed parts which still form a considerable branch of the modern law." [26] As an example "it will be matter of curiosity to observe the great address and subtle contrivance of the ecclesiastics in eluding from time to time the laws in being, and the zeal with which successive parliaments have pursued them through all their finesses: how new remedies were still the parents of new evasions; till the legislature at last, though with difficulty, hath obtained a decisive victory." [27] Quaint and long-disused institutions are discussed with as much interest and detail as if they were still a part of daily practice. Here one reads of queen-gold, the king's aulnager, the king's right to a corody, the disused beer tax, and the old hearth-money.[28] Taxes new and old, in use and out of use are discussed side by side. A whole chapter tells the reader "Of the Ancient English Tenures." [29] Pages are given to discussing the minutiae of the hundred-court, the court of chivalry, and the forest courts.[30]

England's legal past becomes a treasury of material on the potentialities of man. One sees how the illiteracy of the Normans led to the use of wax seals on legal documents; and one can enjoy the spectacle of the "heroic madness of knight-errantry" in the ancient trial by battle.[31] The story of equity is a story of personalities and of the "reason and necessities of mankind"; here one must stop to admire the "pervading genius" of Sir Heneage Finch.[32] Sir Thomas More "puzzled a pragmatical professor in the university of Bruges" with his question "whether beasts of the plow, taken in *withernam* [out of the county or concealed], are incapable of being replevied." [33] No detail is irrelevant for Blackstone's study. In considering whether Sir Ralph Hengham's fine was spent for a clock-house at Westminster, it is interesting to note that " (whatever early instances may be found of the private exertion of mechanical genius in constructing horological machines) clocks came not into common use till a hundred years afterwards, about the end of the fourteenth century." [34] The detailed story of the effort of the Church of Rome to avoid its responsibilities to the state showed how "vain and ridiculous is the attempt to live in society, without acknowledging the obligations which it lays us under." [35] One should pause long enough to understand the noble character of Archbishop Chichele.[36] Equally interesting are the wanderings of those "outlandish persons calling themselves *Egyptians*, or *gypsies*." [37] Was all this a mere rag-bag of facts? It hardly seemed so to an age that believed with Bolingbroke, "Man is the subject of every history; and to know him well, we must see him and consider him, as history alone can present him to us, in every age, in every country, in every state, in life and in death. History therefore of all kinds, of civilized and uncivilized, of ancient and modern nations, in short all history, that descends to a sufficient detail of human actions and characters, is useful to bring us acquainted with our species, nay with ourselves." [38] England's past was, of course, not unique as the source of these "constant and universal principles of human nature." Every day since the Creation and every land from China to Peru had its lessons, if one would but seek them. And Blackstone did seek them.

Except for direct references to the law of Rome, the most frequent references to the laws of other countries and of other ages make use of the *Universal History*. In this characteristic by-product of the eighteenth-century quest for man in general, the numerous collaborators had set out to write a "General History of Mankind." The work, first published in the 1740's, was extraordinarily popular, and went through several editions in the course of the century. It had a long and distinguished list of subscribers, and was of such wide interest that, although it came to more than sixty volumes, it was at least three times pirated and several times translated before the second authorized edition had come from the press.[39] Gibbon himself admitted its decisive influence on him: "My indiscriminate appetite subsided by degrees in the *historic*

line: and since philosophy has exploded all innate ideas
and natural propensities, I must ascribe this choice to the
assiduous perusal of the Universal History, as the octavo
volumes successively appeared." [40]   The work itself rewards examination, as an eloquent expression of the purpose which the Enlightenment set for itself in its study of
the past. "History is, without all doubt," said the Preface,[41] "the most instructive and useful, as well as enter-
taining, part of all literature; more especially when it is
not confined within the narrow bounds of any particular
time or place, but extends to the transactions of all times
and nations." "From these . . . events occurring in history, every judicious reader may form prudent and unerr-
ing rules for the conduct of his life, both in a private and
public capacity." Every attempt was made to enable the
reader to reduce to a common denominator the experiences
of ancient and of modern history. Elaborate comparative
tables described the measures of length, weight, and coin-
age used in Scriptural times, in Greece, and in Rome.[42]
Life in America, Turkey, and China was described in
detail. Not only was there a general plan of Noah's Ark,
but with it a blueprint of its construction, with dimensions
translated into English feet.[43]   In this *Universal History*
the lessons of past and of present were made one; and here
was a treasure-house for Blackstone or any other student
of laws in general.

### 3.   FINDING LAW EVERYWHERE

It is not enough to say that the use of these materials
shows Blackstone's interest in comparative law. For to
the eighteenth-century student of history, and to Blackstone in particular, the study of comparative law was not
merely the study of comparisons. According to Blackstone
somewhere there existed a general principle of law, which
was the perfect form of any rule. This perfect form was

# IV.

## SCRIPTURE Measures of Length.

| | | | | | | | | Engl. | Feet. | Inch. Dec. |
|---|---|---|---|---|---|---|---|---|---|---|
| Digit | | | | | | | | | 0 — | 0,912 |
| 4 | Palm | | | | | | | | 0 — | 3,648 |
| 12 | 3 | Span | | | | | | | 0 — | 10,944 |
| 24 | 6 | 2 | Cubit | | | | | | 1 — | 9,888 |
| 96 | 24 | 8 | 4 | Fathom | | | | | 7 — | 3,552 |
| 144 | 36 | 12 | 6 | $1\frac{1}{2}$ | Ezekiel's Reed | | | | 10 — | 11,328 |
| 192 | 48 | 16 | 8 | 2 | $1\frac{1}{3}$ | Arabian Pole | | | 14 — | 7,104 |
| 1920 | 480 | 160 | 80 | 20 | $13\frac{1}{3}$ | 10 | Schœnus meaſ. line | | 145 — | 11,4 |

# V.

## The LONGER SCRIPTURE Measures.

Note, *The Eaſt uſed another* Span, *equal to* $\frac{1}{3}$ *of a* Cubit.

| | | | | | | Engl. Miles. | Paces. | Feet. Dec. |
|---|---|---|---|---|---|---|---|---|
| Cubit | | | | | | 0 — | 0 — | 1,824 |
| 400 | Stadium | | | | | 0 — | 145 — | 4,6 |
| 2000 | 5 | Sab. Day's Journey | | | | 0 — | 729 — | 3,0 |
| 4000 | 10 | 2 | Eaſtern Mile | | | 1 — | 403 — | 1,0 |
| 12000 | 30 | 6 | 3 | Paraſang | | 4 — | 153 — | 3,0 |
| 96000 | 240 | 48 | 24 | 8 | a Day's Journey | 33 — | 172 — | 4,0 |

merely exemplified and imperfectly reflected in any particular legal system. No one summed up the theory better than did Burke:

Mr. Hastings has no refuge here. Let him run from law to law; let him fly from the common law and the sacred institutions of the country in which he was born; let him fly from acts of parliament, from which his power originated. . . . Will he fly to the Mahomedan law? — that condemns him. Will he fly to the high magistracy of Asia to defend taking of presents? Pad Shâ and the sultan would condemn him to a cruel death. Will he fly to the sophis, to the laws of Persia, or to the practice of those monarchs? I cannot utter the pains, the tortures, that would be inflicted on him, if he were to govern there as he has done in a British province! Let him fly where he will, from law to law; — law (I thank God) meets him everywhere . . . I would as willingly have him tried by the law of the Koran, or the Institutes of Tamerlane, as on the common law or statute law of this kingdom.[44]

In the *Commentaries* we are taken "from law to law" and we meet law everywhere.

Certain uniformities, Blackstone says, are inevitable from the nature of society. "The original power of judicature, by the fundamental principles of society, is lodged in the society at large: but as it would be impracticable to render complete justice to every individual, by the people in their collective capacity, therefore every nation has committed that power to certain select magistrates, who with more ease and expedition can hear and determine complaints." [45] One can clearly perceive that "it is a principle of universal law, that the natural-born subject of one prince cannot by any act of his own, no, not by swearing allegiance to another, put off or discharge his natural allegiance to the former." [46] "The universal law of almost every nation (which is a kind of secondary law of nature) has either given the dying person a power of continuing his property, by disposing of his possession by will; or, in case he neglects to dispose of it, or is not permitted to make any disposition at all, the municipal law of the country then steps in." [47]

The most cursory observation of other legal systems will disclose other uniformities which are dictated by Reason herself. For instance, study of the Jewish law and of the laws of Rome shows the rule, that inheritance shall lineally descend to issue but shall never lineally ascend, to be "almost universally adopted by all nations; and it seems founded on a principle of natural reason." [48] The general structure of law courts is nearly everywhere the same — "the course of justice flowing in large streams from the king, as the fountain, to his superior courts of record; and being then subdivided into smaller channels, till the whole and every part of the kingdom were plentifully watered and refreshed. An institution that seems highly agreeable to the dictates of natural reason, as well as of more enlightened policy; being equally similar to that which prevailed in Mexico and Peru before they were discovered by the Spaniards, and that which was established in the Jewish republic by Moses." [49]

Nor are these broad similarities the only ones. Every institution of English law has an analogy in some other legal system, and Blackstone is quick to find it. Yet he is not particularly concerned with the ways in which legal systems affect each other. There are only occasional references to borrowings, and Blackstone fixes his attention not on these direct influences of one system on another, but rather on the similarities themselves. [50] The revenues of the ancient English queens reveal "a practice somewhat similar to that of the eastern countries." [51] The English rule of safe-conduct for merchants reminds one that "it was a maxim among the Goths and Swedes." [52] In view of a provision of the Petition of Right that no soldier shall be quartered on the subject without his consent, it is interesting that "thus in Poland no soldier can be quartered upon the gentry, the only freemen in that republic."[53] The English rule of liability for fire recalls the "similar principle" of the law of the Twelve Tables at Rome.[54] That a wife cannot be sued without her husband's being a defendant "was also the practice in the courts of Athens."[55] The introduction of the feudal tenures "at once, all over England, by the common consent of the nation," calls to mind that "Pharaoh thus acquired the dominion of all the lands in Egypt, and granted them out to the Egyptians."[56] The custom of borough-English finds an analogy in the ancient laws of Scotland and the present laws of the Tartars.[57] In examining the English definition of an heirloom, one should note that "a very similar notion . . . prevails in the duchy of Brabant."[58] It would be a mistake to suppose that the English rule, which punishes by death the bankrupt who fails to make full discovery, is unique, for a similar provision is made by the laws of Naples.[59] Even such a detail as the statutory penalty of 9 Geo. I, c. 22, for cutting down trees is not without a parallel. "In like manner by the Roman law to cut down trees, and especially vines, was punished in the same degree as robbery." [60]

Blackstone is concerned to show that even those institutions which the student is accustomed to think characteristic of England have analogues in other legal systems. Consider equity, for example. "This distinction between law and equity, as administered in different courts, is not at present known, nor seems to have ever been known, in any other country at any time: and yet the difference of one from the other, when administered by the same tribunal, was perfectly familiar to the Romans; the *jus prætorium*, or discretion of the prætor, being distinct from the *leges*, or standing laws." [61] "Thus, too, the parliament of Paris, the court of session in Scotland, and every other jurisdiction in Europe, of which we have any tolerable account, found all their decisions as well upon principles of equity as those of positive law." [62] One must take care to understand the essential parity of law and equity because "strangers are apt to be confounded by nominal distinctions, and the loose, unguarded expressions to be met with in the best of our writers; and thence to form erroneous ideas of the separate jurisdictions now existing in England." [63] Similarly with trusts. "*Uses* and *trusts* are in their original of a nature very similar, or rather exactly the same: answering more to the *fidei-commissum* than the *usus fructus* of the civil law." [64] A technical trust may be considered "a kind of *peculium*." [65] Forms of action are by no means peculiar to the English law. "The Romans introduced, pretty early, set forms for actions and suits in their law, after the examples of the Greeks. . . . And all the modern legislatures of Europe have found it expedient, from the same reasons, to fall into the same or a similar method." [66] The technicalities of English procedure all have counterparts in Roman Law.[67] "*Selecti judices* bore, in many respects, a remarkable resemblance to our juries," and not even the sacred English jury is unique.[68]

Between interest in analogy and argument by analogy the line is thin, and never obvious. Imperceptibly one passes from the "amusement and instruction" of noting a similarity in some other legal system, to the feeling that somehow the English rule is more authentic or defensible because of the similarity. The English rule seems then to have the respectability of conforming to the norms of the community of world legal systems. Or as Sir William Jones, a follower of Blackstone and a great admirer of his method, explained, "The great system of jurisprudence, like that of the Universe, consists of many subordinate systems, all of which are connected by nice links and beautiful dependencies; and each of them . . . is reducible to a few plain elements." [69] The ancient or foreign rule is first used to explain, and then to justify the English institution. The English policy of guardianship in socage "is warranted by the wise institutions of Solon." [70] With regard to canons of descent "the English law is not singular, but warranted by the examples of the Hebrew and Athenian laws, as stated by Selden, and Petit: though among the Greeks in the time of Hesiod, when a man died without wife or children, all his kindred (without any distinction) divided his estate among them. It is likewise warranted by the example of the Roman laws. . . . It is also conformable to the customary law of Normandy." [71] The English "defence, in its true legal sense, . . . is the *contestatio litis* of the civilians." [72] The study of pleading shows that these "pleas, replications, rejoinders, surrejoinders, rebutters, and sur-rebutters, answer to the *exceptio, replicatio, duplicatio, triplicatio*, and *quadruplicatio* of the Roman laws." [73]

The foreign example can "warrant" or "answer to" the English, because they are both illustrations of the natural rule. So great is this emphasis on the prototype that, even where the foreign counterpart differs from the English institution, Blackstone chooses to consider them not as different rules, but as manifestations of the same rule, which is in one system broadened or narrowed. Thus "'*Pater est quem nuptiae demonstrant,*' is the rule of the civil law; and this holds with the civilians, whether the nuptials happen before or after the birth of the child. With us in England the rule is narrowed, for the nuptials must be precedent to the birth." [74] "The prudent jealousy of our ancestors ordained, that no man of law should be judge of assize in his own county, . . . and a similar prohibition is found in the civil law, which has carried this principle so far that it is equivalent to the crime of sacrilege, for a man to be governor of the province in which he was born, or has any civil connexion." [75] "When I have once gained a rightful possession of any goods or chattels, either by a just occupancy or by a legal transfer, whoever,

either by fraud or force, dispossesses me of them, is guilty
of a transgression against the law of society, which is
a kind of secondary law of nature. . . . The wrongful
taking of goods being thus most clearly an injury, the next
consideration is, what remedy the law of England has
given for it." [76] The "finger of nature" [77] has pointed out
to man certain legal rules; and their validity is independent of acceptance by any age or country, being rooted in
the Nature of Man. Thus, "The *duties* of children to
their parents arise from a principle of natural justice and
retribution." [78] Property remains in a man "by the principles of universal law, till such time as he does some other
act which shows an intention to abandon it." [79] "For the
right of *meum* and *tuum*, or property in lands, being once
established, it follows as a necessary consequence, that
this right must be exclusive." [80] The laws of nature are,
thus, ineluctable principles; there is no way of escaping
their compulsive logic.

From the uniformity of man's nature and the constancy
of God's purpose arises the uniformity of the laws of
nature which makes relevant all information about the
past of English law and the analogous institutions of
ancient Rome and the distant kingdom of Whiddah. [81] It
would be impossible to conceive of a country or an epoch
whose experience could not illuminate these eternal, universal laws. Blackstone inevitably appealed to history.
But, it is important to notice that the very concept of the
uniformity of nature, and of the possibility of a science of
human nature, which stimulated him to this interest in
history led him to an attitude which seemed to ignore the
importance of time and place. Men like Blackstone were
interested in the past because its lessons were indistinguishable from those of the present. Past and present were
merged into Man as the single object of study.

### 4. A CONSERVATIVE NATURAL LAW

The notion of laws of human nature was just one aspect of the much broader concept of a universal law of nature. This larger concept, though also fashionable in the eighteenth century, had had a long and varied history. For the most part, this history had shown the attempt, in the changing vocabulary of different periods, to erect a system of law to which people could appeal against some already existing system. As Ritchie has stated it, "the special characteristic of the appeal to Nature is negation, antagonism; it is an appeal from what exists or from what is proposed, and has therefore at all times been a convenient form of criticism, rather than a good basis for construction." [82] Although Greek Sophists and Roman lawyers had used Natural Law for some constructive purposes, in more recent times, the tendency to employ the doctrine as a tool of criticism had become clearer. [83] Aquinas had used Nature as a court of appeal for "those whose consciences or whose political aspirations were offended by the positive law of their country." [84] For Grotius and Puffendorf the law of nature had been a supra-national authority for controlling the new nation-states. In the hands of Locke, the law of nature had served as the weapon for defending the English revolution. And only a few years after Blackstone wrote his lectures, the doctrine of a law of nature was to be employed in the cause of new revolutions by Rousseau, Paine, and Jefferson. Even Marx might find a place in the tradition of the appeal to Nature. [85]

Strange company for Blackstone, these champions and prophets of revolution. Gierke has described the dynamic tradition:

The natural-law theory of the State . . . served as a pioneer in preparing the transformation of human life; it forged the intellectual arms for the struggle of new social forces; it dis-

seminated ideas which, long before they even approached realization, found admittance into the thought of influential circles,
and became, in that way, the objects of practical effort. In
opposition to positive jurisprudence, which still continued to
show a Conservative trend, the natural-law theory of the State
was Radical to the very core of its being. Unhistorical in the
foundations on which it was built, it was also directed, in its
efforts and its results, not to the purpose of scientific explanation of the past, but to that of the exposition and justification
of a new future which was to be called into existence.[86]

Of what "new future" was Blackstone the prophet? That
the doctrine of Natural Law, as Blackstone stated it,
could be turned to fresh and vigorous uses, was shown
by the future which the *Commentaries* were to have in
America. But if Blackstone was the prophet of these uses,
he was himself unaware of the meaning of his prophecies.
He explained that "as man depends absolutely upon
his Maker for everything, it is necessary that he should,
in all points, conform to his Maker's will. This will of the
Maker is called the law of nature. For as God, when he
created matter, and endued it with a principle of mobil-
ity, established certain rules for the perpetual direction of
that motion, so, when he created man, and endued him
with freewill to conduct himself in all parts of life, he laid
down certain immutable laws of human nature, whereby
that freewill is in some degree regulated and restrained,
and gave him also the faculty of reason to discover the
purport of those laws." [87] "This law of nature, being
coeval with mankind, and dictated by God himself, is of
course superior in obligation to any other. It is binding
over all the globe, in all countries, and at all times: no
human laws are of any validity, if contrary to this; and
such of them as are valid derive all their force, and all
their authority, mediately or immediately, from this
original." [88] Here was as clear a statement of the doctrine
of natural law as one could want. And vigorous enough to

satisfy a Rousseau or a Jefferson. The argument did not differ significantly from that of some of the most influential books on the subject current in Blackstone's day. The general outline had come directly from Puffendorf, whose work on the *Law of Nature and of Nations*, is often cited in the *Commentaries*.[89]

As Blackstone applied this doctrine of natural law to the laws of England it seemed anything but a radical doctrine. Not only was it not used as an authority to which one could resort in an appeal against the existing legal system; on the contrary, it was actually the chief tool of rationalization. Frequently used as a way of subjecting institutions to the test of the critical faculties of the reasoning individual,[90] the concept of nature was for Blackstone a theory for shattering the self-confidence of individual reason, and limiting the range of possible criticism of the laws of England. According to Blackstone's theory the sphere within which man was free to create his own laws was indeed narrow, because the great outlines of the law had been prescribed by Nature. And on all issues of importance, man's laws represented simply an attempt to follow this outline. Man could create only where Nature had failed to declare, but by definition, Nature left no lacunae except in matters of indifference. "There are, it is true, a great number of indifferent points in which both the divine law and the natural leave a man at his own liberty, but which are found necessary, for the benefit of society, to be restrained within certain limits. And herein it is that human laws have their greatest force and efficacy; for, with regard to such points as are not indifferent, human laws are only declaratory of, and act in subordination to, the former." [91] Where human laws were not faithful copies of the law of nature, they were not bad laws, but were rather not laws at all.[92] Man's duty was to disobey the apparent law for the real law, which was the dictate of Nature.[93] Except on these minor "matters of indifference," man must use his reason not for the task of invention, but for discovery.[94] And to complain of what one discovered was like rebuking God.

Whether this theory would leave scope for fundamental criticism of existing legal institutions, depended on what one chose to define as the proper implements of discovery. If man's unfettered reason was entirely free to discover the laws of nature, there could be no assurance that the existing system of English laws would be found to accord fundamentally with the system of Nature. There was, however, a way of defining the mechanism of discovery that avoided dangerous scrutiny. And it was close at hand for Blackstone in his day.

For concern with the problem of theodicy, or the attempt to "justify the ways of God to man," in the late seventeenth and early eighteenth century had led to the construction of many theories to demonstrate the purposive perfection of the world. Everywhere were new brands of optimism. Leibniz, with metaphysical subtlety, developed his theory of the best of all possible worlds. Shaftesbury used the vocabulary of aesthetics.[95] Others, ancestors of the utilitarians, were evolving a theory to identify morality with self-interest. In his ingenious and ironical *Fable of the Bees*, Bernard de Mandeville showed more clearly than the rest how, by the pursuit of their own apparently selfish interests, men were led unwittingly to fulfil the great design of the Universe.[96] Pope's "Essay on Man" in 1733 presented a theodicy in readable form for the layman. One finds a vulgar version of this theory near the middle of the eighteenth century in the cynical prudence of Lord Chesterfield's letters to his son. In the course of these attempts to justify God's ways to man, there emerged the justification of man's ways to man. One of the most important products of the concern with theodicy, was this acceptance of man's selfishness not only as the principle on which men did act, but as the principle on which they ought to act. Through the later statements of Paley and Adam Smith, it was to find its place in the doctrines of utilitarianism and of laissez-faire. But the theory that the pursuit of self-interest was somehow bound up with the natural harmony of the world, had a peculiar usefulness for Blackstone. It was, in fact, the principal notion by which the doctrine of natural law was to be made safe and conservative. He used the current theodicy to limit the range within which man's reason should criticize existing institutions, and to show how restricted was man's right to appeal to Nature against the positive law.

Blackstone came to theodicy from this necessity of fettering man's faculties before they began to destroy where they ought only to admire. The concept of the Mystery of Law was, as we have seen, an essential complement to the concept of the Science of Law if reason was not to be allowed to ask embarrassing questions. Similarly, if the law of nature was not to provide an authority to which men could appeal against the established laws of England, one must find a way of proving the established laws of England fundamentally identical with the laws of nature. And it was by a theological argument that Blackstone established this identity.

True, when God had established the laws of nature, he had given man "the faculty of reason to discover the purport of those laws." [97] "But," the *Commentaries* explain, "if the discovery of these first principles of the law of nature depended only upon the due exertion of right reason, and could not otherwise be obtained than by a chain of metaphysical disquisitions, mankind would have wanted some inducement to have quickened their inquiries, and the greater part of the world would have rested content in mental indolence, and ignorance, its inseparable companion. As, therefore, the Creator is a being not only of infinite *power*, and *wisdom*, but also of infinite *goodness*, he has been pleased so to contrive the constitution and frame of humanity, that we should want no other prompter to inquire after and pursue the rule of right, but only our own self-love, that universal principle of action." [98] In the blind pursuit of their own interests, therefore, men stumbled along the path of natural law. The harmony of the world had come from the design of God and not from the intentions of men. Man, realizing that "his reason is corrupt, and his understanding full of ignorance and error," [99] must reach his knowledge of the laws of nature, through revelation, and through the dictates of his own self-love.

## 5. SELF-LOVE, HISTORY, AND GOD'S DESIGN

But where was the student to look for the definition of the specific laws of nature? Where did Blackstone himself look? Surely not to the vagaries of any "chain of metaphysical disquisitions"; certainly not to the fruits of abstract speculation. These would make man the dupe of his own feeble reason. And the wisdom of God had created the world so that man was not driven to reliance on such a weak resource. There was at hand, however, a guide to the laws of nature which was clear and reliable, — the laws of England.

By studying the existing institutions, and how they had come to be what they were, one could see declared with dramatic clarity the particular laws that man's self-love had led him to produce. These institutions might sometimes lack the attractive simplicity of the creations of doctrinaire reason. But they had the greater authenticity of being the actual creatures of man's pursuit of his own interest. Through continued use they had been shown not inconsistent with the practical demands of man's self-love. Careful study of the rules of English law would show how they were answers to man's needs, how they had served as the means for attacking obstacles to man's happiness. Was this not, after all, the surest sign that they were laws prescribed by Nature herself? Thus, for example, one could see that "when property came to be vested in individuals by the rights of occupancy, it became necessary for the peace of society, that this occupancy should be continued, not only in the present possessor, but in those persons to whom he should think proper to transfer it; which introduced the doctrine and practice of alienations, gifts and contracts. But these precautions would be very short and imperfect, if they were confined to the life only of the occupier; for then, upon his death, all his goods would again become common, and create an infinite variety of strife and confusion. The law of very many societies has therefore given to the proprietor a right of continuing his property after his death, in such persons as he shall name; and, in defect of such appointment or nomination, or where no nomination is permitted, the law of every society has directed the goods to be vested in certain particular individuals, exclusive of all other persons." [100] This kind of explanation, which could be repeated for nearly every rule of English law, was the best evidence to man's feeble faculties that here was a prescription of the law of nature.

The uniformity of human nature made it possible, moreover, to refer to other legal systems to find the rationale of the English rule. "Idleness in any person whatsoever is also a high offence against the public economy. In China it is a maxim, that if there be a man who does not work, or a woman that is idle, in the empire, somebody must suffer cold or hunger: the produce of the lands not being more than sufficient, with culture, to maintain the inhabitants: and therefore, though the idle person may shift off the want from himself, yet it must in the end fall somewhere. The court also of Areopagus at Athens punished idleness, and exerted a right of examining every citizen in what manner he spent his time. . . . The civil law expelled all sturdy vagrants from the city: and, in our own law," all idle persons and vagabonds are punished.[101]

Experience whether of China, Athens, or ancient England, was, after all, the best test of whether rules were designed to serve man's happiness. Only by the study of origins could one see the particular needs which existing rules had been made to serve. And, of course, this meant that the student's access to the laws of nature was as limited as the data of history. The student aware of these limitations would "at this distance of time" simply presume that the ancient rule would never have been introduced without a good reason.[102] The past was, then, the court of appeal for the institutions of the present; it alone had the answer to the question whether a present law had been designed to meet a need. Thus Blackstone invested what had been simply an expedient solution of a problem with the inevitability of an absolute prescription of Nature.

The identification of the principle of self-love with the law of nature also provided a convenient way of avoiding what otherwise might have been an embarrassing paradox. If the laws of nature were immutable and universal, how did it happen that the laws of states had changed, and yet the changes had not made the laws of these states contrary to the natural law? How did it happen that, although so many institutions seemed to be invented, yet the laws of nature could only be discovered? The answer of the *Commentaries* was clear. Invention and discovery, to a believer in the harmony of man's selfishness with the purpose of the Universe, were not separate processes. When, in the course of experience, the great men of England's past had been confronted with obstacles to their happiness and had devised means for overcoming them, they had devised what the law of nature had intended them to devise; they had, in other words, discovered by experience, what God himself had invented as the weapons against these obstacles.[103]

By showing how laws had been the creatures of environment, Blackstone further showed how inevitable were existing laws wherever or whenever they existed. "People are apt to be angry at the want of simplicity in our laws: they mistake variety for confusion, and complicated cases for contradictory. They bring us the examples of arbitrary governments, of Denmark, Muscovy, and Prussia; of wild and uncultivated nations, the savages of Africa and America; or of narrow domestic republics, in ancient Greece and modern Switzerland; and unreasonably require the same paucity of laws, the same conciseness of practice, in a nation of freemen, a polite and commercial people, and a populous extent of territory. . . . Again; were we a poor and naked people, as the savages of America are, strangers to science, to commerce, and the arts as well of convenience as of luxury, we might perhaps be content, as some of them are said to be, to refer all disputes to the next man we meet upon the road, and so put a short end to every controversy. For in a state of nature there is no room for municipal laws; and the nearer any nation approaches to that state the fewer they will have occasion for. When the people of Rome were little better than sturdy shepherds or herdsmen, all their laws were contained in ten or twelve tables; but as luxury, politeness, and dominion increased, the civil law increased in the same proportion; and swelled to that amazing bulk which it now occupies, though successively pruned and retrenched by the emperors Theodosius and Justinian. . . . In like manner we may lastly observe, that, in petty states and narrow territories, much fewer laws will suffice than in large ones, because there are fewer objects upon which the laws can operate. The regulations of a private family are short and well known; those of a prince's household are necessarily more various and diffuse." [104] Change and growth had been required by the very laws of nature. Dr. Johnson had written, in 1753, in Number 95 of *The Adventurer*:

Thus love is uniform, but courtship is perpetually varying: the different arts of gallantry, which beauty has inspired, would of themselves be sufficient to fill a volume; sometimes balls and serenades, sometimes tournaments and adventures, have been employed to melt the hearts of ladies, who in another century have been sensible of scarce any other merit than that of riches, and listened only to jointures and pin-money.

What Dr. Johnson wrote of love, Blackstone might have written of legal systems for, according to the *Commentaries*, Law is uniform, though legal systems are perpetually varying. But this was the inexorable change of time and the seasons. One could as reasonably complain of the complexity of the laws of a country of England's luxury, politeness, and dominion, as one could reproach the northern weather.[105]

The determinism which had made the legal system of any country, in God's design, the product partly of climate and of the stage of social development, also made it the product of its innate "spirit" or "genius." First there was, of course, the "genius" of the people themselves. For example, the oriental practice of accompanying petitions by presents to the officers of government was "calculated for the genius of despotic countries." [106] The "genius of the Roman people" had led them to treat merchants differently from the way they were treated in England.[107] The English county courts showed a "plan entirely agreeable to the constitution and genius of the nation." [108] Moreover, the legal system itself in each country contained an essence which sought expression. One could discover the "spirit" or "genius" of the law only by examining the law itself, yet somehow one could estimate how well particular rules expressed the essential nature of the law. The abolition of purgation and of the old method of trying contempts earned Blackstone's approval for its clear expression of the genius of English law.[109] The power of impressing seamen, if it resides anywhere in England, must, from the "spirit of our constitution" reside in the crown alone.[110] The genius of a people and the spirit of their laws, expressed in the time-tested rules of the legal tradition, were, of course, themselves the product of the laws of nature.[111]

Blackstone insists that the laws of nature are "binding over all the globe, in all countries, and at all times." [112] Much of the time it would seem that the laws of nature, like physical laws, could not be evaded. Thus, for instance, that "credulity and superstition will, in all ages and in all climates, produce the same or similar effects" explains the use of the "corsned" in early English trials.[113] Again, "There is an active principle in the human soul, that will ever be exerting its faculties to its utmost stretch, in whatever employment, by the accidents of time and place, the general plan of education, or the customs and manners of the age and country, it may happen to find itself engaged." [114] What praise, then, did the English law deserve for obeying rules which no legal system could disobey? Was it any more admirable for the laws of England to accord with the inevitable laws of human nature than it was for any man to obey the inevitable laws of gravitation? The answer to this question was for Blackstone not difficult. It was, in fact, the very inevitability of the laws of human nature that made the accordance of English laws with them so admirable. Where any apparently human institutions could be shown to have somehow a superhuman fixity and permanence, this was itself an object of wonder. The kind of feeling of awe which men have had for the ancient pyramids, or which has made some admiring critics call Shakespeare a "force of nature" was the feeling of Blackstone and his fellow-admirers of English laws. Here were institutions which man seemed to have created, and yet which had immanent in them the never-changing quality of God.

## 6. THE CONVENIENT AMBIGUITY OF THE LEGAL WORLD

Blackstone was also able to avoid the appearance of praising the inevitable by his use of an ambiguity which lurked in the very concept of Nature. To be sure, the writers of the great texts on natural law, and especially those on whom the *Commentaries* relied, had been careful to distinguish between the positive establishments of individual countries, and the admirable exhortations of Nature herself. As Puffendorf had explained, "That Notion of extracting the Law of Nature from the Manners and Customs of the World, is accompanied with this farther Inconvenience; that 'tis almost impossible to find any Nation, which is govern'd purely by Natural Law." [115] And in his Introduction to the *Commentaries*, Blackstone had made a similar distinction. Yet in his discussion of the laws of England themselves, he generally failed to distinguish between Nature meaning the world as it was and Nature meaning the world as it ought to be.

And for this confusion Blackstone had ample authority. Puffendorf had explained that "all Civil Laws do either presuppose or include the chief Heads of the Law of Nature, those by which the Safety of Mankind is secur'd: Neither are these in the least injur'd or impair'd by the particular Ordinances, which each Commonwealth finds a Necessity for superadding, for its separate Interest and Benefit." [116] But how was one to apply the distinction between laws natural and laws merely positive? The valid rules of both kinds were the rules that would serve the interests of men. For, in the words of Puffendorf, "there seems no way so directly leading to the Discovery of the

Law of Nature, as is the accurate Contemplation of our Natural Condition and Propensions"; since man's self-love is his strongest inclination, the foundation of all law is its tendency to man's preservation.[117] Any law even "positive" which is against the interest of society is thus by definition contrary to Nature. It was not possible, therefore, to distinguish between the actual institutions of society and the ideal requirements of Nature by the ends that they served. Both served the same end, which was man's happiness.

The science of human nature, as we have seen, insisted on the identification of English laws with the laws of nature. According to this notion, the laws of England were part of the data from which one derived natural laws. As one could discover what the laws of England were by examining the laws of nature, so one could discover the laws of nature from looking at the laws of England.[118] In all the rules of English law Blackstone therefore sought the principles of human nature, and it was not hard to find in every English institution an example of a natural rule. By this technique he made it seem as clear a part of Nature's design that murder should be a crime, as that the newborn swan should belong equally to the owner of the cock-swan and the owner of the hen-swan.[119]

But it would seem important finally to know whether "Nature" was simply the sum of everything one saw about him, or was the sum of all things good and desirable. Was natural law a set of descriptive or of prescriptive rules? In the *Commentaries*, it was at the same time both. The conflict between science and religion, between the desire to explain and the fear of demanding explanation, was resolved in the notion of natural law, not by making of natural law a coherent and consistent doctrine, but by allowing it to be two different things at once. Yet to Blackstone, who liked to identify the existing laws of England with laws as they always ought to be, this ambiguity was not a contradiction. Nature was at once things as they were and things as they ought to be. One had to study the rules of Nature to be certain that things as they were would not be allowed to deviate from the natural ideal. And this, despite the fact that everywhere and at all times the world was demonstrating that it was impossible for human action to deviate in the smallest measure from the rules of Nature.

The science of human nature, as we have seen, identified the characteristics of the legal system with the essential qualities of man's nature. The doctrine of natural law now equated all law that was really law with the inescapable design of the Universe. Here, clearly, the difference between law as description and law as prescription had vanished. The world as it was, the world as it ought to be, and the world as it must be, all became one world. And in that world Blackstone contemplated the laws of England.

## CHAPTER THREE

# THE TENDENCY
# OF HISTORY

## I. MAN'S PLACE IN LEGAL HISTORY

IT WAS EASY for Blackstone to talk about the laws of
nature without making clear whether he was discussing the past, the present, or the future; or, indeed,
whether he was simply describing an ideal condition
which had never been and could never be anywhere on
this earth. He imagined the law to exist in a timeless
realm where somehow the actual and the ideal were
merged in the conception of a beneficent Providence.
Such an attitude might seem to us today to destroy the
importance of chronology. It might seem to make im-
pertinent any attempt to break down the uniformity of
Man and the permanence of God into the daily accidents
of change. Yet in eighteenth-century England, the conceptions of natural law and of the science of human
nature did not destroy the problem of the tendency of
history; instead, they made that problem inescapable. If
history was philosophy teaching by examples, it must
have something to teach. The notion of natural law
which had made God the Master of history had made it
impossible for history to be a blind, amoral process. There
must be direction: one must be able, by the mere examination of the past, to ascertain moral values and describe change as a movement toward or away from those
values. Moreover, it was necessary to know the values

that might be realized in history, and whether they were tending to be realized. Man had to know whether the processes of time moved naturally toward the proper goal, and if they did not, he had to know whether he could do anything to encourage the desired movement.

The notion of natural law in the eighteenth century had connected the process of history with all man's values. And it was necessary to have some set of ideas which would enable man to satisfy both aspects of the conception of natural law: the idea of the law of nature as a prescriptive rule which man ought to try to obey; and the idea of the law of nature as a descriptive rule which man could not disobey if he tried. A simple dogma, which would insist that history showed man to be entirely free to bring his world into accord with the Divine plan, would have left to man's reason a dangerously large role; on the other hand, to assert that history showed that man had no freedom to affect the course of events, but was entirely ruled by a rigid Providence, might have destroyed a principal reason for studying history at all. Blackstone in fact tried to escape from this dilemma through a theory of the tendency of history that admitted in a limited way both the prescriptive and the descriptive notions of natural law.

This theory seems to rest on two apparently contrary axioms, which Blackstone used to complement each other. The first axiom stated the laws of nature to be rules which man was free to disobey, but which he must study in order that he might make the world more like its ideal. One form which this notion took in the eighteenth century — and a form used by Blackstone — was the doctrine of primitivism. This was the doctrine that in his original state of nature man was good and the world was good, and that he had degenerated into civilization. In the light of this first axiom, the purpose of the study of history was to enable man to discover and recover some of his lost innocence. The second axiom, on the contrary, stated history to be an inevitable process, obeying the laws of the God of nature, and leading man to a goal which no action of his own could prevent him from reaching. By this notion, man was not free to make himself either more, or less, blessed, but was forced with mechanical certainty to obey the rules set for him by his Creator. Beginning with the concept of a beneficent God, Blackstone, like many other men in the eighteenth century, described this axiom by the idea of progress. And since the movement of history had been determined by a wise Providence, the intervention of man's conscious purposes might interfere with progress, but could hardly hasten it.

Blackstone fitted together these two seemingly dissident axioms into a theory that justified English law as it was and warned man to be wary of rash attempts to reform it. Any attempt to change institutions was, by the notion of primitivism, restricted to the narrow sphere of man's attempting to recover some of his lost virtue. And since progress was one of Nature's inescapable laws, men were justified in the belief that if they simply did not meddle with institutions the result was certain to be good. But before we can understand the mosaic of these ideas, it is necessary to consider in turn the popular meaning both of primitivism and of progress, and to see in each case how the doctrine was applied in the *Commentaries* to the laws of England.

## 2. THE PRIMITIVE LAW AND MAN'S LOST INNOCENCE

Although the notion of primitivism had been current long before the seventeenth century,[1] the Enlightenment, in its quest for the laws of nature, found a particular significance in the study of man's primitive state. If one sought the key to man's behaviour at all times and in all places, where could one look with more profit than to man's earliest condition, before the accretions of civilization had created superficial differences between men? Modern scholars have classified the notions of primitivism of this period into "chronological primitivism" which described man's degeneration historically; and "cultural primitivism" which found the primeval virtues in the primitive and simple societies of all ages. However important this distinction may be for defining the attitudes of professional philosophers in the seventeenth and the eighteenth centuries, for most laymen, and certainly for Blackstone, the difference was an unimportant one.[2] For our purposes it is desirable to give the notion no greater precision than it seems to have in the *Commentaries*. We shall therefore deal with primitivism as the idea that the natural virtues of man and of society were clearest in man's primitive condition while we allow the word "primitive" to include the chronological-cultural ambiguity. As a seventeenth-century writer had explained:

Those Nations that have more of Art and Improvement amongst them, have so painted Natures face, have hung so many Jewels in her eare, have put so many bracelets upon her hand; they have cloth'd her in such soft and silken raiment, as that you cannot guesse at her so well, as you might have done, if she had nothing but her own simple and neglected beauty: you cannot taste the Wine so well, because they have put Sugar into it, and have brib'd your palate. So that the learned *Salmasius* will scarce go about to fetch the Law of Nature from the Jewes principally; you see he chooses to fetch it rather from a Scythian, from a Barbarian; there he shall see it without any glosses, without any Superstructures, without any carving and gilding.[3]

The conception of the law of nature seems to have had a sort of contagious ambiguity, and since men were using the search for the primitive as a way of discovering man's natural virtues, the distinctions between past and present, actual and ideal, were seldom clearly drawn.

The surest guide to every man's conduct came to be considered his "primitive," that is, his natural or direct reactions, wherever or however he might express them. Thus, there was no paradox in the Age of Reason turning for its example of virtue to the untutored savage. For every man's first and most direct feelings were his best mentor. As Shaftesbury wrote in 1709:

No sooner are actions viewed, no sooner the human affections and passions discerned . . . than straight an inward eye distinguishes, and sees the fair and shapely, the amiable and admirable, apart from the deformed, the foul, the odious, or the despicable. How is it possible, therefore, not to own "that as these distinctions have their foundation in Nature, the discernment itself is natural, and from Nature alone "? [4]

He might have added the question: Who should be better able to discern these distinctions than the man closest to Nature, that is, primitive man?

But in the eighteenth century, these philosophical grounds of interest in primitive man were not the only ones. While explorers eagerly searched the southern Pacific Ocean for the legendary *Terra Australis*, geography was a developing science. Lord Anson completed his famous voyage around the world in 1744, and just four years afterward his chaplain published its thrilling story. Within the next fifty years the many voyages of Captain Cook and others were to focus popular attention on the land of the savage.[5] Near the end of the period, Boswell summed up this growing interest, "The difference between the savage and the civilized state of man has been much considered of late years, since so many discoveries of distant regions and new nations have been made under his present majesty's patronage." [6] England was seeing primitive man in the flesh. Peter the Wild Boy, found in the woods near Hanover some years earlier, was in the mid-century still living in England. In 1768, Lord Monboddo

The Happiness of Primitive Man

made available to English readers the *Account of a Savage Girl* who had been discovered in the wilderness of Champagne. Captain Cartwright, in 1772, brought back from Labrador a family of five Eskimos to become the cynosure of London. Omai, the gentle South Sea Island savage, a trophy of Captain Cook's second voyage to the Pacific, was an even greater sensation; he was painted by Reynolds and became the darling of Lady Sandwich. It was easy to see, effete London had much to learn from him, as it had been learning from many other savage visitors during the eighteenth century.[7]

The American Indian provided abundant examples of the life of nature; men of letters used them until the Noble Savage became a familiar figure.[8] The old argument between the Ancients and the Moderns, which had been dramatized in the late seventeenth-century Battle of the Books, was restated now as the conflict between Simplicity and Luxury. Popular literature was full of the beauties of the simple life,[9] and Lord Monboddo and Rousseau provided philosophies to show what man had lost as he became civilized. In "The Bard," in 1757, Gray sought to recapture the eloquence and the imagination that "without respect of climates . . . reigns in all nascent societies of men, where the necessities of life force everyone to think and act much for himself."[10] The vogue of the ancient bard and eloquent savage grew. Macpherson and Chatterton sought fame by forging poems supposed to be the work of a simpler age. In 1765 Percy published his *Reliques of Ancient English Poetry*, and his was but one of many such collections. Goldsmith declared in 1770, in his introductory letter, that he had written "The Deserted Village" to "inveigh against the increase of our luxuries." On all sides, philosophers and poets were wistfully admiring the simple perfection of primitive life.

For the student of law, concerned with the past, and eager to find the essence of the laws of England, the doctrine of primitivism clearly had its uses. "The common law of England," wrote Blackstone, "has fared like other venerable edifices of antiquity, which rash and inexperienced workmen have ventured to new-dress and refine, with all the rage of modern improvement. Hence, frequently its symmetry has been destroyed, its proportions distorted, and its majestic simplicity exchanged for specious embellishments and fantastic novelties. For, to say the truth, almost all the perplexed questions, almost all the niceties, intricacies and delays (which have sometime disgraced the English, as well as other, courts of justice) owe their original not to the common law itself, but to innovations that have been made in it by acts of parliament." [11] Looking back to the times of ancient simplicity, one saw the institutions in their "pristine proportions and splendour." [12] Before "the various necessities of mankind" had induced judges to complicate the laws, one could have seen the "rigour and simplicity of the rules of the common law." [13] But there was a natural tendency for institutions to become corrupted. Examining the old county courts, one of the more remarkable features of the Saxon law, it was clear that "the decisions and proceedings therein were much more simple and unembarrassed; an advantage which will always attend the infancy of any laws, but wear off as they gradually advance to antiquity." [14] "In a nation of freemen, a polite and commercial people, and a populous extent of territory," there was a certain inevitable complexity not found among the institutions of "wild and uncultivated nations." [15]

Yet that pristine simplicity was not entirely beyond recall. The mere possibility of bringing English law a little more into accord with the ancient simple plan justified the study of history, and of the original pattern of the law. "This is a faithful sketch of the English juridical constitution, as designed by the masterly hands of our forefathers, of which the great original lines are still

strong and visible; and, if any of its minuter strokes are
by the length of time at all obscured or decayed, they may
still be with ease restored to their pristine vigour: and
that not so much by fanciful alterations and wild experiments (so frequent in this fertile age), as by closely ad-
hering to the wisdom of the ancient plan, concerted by
Alfred, and perfected by Edward I; and by attending to
the spirit, without neglecting the forms, of their excellent and venerable institutions." [16]  The history of English
law was, then, a story of how simple Saxon virtue had been
corrupted by Norman subtlety: "Statute after statute
has in later times been made, to pare off these troublesome excrescences [of Norman practitioners], and restore
the common law to its pristine simplicity and vigour; and
the endeavour has greatly succeeded: but still the scars
are deep and visible; and the liberality of our modern
courts of justice is frequently obliged to have recourse to
unaccountable fictions and circuities, in order to recover
that equitable and substantial justice, which for a long
time was totally buried under the narrow rules and fanciful niceties of metaphysical and Norman jurisprudence." [17]
The most precious ingredients in the common law, although they might seem to have been added at some later
time, were in fact the rediscovered remnants of the law's
original virtue. Thus, for example, "the liberties of Englishmen are not (as some arbitrary writers would represent
them) mere infringements of the king's prerogative, ex-
torted from our princes by taking advantage of their
weakness; but a restoration of that ancient constitution,
of which our ancestors had been defrauded by the art and
finesse of the Norman lawyers, rather than deprived by
the force of Norman arms." [18]  Trial by jury was one of the
most valuable relics of the primeval Saxon heritage, and
"to restore it to its ancient dignity, if at all impaired by
the different value of property, or otherwise deviated from
its first institution," was the duty of every Englishman.[19]

The modern law was merely a pale reflection of the magnificent original. And therefore, Blackstone found it necessary to warn the reader, "Nor have its faults been concealed from view, for faults it has, lest we should be tempted to think it of more than human structure; defects, chiefly arising from the decays of time, or the rage of unskilful improvements in later ages." [20] The excellence of that primitive structure was one of the chief reasons why the common law must command our reverence. Yet primeval times were so far in the past, and the pristine shape of the law had been so mangled by awkward attempts to remodel it, that the best one could do was to imagine the perfection that must have been. One had to try, for example, to see the feudal system as "what originally was a plan of simplicity and liberty," although in later times from it "the most refined and oppressive consequences were drawn" and "from this one foundation, in different countries of Europe, very different superstructures have been raised." [21] "So that the wise and equitable provision of the statute Westm. 2, 13 Edw. I, c. 24, for framing new writs when wanted, is almost rendered useless by the very great perfection of the ancient forms. And, indeed, I know not whether it is a greater credit to our laws to have such a provision contained in them, or not to have occasion, or at least very rarely, to use it." [22] This perfection was the Holy Grail of the legal historian.

Nostalgia for the ancient common law carried with it the conviction that every particular rule in the primitive system must have been founded in reason; in short, that "the wisdom of our ancient law determined nothing in vain." [23] Belief that the whole legal system was reducible to principles, the fundamental tenet of Blackstone's Science of Law, carried with it the primitivistic conviction that the original form of the legal system had been one of pure and rational simplicity. This helps explain the passage which we have already quoted, where the *Commen-*

*taries* declared, "Whenever a standing rule of law, of which the reason perhaps could not be remembered or discerned, hath been wantonly broken in upon by statutes or new resolutions, the wisdom of the rule hath in the end appeared from the inconveniences that have followed the innovation. The doctrine of the law then is this: that precedents and rules must be followed, unless flatly absurd or unjust: for though their reason be not obvious at first view, yet we owe such a deference to former times as not to suppose that they acted wholly without consideration." [24] The laws relating to the poor, for example, "notwithstanding the pains that have been taken about them . . . still remain very imperfect, and inadequate to the purposes they are designed for: a fate that has generally attended most of our statute laws, where they have not the foundation of the common law to build on." [25] On the other hand, when we examine the system of English courts, securely founded in ancient practice, "upon the whole, we cannot but admire the wise economy and admirable provision of our ancestors, in settling the distribution of justice in a method so well calculated for cheapness, expedition, and ease." [26] The earliest legal rules thus were the most effective.

And yet these provisions of the earliest common law could often be understood only by reference to the remarkable character of the Englishmen of those days. For instance, the earliest Englishmen had made the rule that "on every return-day in the term, the person summoned has three days of grace, beyond the day named in the writ, in which to make his appearance. . . . For our sturdy ancestors held it beneath the condition of a freeman to appear, or to do any other act, at the precise time appointed." [27] The conclusion was that "when, therefore, a body of laws, of so high antiquity as the English, is in general so clear and perspicuous, it argues deep wisdom and foresight in such as laid the foundations, and great care and circumspection, in such as have built the super-structure." [28] Every day Englishmen were profiting from the prescience of their forefathers.

The bungling efforts of modern Englishmen were responsible for the defects in daily practice. Thus, the "special plea" was "originally intended to apprise the court and the adverse party of the nature and circumstances of the defence, and to keep the law and the fact distinct." This was an excellent purpose, and the special plea would have been a good enough device had not the "science of special pleading" been "frequently perverted to the purposes of chicane and delay." As a result the old rules of pleading had to be changed.[29] There were "a few unworthy professors" of the law who practised chicane "and who to gratify the spleen, the dishonesty, and the wilfulness of their clients, may endeavour to screen the guilty, by an unwarrantable use of those means which were intended to protect the innocent." [30] Difficulties in early equity were due, not to any defect in the system, but to ignorance of the law, and to men's overpowering ambitions.[31] The primitive perfection of the law must therefore not be confused with the works of the men who were only partly willing or able to discover it.

Blackstone's primitivism therefore urged the return to the simplicity of the times before there had been much history; it advocated distrust of the accretions of time and experience, appealing from the present to the past. But there was another kind of appeal to the past which we find in the *Commentaries*, and which was crucial to the argument in favor of the existing English legal system. This was the doctrine of traditionalism. To be sure, traditionalism, like primitivism, appealed to the past. It appealed to the past because, in apparent contradiction to primitivism, it asserted that those very accretions of time and experience, confused though they might seem, contained the wisdom which man should seek to embody in law.

Blackstone, like Burke after him, was saying that institutions, from the mere fact that they had long existed, had some claim to reverence and to preservation. Conflicting though the notions of primitivism and traditionalism might appear to us today, the *Commentaries* passed easily from one to the other and, in fact, sometimes seemed to confuse them both into a single doctrine. By not insisting on the distinction between primitivism and traditionalism, Blackstone again discouraged modern man from wanting to change drastically the laws handed down to eighteenth-century Englishmen. The *Commentaries* insisted that "our admirable system of laws" had been "built upon the soundest foundations, and approved by the experience of ages." [32]   The sanction of Time was a mysterious and, in a sense, an aesthetic sanction. For England's system of remedial laws could be compared to "an old Gothic castle," full of much that was magnificent and venerable; [33] and, like all tradition, it deserved respect.

Indeed, all the virtues of tradition seemed to be inherent in the very definition of the English common law because, after all, the common law was rooted in custom. The definition of the common law as custom, at the same time that it allowed Blackstone to attribute to the law the virtues of those early times in which English law had originated, permitted him to find in the law the accumulated wisdom of all the ages since. And who would dare to set his private stock of wisdom against the accrued capital of wisdom of all the past? This double use of the concept of custom in the *Commentaries* to include the idea both of primitivism and of traditionalism was indicated by the description of "those ancient and invariable maxims '*quae relicta sunt et tradita.*'" [34] Maxims contained something of the earliest virtue of the law since they had been "*relicta*" by the earliest age; they deserved respect for being the accumulated experience that had been "*tradita*," handed down from century to century. "Custom, which is the life of the common law," derived much of its validity from the presumption in favour of the products of experience.[35] One should not be over-eager, for example, to change the jurisdiction of the spiritual courts because "should an alteration be attempted, great confusion would probably arise, in overturning long-established forms, and new-modelling a course of proceedings that has now prevailed for seven centuries."[36] Thus, despite the apparent conflict between the two ideas, Blackstone used traditionalism to complement primitivism in limiting man's freedom to change the law.

### 3. THE PROMISE OF LEGAL PROGRESS

But primitivism, even though tempered by some respect for tradition, might become a philosophy of reform, or, still worse, of revolution. Primitivism and reform had been old companions.[37] The development of the word "radical" from the Latin *radix* meaning "root" shows how closely associated are the ideas of primitivism and anti-conservatism. Many of the radical movements in Christianity had been those which appealed to the primitive church. And before the end of the eighteenth century, revolutionaries in America and France were to demand the rights which they conceived men to have had in their earliest condition. But it is difficult to draw revolutionary implications out of Blackstone's primitivism, because the *Commentaries* were careful to show that the attempt to improve the law was not merely dangerous but also, in a sense, futile.

Blackstone demonstrated this by showing that through all legal history there ran a mysterious purpose which was of its own force improving institutions. This Providence was, moreover, at once so mysterious and so powerful that in comparison men were bound to be either bungling or insignificant. The doctrine by which the *Commentaries* asserted this was a theory of progress. This was Black-stone's way of giving man optimism, and at the same time faith and quietism. The belief in the idea of progress which had in the seventeenth century sprung from man's new confidence in his reason, was, before the eighteenth century ended, to be used by Blackstone for the very purpose of discouraging men from exercising a critical reason upon institutions.

Before the eighteenth century, there had been no general acceptance in England of the possibility of the indefinite progress of civilization.[38] But in the flush of discovery of new powers of reason, the Enlightenment was unwilling to set a limit to the possibilities of the future. Writing soon after Blackstone, the radical Joseph Priestley explained what the consequences of the division of labour might be:

Nature, including both its materials and its laws, will be more at our command; men will make their situation in this world abundantly more easy and comfortable; they will probably prolong their existence in it and will grow daily more happy. . . . Thus, whatever was the beginning of the world, the end will be glorious and paradisiacal beyond what our imaginations can now conceive. Extravagant as some people may suppose these views to be, I think I could show them to be fairly suggested by the true theory of human nature and to arise from the natural course of human affairs.[39]

Even Gibbon, whose lifework was to record the decline of one of the greatest civilizations of the past, was careful to indicate that the moral of his story was not pessimism. "Yet the experience of four thousand years should enlarge our hopes, and diminish our apprehensions; we cannot determine to what height the human species may aspire in their advances towards perfection; but it may safely be presumed that no people, unless the face of Nature is changed, will relapse into their original barbarism."[40] Bravely refusing to be discouraged by the shattered fragments of the Roman Empire, he wrote, "Since the first discovery of the arts, war, commerce, and religious zeal have diffused, among the savages of the Old and New World, those inestimable gifts: they have been successively propagated; they can never be lost. We may therefore acquiesce in the pleasing conclusion that every age of the world has increased, and still increases, the real wealth, the happiness, the knowledge, and perhaps the virtue, of the human race." [41] Adam Smith, who in many ways expressed the assumptions of his day, writing before 1776, pointed to "the causes of improvement in the productive powers of labour" and showed how the principle of the division of labour, if extended, could produce a boundlessly expanding prosperity for mankind. So important was the conception of progress in his economics that he declared, "It is in the progressive state, while the society is advancing to the full acquisition rather than when it has acquired its full complement of riches, that the condition of the labouring poor, of the great body of the people, seems to be the happiest and the most comfortable. It is hard in the stationary, and miserable in the declining state. The progressive state is in reality the cheerful and the hearty state to all the different orders of the society. The stationary is dull; the declining melancholy." [42] According to this doctrine, progress was not merely the desirable movement toward a better condition; it was necessary if society was to continue as happy as it had been.

Yet the eighteenth-century theory of progress was not always simple. Many thinkers evolved their own doctrines to prove the promise of the future. Adam Ferguson, the pioneer sociologist, could not be satisfied with a naïve doctrine of inevitable and infinite perfectibility.[43] He could see history only as a cyclical process. Yet even he proposed an evolutionary theory which would justify optimism for the improvement of man's understanding, though no particular society could permanently embody the struggle toward that better state.[44] In his *History of Civil Society* in 1767, he wrote, "When nations succeed one another in the career of discoveries and inquiries the last is always the most knowing. Systems of science are gradually formed. The globe itself is traversed by degrees, and the history of every age, when past, is an accession of knowledge to those who succeed. The Romans were more knowing than the Greeks; and every scholar of modern Europe is, in this sense, more learned than the most accomplished person that ever bore either of those celebrated names." [45] "Destined to cultivate his own nature, or to mend his situation, man finds a continual subject of attention, ingenuity, and labour. . . . His faculties are strengthened by those very exercises in which he seems to forget himself. . . . He suits his means to the end he has in view, and, by multiplying contrivances, proceeds by degrees, to the perfection of his arts." [46] "The steps which lead to perfection are many and we are at a loss on whom to bestow the greatest share of our praise; on the first or on the last who may have borne a part in the progress." [47]

While philosophers were inventing new theories of progress, many popularizers were at work, and they were neither able nor willing to adapt their statements to the distinctions of philosophy.[48] Moreover, in the mid-eighteenth century, it was hardly necessary for the layman to be urged by metaphysics to believe in a doctrine of progress. Any man who was alert to the growth of science, the improvement of commerce, and the new techniques of agriculture would have had to invent a theory of progress for himself if there had not been philosophers to make one for him. And the eighteenth-century idea of progress, in its most popular form, was simply the notion that man, by the exercise of his reason, might continue to achieve indefinite improvements in his condition.

But, for Blackstone's purpose, this simple form of the idea was not quite satisfactory. As we shall see, the *Commentaries* insisted on showing that progress was not merely possible, but was inevitable. In this way, Blackstone employed the very doctrine that was being used by others as their principal argument for experiment and action, to encourage the student of English law confidently to place his faith in a self-moving Providence.[49]

For all that Blackstone had said about the degeneration of man into civilization, he now assumed an inevitable tendency toward the improvement of man's condition. Accordingly, he often chronicled English legal history as the mere story of the automatic improvement of institutions. To be sure, modern institutions might sometimes seem confused, but man's nature was complex and the life of an eighteenth-century Englishman was not the simple life of his brave Saxon ancestor. Belief in progress made Blackstone view the barbarous state of men who lived before the eighteenth century with pity, and sometimes with contempt. He called the thirteenth century "those days of bigotry." [50] He was tolerant of Coke because of the "pendantry and quaintness of the times he lived in."[51] The distinctions of the law of descent "were sufficient to puzzle the understandings of our brave, but unlettered ancestors."[52] He looked back on the "very early times, before our constitution arrived at its full perfection," and could understand the defects which English law had shown in "those rude and unlettered ages."[53] The strong anti-papist sentiment of his time provided Blackstone with another epithet of contempt for the past, which he called the "dark ages of monkish superstition and civil tyranny."[54] Thus, "oaths being of a sacred nature, the logic of those deluded ages concluded that they must be of ecclesiastical cognizance."[55] According to the *Commentaries*, "To keep the laity in the darkest ignorance, and to monopolize the little science, which then existed, entirely among the monkish clergy, were deep-rooted principles of papal policy."[56] To demonstrate the excellence of the current laws of heresy, he explained, "I only mean to illustrate the excellence of our present establishment, by looking back to former times."[57] More than one unfortunate and evil practice, like the ancient "corsned," had "sprung from a presumptuous abuse of revelation in the ages of dark superstition."[58]

To be sure, there had been no age in the past to equal Blackstone's "enlightened age." But how could one know that there would be no better era in the future? Indeed one could not. The very arguments which were used to prove that the present must be superior to the past, could be used to prove that the future must be superior to the present. Thus, as Blackstone wrote, "The advantages that might result to the science of the law itself, when a little more attended to in these seats of knowledge, perhaps, would be very considerable. The leisure and abilities of the learned in these retirements might either suggest expedients, or execute those dictated by wiser heads, for improving its method, retrenching its superfluities, and reconciling the little contrarieties which the practice of many centuries will necessarily create in any human system."[59] English lawyers might even in the course of time, following the example of their predecessors, develop new devices for fulfilling the ancient purposes of law. Although the Romans must be given "the honour of originally inventing" the corporation, "our laws have considerably refined and improved upon the invention, according to the usual genius of the English nation."[60] The history of benefit of clergy showed how "experience having shown that so very universal a lenity was frequently inconvenient, and an encouragement to commit the lower degrees of felony," the old rules had been altered by statute.[61]

And the history of every department of the law revealed this gradual improvement. "Thus the wager of law was

never permitted, but where the defendant bore a fair and
unreproachable character; and it also was confined to
such cases where a debt might be supposed to be discharged
or satisfaction made in private without any witnesses to
attest it: and many other prudential restrictions accompanied this indulgence. But at length it was considered,
that (even under all its restrictions) it threw too great a
temptation in the way of indigent or profligate men; and
therefore by degrees new remedies were devised, and new
forms of action were introduced, wherein no defendant is
at liberty to wage his law. So that now no plaintiff need
at all apprehend any danger from the hardiness of his
debtor's conscience, unless he voluntarily chooses to rely
on his adversary's veracity, by bringing an obsolete, instead of a modern action." [62] Advances seemed sometimes
to come from the invention of entirely new devices. The
action on an implied contract for a judgment debt "seems
to have been invented, when *real* actions were more in use
than at present, and damages were permitted to be re-
covered thereon; in order to have the benefit of a writ of
*capias* to take the defendant's body in execution for those
damages, which process was allowable in an action of
debt . . . but not in an action real." [63] The church, for
instance, "had the honour of inventing those fictitious
adjudications of right, which are since become the great
assurance of the kingdom, under the name of *common
recoveries.*" [64] Changes in the forms of legal institutions
were, in a sense, inevitable, since there was a vital force
in the common law which would not leave justice undone
and wrongs unrequited. And "all oppressions which may
happen to spring from any branch of the sovereign power,
must necessarily be out of the reach of any *stated rule* or
*express legal* provision; but, if ever they unfortunately
happen, the prudence of the times must provide new remedies upon new emergencies." [65] Changes had emerged
from "the nature of traditional laws in general; which,

being accommodated to the exigencies of the times, suffer by degrees insensible variations in practice." [66]

Still, progress had sometimes been halting; the accidents of history made some periods more progressive than others. From the time of Edward I to that of Henry VII "the civil wars and disputed titles to the crown gave no leisure for farther juridical improvement." [67] Edward I's thirteen years of reform had done more than many centuries since.[68] Because changes in the common law had been due to what "the humour or necessity of subsequent times hath occasioned," [69] it was not reasonable to expect that the rate of improvement should be constant.

In order to justify the Science of Law, however, Blackstone had to show that there was opportunity and hope for improvement even in his own time. And he took care to point out some of the areas where improvements could still be made. The English criminal law, for example, has "some particulars that seem to want revision and amendment." [70] "And if the whole of this plan [for penitentiary houses] be properly executed, and its defects be timely supplied, there is reason to hope that such a reformation may be effected in the lower classes of mankind, and such a gradual scale of punishment be affixed to all gradations of guilt, as may in time supersede the necessity of capital punishment, except for very atrocious crimes." [71] Since progress in the past had proceeded at an irregular rate, progress in the present and the future might not always go ahead at top speed. But these minor modifications of the theory of progress could not obscure the fundamental assumption on which Blackstone worked: the direction of development was inevitably towards a better form of law. So important was this axiom in Blackstone's scheme, that he closed the *Commentaries* with his chapter, "Of the Rise, Progress and Gradual Improvements of the Laws of England."

## 4. THE AUTOMATIC IMPROVEMENT OF
## THE LAW

The form which the *Commentaries* gave to the idea of progress left the social scientist no hope for an expanding role in shaping institutions. Blackstone held out to the student of law the unsatisfying certainty of being a powerless spectator of a happy story. For progress was automatic. "And here I cannot but again admire the wisdom of suffering time to bring to perfection new remedies, more easy and beneficial to the subject." [72] The fundamental maxims of the law "have been and are every day improving, and are now fraught with the accumulated wisdom of ages." [73] The doctrine of the inevitability of progress, once accepted, provided a convenient way to understand many otherwise inexplicable past changes in the common law.

To explain these changes one had merely to look for the improvement that any reasonable man at the time would have desired. And where the materials of history were scanty, one could speculate on what kind of evil the new rule had been made to remedy. The interpretation of the past might thus become a quest for the true and good reasons which one could be certain had existed. "And perhaps the true reason why these [beasts of the plough] and the tools of a man's trade were privileged at the common law, was because the distress was then merely intended to compel the payment of the rent, and not as a satisfaction for its non-payment: and therefore, to deprive the party of the instruments and means of paying it, would counteract the very end of the distress." [74] To understand why the law came to be less lenient to the man who killed in self-defence one could also conjecture: "The law besides may have a farther view, to make the crime of homicide more odious, and to caution men how they venture to kill another upon their own private judgment." [75] The past thus showed the changes in law to be rooted in the changing needs of man.

This was well enough for the past, but what of the future? Did this not imply that there still remained a freedom to change the law whenever a good reason seemed to exist? Blackstone was careful to avoid this implication. Because progress was inevitable, it was all the more important that the student of the law should not meddle with institutions lest by his meddling he somehow disturb the beneficent processes of an all-wise Providence. "But, as these formal and orderly parts [of a deed] are calculated to convey that meaning in the clearest, distinctest, and most effectual manner, and have been well considered and settled by the wisdom of successive ages, it is prudent not to depart from them without good reason or urgent national necessity." [76] As one surveyed the history of English law, one saw how the innovations had resulted in "improving the texture and wisdom of the whole by the accumulated wisdom of divers particular countries." [77] "Though upon comparison we plainly discern the alteration of the law from what it was five hundred years ago, yet it is impossible to define the precise period in which that alteration accrued, any more than we can discern the changes of a bed of a river, which varies its shores by continual decreases and alluvions." [78] The student thus had to feel humble and reverent toward the tendency of history, for that tendency was no less a part of the laws of nature than was the prohibition of murder. Though he might be sincere in his desire to hasten progress, man had to be aware that he was treading sacred ground and had better leave the laws of nature and of history to work themselves out.

These laws of history had many aspects which to the modern reader might seem contradictory. But their context in the *Commentaries* fitted them together into a defence of the English legal system. Primitivism served the need for a doctrine to justify man's active attempt to improve his condition; but limited by traditionalism, it was prevented from becoming a dangerously radical doctrine. By thus defining the sphere of man's reason as the realm of reducing the evils which man had brought upon himself, Blackstone limited man's ability and discouraged his desire to make drastic changes. On the other hand, man was not doomed to the pessimistic belief that his institutions were every day becoming worse. Man's hope lay in the very fact that, despite his bungling weakness, a beneficent God had ordered the world and had made somehow, an inevitable progress. Optimism and quietism were introduced together, and in the *Commentaries* they were inseparable.

Blackstone's discussion of the tendency of history had, however, revealed some of the formal qualities which he thought were admirable, and which he wished the reader to think admirable in English law. The law, as he was to show, retained even in its modern form something of the orderly and natural simplicity which had been characteristic of man's primitive condition. And modern English law revealed how the primitive simplicity of nature had been improved by the nice arrangements of art. But the appeal of these ideas to the eighteenth-century lawyer was, of course, affected by the current notions of aesthetics.

# CHAPTER FOUR

# THE USE OF AESTHETICS

## I. THE AESTHETIC APPEAL IN NATURE

THE STARTING POINT of aesthetics for Blackstone's eighteenth-century reader was, as might have been expected, the concept of nature. Only by beginning with a study of the laws of nature could one ever discover the laws of aesthetics. Nature herself contained the rules of art; and as the God of nature had made the world wisely, it was inconceivable that he should not have made it beautifully. Thus, Alexander Pope wrote in his "Essay on Criticism":

> First follow Nature, and your judgment frame
> By her just standard, which is still the same;
> Unerring NATURE, still divinely bright,
> One clear, unchang'd and universal light,
> Life, force, and beauty, must to all impart,
> At once the source, and end, and test of Art.[1]
> Those RULES of old, discover'd, not devis'd,
> Are Nature still, but Nature methodiz'd;
> Nature, like Liberty, is but restrain'd
> By the same Laws which first herself ordain'd.[2]

Since the laws of England, according to Blackstone, so clearly and inevitably expressed the laws of nature, it was not surprising that the reader of the *Commentaries* should see described in the English legal system everything that was aesthetically satisfactory.

But the ambiguity of the concept of nature affected also the notions of aesthetics which one was to derive from nature. The eighteenth-century mind often seemed undecided whether the rules of aesthetics were God's prescription for making the world beautiful, or merely a description of how everything in the world was naturally already in some sense beautiful. Hogarth, for example, in his *Analysis of Beauty* in 1753, used his notion of the "S" curve to describe the combination of order and disorder that one found in nature and that the true artist must try to imitate.[3] In describing Harrison's recently invented clock, he declared:

But in Nature's machines how wonderfully do we see beauty and use go hand in hand. Had a machine for this purpose been Nature's work, the whole and every part might have had exquisite beauty of form without danger of destroying the exquisiteness of its motion, even as if ornament had been the sole aim, its movement too might have been graceful, without one superfluous tittle added for either of these lovely purposes . . . this is that curious difference between the fitness of Nature's machines (one of which is man) and those made by mortal hands.[4]

In 1759, Burke too, sought materials for his aesthetic in the study of nature.

Yet if aesthetic theory in the eighteenth century was to leave any scope for man's creative efforts, it had to assume that the laws of aesthetics were prescriptive as well as descriptive, and that, somehow, by following them man could increase the quantity of beauty in the world. Some writers emphasized this aspect of aesthetics by saying that the world of nature which man found around him on this earth was not in fact as aesthetically attractive as it might be. A writer whose works were popular in England until near the end of the eighteenth century had clearly pointed out this fact. Writing in his *Sacred Theory of the Earth* in

1684, Thomas Burnet had said, "If the sea had been drawn round the earth in regular figures and borders, it might have been a great beauty to our globe."[5] The stars, too, might have been better arranged, for "they lie carelessly scattered, as if they had been sown in Heaven like seed in handfuls and not by a skillful hand neither." The effect would have been much more beautiful "if they had been placed in rank and order, if they had been all disposed into regular figures, and the little ones set with due regard to the greater; then all finished and made up into one fair piece or great composition according to the rules of art and symmetry." [6] But why was the world not to be found in this excellent condition? The explanation was not difficult. As "it would have cost no more to have made things in better order, nay, it would have been more easy and more simple," the earth must have been originally created in fine proportion, but its present irregularities must have been due to man's wickedness and the ensuing wrath of God.[7]

Still, man was not compelled to leave disorder in the world. One of his rational attributes was his ability somehow to discover in nature the rules which ought to be obeyed. And the eighteenth century, in its quest for the laws of nature, thus sought the laws of beauty. To discover the kind of aesthetic qualities which the eighteenth-century mind might have found in Blackstone's description of the English legal system it is necessary to define, in a general way, the popular notions of aesthetics. We should carefully preserve the "natural" ambiguity in the laws of aesthetics, and must avoid giving the ideas greater precision than they would have had to the ordinary reader. Whatever the nice distinctions of the professional writers on the subject, we will be concerned only with the main concepts which appear to have been current. For these ideas, however, we will not be able to go to a specialized literature of "aesthetics." Aesthetics as a separate study was only beginning to develop in the eighteenth century. Dr. Johnson's *Dictionary* did not contain "aesthetics," and apparently the word was not in general use until near the middle of the nineteenth century.[8] Nevertheless the leading aesthetic ideas of Blackstone's time can be discovered by the inductive method of examining artistic taste, and by making use of a few of the numerous contemporary treatises on rhetoric. Although "rhetoric" was defined by Dr. Johnson as "the act of speaking not merely with propriety, but with art and elegance," the study of the subject amounted to more than this, and it actually was one of the principal rubrics under which people discussed aesthetic problems.

In the eighteenth century, the search for the laws of aesthetics expressed the new-found confidence of the Enlightenment, and writers justified their work by defending man's new rational instruments. As Thomas Sheridan wrote in his *Lectures on Elocution* in 1762, "Is it not amazing to reflect, that from the creation of the world, there was no part of the human mind clearly delineated, till within the last sixty years? when Mr. Locke arose, to give us a just view, of one part of our internal frame, 'the understanding,' upon principles of philosophy founded on reason and experience." [9] And many of the English writers of the eighteenth century, by appealing to experience, arrived at a bold distinction that was to be central in the discussion of aesthetics.

This central distinction was sharply described in 1759 in Edmund Burke's *Inquiry into the Origin of our Ideas of the Sublime and the Beautiful*. "Sublime objects are vast in their dimensions, beautiful ones comparatively small: beauty should be smooth and polished; the great, rugged and negligent. . . . Beauty should not be obscure; the great ought to be dark and gloomy: beauty should be light and delicate; the great ought to be solid, and even massive." [10] Though the subtleties of Burke's psychology were not generally accepted, the popular mind did seize upon the easy distinction between "sublimity" and "beauty." James Beattie, writing later in the century, summed up this attitude when he insisted that the sublime and the beautiful "both indeed give delight; but the gratification we derive from the one is different from that which accompanies the other." [11] The difference was explained by Hugh Blair in 1783 when he said in his *Lectures on Rhetoric and Belles Lettres:*

Beauty, next to Sublimity, affords, beyond doubt, the highest pleasure to the imagination. The emotion which it raises, is very distinguishable from that of Sublimity. It is of a calmer kind; more gentle and soothing; does not elevate the mind so much, but produces an agreeable serenity. Sublimity raises a feeling, too violent, as I showed, to be lasting; the pleasure arising from Beauty admits of longer continuance.[12]

In the popular vocabulary, "beauty" represented the attempt to recover some of the orderliness that must have existed originally in God's plan for the Universe. Thus the neo-classic order of Christopher Wren's Cathedral, and the strait heroic couplets of Dryden and Pope embodied the rational aspirations of the Enlightenment. In the early eighteenth century, the notion of order and intelligibility as the touchstones of "beauty" was current. Although Pope had died in 1744, the cult of order certainly did not die with him. The English countryside everywhere bore signs of this notion of "beauty." Burnet's plan for the cosmos was reproduced, in small, in the English country garden. Vauxhall was divided into oblong groves by straight walks intersecting at right angles. A rotunda at Ranelagh, opened in 1742, had a still more formal setting, the octagonal basin marking the axes of a symmetrical and monotonous design.[13] Art showed the neatness and order which illustrated the neo-classic equation of proportion and beauty.

"Sublimity" was also an easily comprehended idea. Drawing on Longinus, who had found the source of elevated language in "the power of forming great conceptions" and "vehement and inspired passion," [14] men attributed to the sublime the power of inspiring awe. When man felt overpowered, and saw an object greater than himself, this was likely to be the sublime. Buffon in France was saying that "the sublime is to be found only in lofty subjects"; [15] and Blair in England declared, "All vastness produces the impression of sublimity," [16] and explained, "A great mass of rocks, thrown together by the hand of nature with wildness and confusion, strike the mind with more grandeur, than if they had been adjusted to one another with the most accurate symmetry." Significantly, the most common examples of sublimity were drawn from the works of Nature herself. Burke and Lord Kames, like many others, also had described the beautiful as the small, the neat, and the comprehensible; the sublime as the large, the disordered, and the awe-inspiring.[17]

Of course the greatest works of art would combine both of these qualities, the neat intelligibility of beauty and the vast awesomeness of sublimity. Since the artist was to imitate nature, he must naturally attain as best he could all the qualities of nature. In many of the works of the mid-eighteenth century, artists tried to embody both of these qualities. Thomas Gray used the neo-classic elegy to describe the primitive virtues of an ancient bard; Goldsmith employed the artifices of the couplet in depicting the rude charm of country life. Even before Ranelagh had been built, many gardens showed an affected naturalism. Men were trying to reveal the "sublimity" of nature by using the neat devices of "beauty." [18]

Since the works of nature were supposed to embody the qualities both of "sublimity" and of "beauty," it was inevitable that the English legal system, itself derived from the law of nature, should illustrate these qualities.

When the *Commentaries* showed the close accord of English laws with the laws of nature, they were thus simultaneously proving to the eighteenth-century mind that English law had the aesthetic virtues of nature. And the converse of this also seemed true: if the English legal system could be shown to be at once "beautiful" and "sublime," this would reënforce the presumption that these institutions were part of Nature's scheme.

## 2. THE ORDERLY BEAUTY OF THE LAW

In describing how the prevalent assumptions of aesthetics affected the meaning of the *Commentaries*, it is important at the outset to understand that we are not talking about any conscious purpose on Blackstone's part to employ the aesthetic vocabulary of his day in rationalizing English law. We will, rather, consider Blackstone's work from the point of view of an eighteenth-century reader to see what kind of aesthetic appeal the legal system as described in the *Commentaries* might have had for him. Blackstone did, of course, intend his description of English law to persuade the reader of its excellence. And his graceful and sometimes eloquent style, already amply illustrated by our quotations, was certain to have some effect on the reader. Perhaps Blackstone actually was in some instances consciously employing the assumptions of his day to make the legal system appear aesthetically attractive, and hence more acceptable to his reader. But we are not mainly concerned with this question; we are interested, rather, in ascertaining the meaning of the *Commentaries* in his time.

Some of the qualities, like simplicity and symmetry and awesomeness, which the *Commentaries* persuasively described, were in a sense merely the qualities which men have always found aesthetically appealing. It is no part of our purpose to demonstrate that these ideas were unique to the eighteenth century. We will, however, want to see how some of these universally appealing qualities were described in the eighteenth century, and how English institutions, as they were described in the *Commentaries*, appealed aesthetically to a reader of the time.

To find the qualities of the "beautiful" in the English law which Blackstone described was surely not difficult. For in the first place, Nature had created unity and reduced the whole of the legal system to one simple principle. A beneficent Providence, by having "so inseparably interwoven the laws of eternal justice with the happiness of each individual, . . . has not perplexed the law of nature with a multitude of abstracted rules . . . but has graciously reduced the rule of obedience to this one paternal precept, 'that man should pursue his own true and substantial happiness.'" [19] Since simplicity was the first quality of God's plan for the world, it would be blasphemy — no less than impugning the competence of the Creator — to deny such a quality to the laws of England. The general arrangement of the *Commentaries* made clear this quality of simple order. Blackstone had complained that "Fitz-Herbert and Brooke, and the subsequent authors of abridgements, have chosen a method, the least adapted of any to convey the rudiments of a science, namely, that of the alphabet." [20] The order of the alphabet seemed to Blackstone to be complex and artificial; he chose rather to arrange the common law according to the simple and symmetrical order which seemed to inhere in the nature of the law itself. Hence, he divided his work into four books remarkably equal in length.[21] The first two books contained "Rights"; the second two books contained "Wrongs," because "the primary and principal objects of the law are RIGHTS, and WRONGS. In prosecution, therefore, of these commentaries, I shall follow this very simple and obvious division; and shall, in the first place, consider the *rights* that are commanded, and secondly the *wrongs* that are forbidden, by the laws of England." [22] Not only did this division have the attractiveness of duality; it also had the appeal of unity. Right and wrong were the obverse and reverse of a single concept: it was impossible to conceive a right without a wrong, and vice versa.[23] Within each half of the *Commentaries* there was also a symmetry. In the first two books "Persons" were balanced against "Things"; in the second two books "Private" wrongs were balanced against "Public." [24] This "natural order," this charm of simple symmetry in English law as a whole was, moreover, to be found equally in the examination of any part. Since Blackstone had defined his work as the "task of examining the great outlines of the English law, and tracing them up to their principles,"[25] he had assumed some kind of unity.

But Blackstone often found a further, more complex harmony, the beauty of a pattern of numbers. Where others might have seen confusion, Blackstone artfully revealed a numerical simplicity. "Children are of two sorts; legitimate, and spurious or bastards, each of which we shall consider in their order." [26] "The people . . . are divisible into two kinds; the clergy and laity." [27] "The queen of England is either queen *regent*, queen *consort*, or queen *dowager*." [28] "The three great relations in private life are, 1. That of *master and servant*; which is founded in convenience. . . . 2. That of *husband and wife*; which is founded in nature, but modified by civil society. . . . 3. That of *parent and child*, which is consequential to that of marriage, being its principal end and design. . . . But, since the parents . . . may be snatched away by death before they have completed their duty, the law has therefore provided a fourth relation; 4. That of *guardian and ward*, which is a kind of artificial parentage, in order to supply the deficiency, whenever it happens, of the natural. Of all these relations in their order." [29] Many departments which to the uninitiated might have seemed chaotic were thus reduced to order by the simple expedient of subdividing them into numbered classes. To have said that there were "many" crimes would have made this branch of the law seem a mere miscellany; but Blackstone said that there were *five* kinds. By defining the fifth "species of offence" as "those against the public *police* or *economy*," Blackstone gave the whole criminal law an appearance of simplicity, although, as he explained, "this head of offences must therefore be very miscellaneous, as it comprises all such crimes as especially affect public society, and are not comprehended under any of the four preceding species." [30] "Miscellaneous," indeed! It included such topics as the laws concerning unwholesome provisions, the crime of bigamy, and the statutes against gypsies.[31] It was also possible to subdivide ouster of the freehold into five methods by making the fifth a residuary class.[32] Enumeration, a useful tool for all sciences, in Blackstone's hands demonstrated the clear simplicity of English law.

Institutions which did not fit into one class or another were not allowed to disturb the symmetry of the whole. They were explained, rather, as partaking of the qualities of several classes. Thus Blackstone described the estate of a "tenant in tail after possibility of issue extinct" as "of an amphibious nature, partaking partly of an estate-tail, and partly of an estate for life." [33] Chattels real were "of a mongrel, amphibious nature, originally endowed with one only of the characteristics of each species of things; the immobility of things real, and the precarious duration of things personal." [34] In this manner any rules which might have appeared to confuse the neat system were themselves used in the *Commentaries* to give greater sharpness to the divisions already made; for in calling a rule "amphibious" one presupposed two clear types of which the rule was a mixture.[35]

In addition to the ordinary device of number, the *Commentaries* enlisted the vocabulary of Roman law, — even

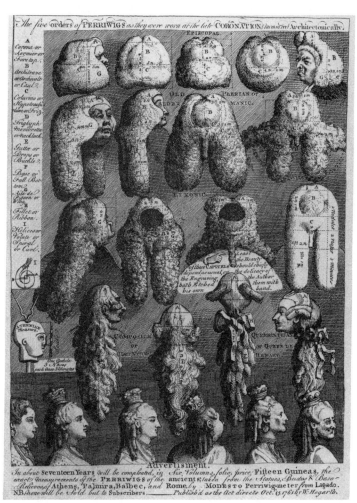

HOGARTH ON THE ART OF CLASSIFICATION

for those parts of the law which were most peculiarly English. "Valuable considerations" in English law were classified under the four species into which they were divided by the civilians, although these species had no organic relation to the English rules.[36] A qualified property in creatures *ferae naturae* may be obtained "either *per industriam, propter impotentiam,* or *propter privilegium."* [37] The Roman simplicity confirmed the English.

This orderly beauty was revealed not merely by coordinate classifications, but also by a hierarchical arrangement of legal rules. The distinctness of the stages between "lowest" and "highest" was witness to the neat attractiveness of the rules of English law.[38] Thus, because the civil courts had a "gradual subordination to each other," Blackstone began by describing the lowest and gradually ascended to the highest.[39] Titles to property were arranged according to the steps toward perfection of title; therefore he could say that where the tenant had an apparent right of possession, his title was "advanced one step nearer to perfection." [40] Blackstone explained that "surrender is the falling of a less estate into a greater." [41] In treason and trespass there were no accessories but only principals, "the same rule holding with regard to the highest and lowest offences, though upon different reasons. In treason all are principals, *propter odium delicti*; in trespass all are principals, because the law, *quae de minimis non curat,* does not descend to distinguish the different shades of guilt in petty misdemeanors." [42] Some crimes and misdemeanors were "either too high or too low to be included within the benefit of clergy." [43]

But neat, coördinate classes and sharply ascending stages were not the only qualities of beauty in a doctrinal system. As important as these was fitness, the suitability of an epithet or rule to the object to which it was being applied. The common law, to be sure, had the pervading appropriateness to man's nature which was to be found in

all God's handiwork: this was the suitability of a reasonable system to the creatures of a rational God. And Blackstone was quick to discover fitness in every part of the law.
He observed "the foundation and justice of forfeitures for
*crimes and misdemeanors*, and the several degrees of those
forfeitures proportioned to the several offences." [44] Retaliation was a less fitting punishment for crimes of
commission than for crimes of intention.[45] As "it is impossible that government can be maintained without a due
subordination of rank," [46] the common law proportioned
the legal rules to the deserts of each stage in the social
scale. There were many other ways of showing this fitness
of legal consequence to fact. Thus, conditional feuds were
"strictly agreeable to the nature of feuds." [47] Everywhere
in the law there was a natural and proportionate fitness.

The beautiful simplicity of the common law was further
demonstrated by Blackstone's frequent use of the maxim
for stating a legal rule. "When a vicar is instituted, he
. . . takes, if required by the bishop, an oath of perpetual
residence; for the maxim of law is, that *vicarius non habet
vicarium*." [48] "If an innkeeper's servants rob his guests,
the master is bound to restitution: for as there is a confidence reposed in him, that he will take care to provide
honest servants, his negligence is a kind of implied consent
to the robbery; *nam qui non prohibet, cum prohibere possit,
jubet*." [49] Sometimes in Latin, sometimes in English, the
maxim always helped reduce a chaos of particular examples
to the simple order of a terse and obvious rule. It served
the purpose for the student of the law that the heroic
couplet served for the writer of poetry. Both showed the
materials cast in sharp simplicity.

Related to the concepts of order and simplicity in the
eighteenth century was the concept of balance. The
equilibrium of neo-classic architecture and of Gibbon's
sentences had its counterpart in every structure that the
period called beautiful. Physics coöperated with aesthe-

tics to encourage the use of balance in describing institutions. It has been suggested that "the curve of acceptance of the theory of balanced government in England corresponds to the curve of acceptance of classical, system-building, *a priori* thought. For however much the government in the seventeenth and eighteenth centuries may have approximated a government of equal, balanced estates, the terms used to justify it were taken from the realm of mathematics and physics." [50] Montesquieu, to whom the *Commentaries* frequently referred, had shown the balance of forces in the English constitution. [51] Blackstone himself explained that "like three distinct powers in mechanics, they [Crown, Lords, and Commons] jointly impel the machine of government in a direction different from what either, acting by itself, would have done; but at the same time in a direction partaking of each, and formed out of all; a direction which constitutes the true line of the liberty and happiness of the community." [52] "It was necessary, for preserving the admirable balance of our constitution, to vest the executive power of the laws in a prince." [53] "There presides over all one great court of appeal, which is the last resort in matters both of law and equity; and which will therefore take care to preserve an uniformity and *equilibrium* among all the inferior jurisdictions." [54] This metaphysical use of the idea of balance was not easily distinguished from the idea of moderation, and the *Commentaries* used the two interchangeably. By setting up suitable alternatives, Blackstone was able to define any rule as a moderate one: "The laws of England, more wisely, have steered in the middle between both extremes: providing at once against the inhumanity of the creditor, who is not suffered to confine an honest bankrupt after his effects are delivered up; and at the same time taking care that all his just debts shall be paid, so far as the effects will extend." [55] "And herein indeed consists the true excellence of the English government, that all the parts of it form a mutual check upon each other." [56] The simplicity, symmetry, and balance, all to be found in the laws of England, were the gamut of the "beautiful" in the eighteenth-century aesthetic.

The more one inquired, the clearer it became that these orderly virtues permeated the law. The *Commentaries* showed "the great plan of the English constitution, wherein provision is wisely made for the due preservation of all its parts." [57] In describing the fiction of equity that "what ought to be done shall be considered as being actually done," Blackstone explained that "this fiction is so closely pursued through all its consequences, that it necessarily branches out into many rules of jurisprudence, which form a certain regular system." [58] The student must be wary of neglecting ancient rules lest he fail to discover the nice order that lay in them. He observed of the ancient rules "how closely they are connected and interwoven together, supporting, illustrating, and demonstrating one another." [59] Blackstone agreed with Coke that "whoever considers how great a coherence there is between the several parts of the law, and how much the reason of one case opens and depends upon that of another, will, I presume, be far from thinking any of the old learning useless." [60] So eager was he to show the coherence of the whole system that instead of accepting the more usual view that equity was supplemental to the law, the *Commentaries* treated law and equity as theoretically one, — simply different qualities of the same essence.[61] It was clear to Blackstone that England had a "constitution, in theory the most *beautiful* of any, in practice the most approved, and, I trust, in duration the most permanent. It is the duty of an expounder of our laws to lay this constitution before the student in its true and genuine light: it is the duty of every good Englishman to understand, to revere, to defend it." [62]

Since the English constitution was already "the most

beautiful of any," rash attempts to improve it could surely not be fruitful. In describing Blackstone's Mystery of Law we saw how he advised against change, and that advice is equally relevant here. "How difficult and hazardous a thing it is, even in matters of public utility, to depart from the rules of the common law; which are so nicely constructed and so artificially connected together, that the least breach in any one of them disorders for a time the texture of the whole." [63] The artificial subtleties of Norman jurisprudence had undone the simple beauty which it was now taking centuries to restore.[64] The history of the common law showed that "frequently its symmetry has been destroyed, its proportions distorted, and its majestic simplicity exchanged for specious embellishments and fantastic novelties." [65] An uninformed attempt to create orderly beauty in the law was perilous; men dared not change a rule lest they unbalance a symmetry which was still hidden from them, and which might always remain unrevealed.[66] Moreover, any such attempt was unnecessary because of the natural aesthetic virtues of the law. Legal study, therefore, should seek simply to discover the beauties of the legal system. Even the concept of beauty, which in much of the thought of the eighteenth century seemed to be equated with that part of aesthetic appeal which was due to intelligibility and rationality, seemed to be employed in the *Commentaries* to discourage the effort at reform. When Blackstone found "beauty" in the legal system it became an anti-rational, almost a mystical, concept. But there was at hand in the aesthetic vocabulary of the day another notion more directly suited for describing in the legal system its awesomeness and ultimate unintelligibility.

## 3. THE SUBLIME OBSCURITY OF THE LAW

In the mid-eighteenth century, when Blackstone was writing his *Commentaries*, there was a great vogue for the concept of the "sublime." In the popular vocabulary, while "beauty" stood for simplicity, order, and clarity, "sublimity" stood for complexity, disorder, and obscurity. Although, to be sure, all disordered and obscure objects would not have been considered sublime, everything that was considered sublime had to be somewhat disordered and obscure. In 1763, Lord Kames said, in his *Elements of Criticism*, that "the delightful emotion of grandeur, depends little on order and regularity; and when the emotion is at its height by a survey of the greatest objects, order and regularity are almost totally disregarded." [67] Hugh Blair, writing later in the century in his *Lectures on Rhetoric and Belles Lettres*, described the emotion similarly:

Disorder too, is very compatible with Grandeur; nay, frequently heightens it. Few things that are strictly regular, and methodical, appear sublime. We see the limits on every side; we feel ourselves confined; there is no room for the mind's exerting any great effort. Exact proportion of parts, though it enters often into the beautiful, is much disregarded in the Sublime.[68]

Now, for all that Blackstone had written of the orderliness of the law, he was to give his readers ample evidence in the legal system of the disorder which Kames and Blair equated with sublimity. Indeed the irregularity was as manifold as human events themselves, and ultimately was founded in nature. "We are now to proceed to the cognizance of private wrongs; that is, to consider in which of the vast variety of courts . . . every possible injury that can be offered to a man's person or property is certain of meeting with redress." [69] Since the law of the land offered a remedy for "every possible injury," [70] legal remedies could not be confined to the narrow symmetry of an orderly system: "We have now gone through the whole circle of civil injuries and the redress which the laws of England have anxiously provided for each. In which the student cannot but observe that the main difficulty which attends their discussion arises from their great variety, which is apt at our first acquaintance to breed a confusion of ideas, and a kind of distraction in the memory. . . . This difficulty, however great it may appear at first view, will shrink to nothing upon a nearer and more frequent approach. . . . And, such as it is, it arises principally from the excellence of our English laws; which adapt their redress exactly to the circumstances of the injury, and do not furnish one and the same action for different wrongs, which are impossible to be brought within one and the same description." [71] Since "the prudence of the times must provide new remedies upon new emergencies," [72] the sublime intricacy of the common law was proportioned not merely to the complexity of experience at any particular time, but also to the changing complexities of history. In describing the development of equity, Blackstone observed that "in the course of a century this mighty river hath imperceptibly shifted its channel." [73] Rigid minds that demanded a "general and positive" rule for the King's prerogative were in danger of "forgetting how impossible it is, in any practical system of laws, to point out beforehand those eccentrical remedies, which the sudden emergence of national distress may dictate, and which that alone can justify." [74] Thus, our ancestors "endeavoured, by a series of minute contrivances, to accommodate such personal actions as were then in use to all the most useful purposes of remedial justice." [75] All this was not the complexity of confusion so much as the complexity of grandeur, — the law reflecting the infinite variety of experience.

Lawyers who had insisted on a strait adherence to simple rules had sometimes interfered with the proper expression of this virtue. "The courts were formerly very nice and curious with respect to the nature of the defence, so that if no defence was made, though a sufficient plea was pleaded, the plaintiff should recover judgment. . . . But

of late years these niceties have been very deservedly discountenanced: though they still seem to be law, if insisted on." [76] The *Commentaries* noted the "sufferings"
of suitors as the result of the narrowness of judges in restricting amendments to pleading.[77] To be sure, "there
is an active principle in the human soul, that will ever be
exerting its faculties to its utmost stretch, in whatever
employment . . . it may happen to find itself engaged." [78]
But this active principle, when unrestrained as it was in
Norman times, had produced unfortunate consequences.
For Blackstone explained, as we have already seen, "the
liberality of our modern courts of justice is frequently
obliged to have recourse to unaccountable fictions and
circuities, in order to recover that equitable and substantial
justice, which for a long time was totally buried under the
narrow rules and fanciful niceties of metaphysical and
Norman jurisprudence." [79]

But unlike the "fanciful niceties," the "sublime" variety which was natural to English law, was something to
be treasured.  To attack it, or to attempt to remove rules
that seemed to disturb its symmetry, was to hazard an
essential virtue of the laws of England.  For complexity
was needed to suit the remedy to the injury.[80]  "But this
intricacy of our legal process will be found, when atten-
tively considered, to be one of those troublesome, but not
dangerous evils, which have their root in the frame of our
constitution, and which, therefore, can never be cured,
without hazarding every thing that is dear to us," since,
"in free states, the trouble, expense, and delays of judicial
proceedings are the price that every subject pays for his
liberty." [81] The multifariousness of English laws was thus
a badge of social progress.[82]

This complexity was something apparent to man's
reason; he could see, and, in a measure, understand it.
But much of the law was obscure, as Blackstone admitted;
indeed, so obscure that man might not even be able fully

to comprehend its complexity. This quality, however, certainly did not detract from the "sublimity" of the legal system. As Hugh Blair said:

Obscurity . . . is not unfavourable to the Sublime. Though it render the object indistinct, the impression, however, may be great; for, as an ingenious Author has well observed, it is one thing to make an idea clear, and another to make it affecting to the imagination; and the imagination may be strongly affected, and, in fact, often is so, by objects of which we have no clear conception. Thus we see, that almost all the descriptions given us of the appearances of supernatural Beings, carry some Sublimity, though the conceptions which they afford us be confused and indistinct. Their Sublimity arises from the ideas, which they always convey, of superior power and might, joined with an awful obscurity. . . . In general, all objects that are greatly raised above us, or far removed from us, either in space or in time, are apt to strike us as great. Our viewing them, as through the mist of distance or antiquity, is favourable to the impression of their Sublimity.[83]

Burke had explained that "there are reasons in nature, why the obscure idea, when properly conveyed, should be more affecting than the clear. It is our ignorance of things that causes all our admiration, and chiefly excites our passions." [84] As the "obscurity" which surrounded man's notion of the Supreme Being came from the imperfection of man's feeble understanding and not from any indefiniteness in the objective nature of God, so in the common law the obscurity was a subjective and not an objective one.

Some apparent obscurity in the law came from the difficulty of historical precision. This was because "the maxims and customs . . . are of higher antiquity than memory or history can reach: nothing being more difficult than to ascertain the precise beginning and the first spring of an ancient and long established custom." [85] "It is morally impossible to trace out with any degree of accuracy, *when* the several mutations of the common law were made, or what was the respective original of those several customs we at present use, by any chemical resolution of them to their first and component principles. . . . First, from the nature of traditional laws in general; which, being accommodated to the exigencies of the times, suffer by degrees insensible variations in practice: so that, though upon comparison we plainly discern the alteration of the law from what it was five hundred years ago, yet it is impossible to define the precise period in which that alteration accrued, any more than we can discern the changes of a bed of a river, which varies its shores by continual decreases and alluvions. Secondly, this becomes impracticable from the antiquity of the kingdom and its government." [86] But the greater part of the obscurity of the law was derived from the very complexity of experience and the perfection with which the common law expressed that complexity. And this was not merely the obscurity of history. It was the obscurity of prophecy, for it was the indefiniteness of an institution which had to adapt itself to the indefinable necessities of the future.

Blackstone, summing up the obscure complexity of English law, used one of the principal eighteenth-century symbols of the "sublime." "Gothic" was being generally employed to describe the kind of aesthetic experience which had the "sublime" elements of disorder and grandeur.[87] And the *Commentaries* said, "Our system of remedial law resembles an old Gothic castle, erected in the days of chivalry, but fitted up for a modern inhabitant. The moated ramparts, the embattled towers, and the trophied halls, are magnificent and venerable, but useless, and therefore neglected. The inferior apartments, now accommodated to daily use, are cheerful and commodious, though their approaches may be winding and difficult." [88] Since Blackstone was interested in developing the qualities "of the heart," which meant "affectionate loyalty to the king, a zeal for liberty and the constitution, a sense of

The Sublime and the Beautiful in a Single Garden: An Artificial Ruin and a Neo-Classical Pavilion

real honour, and well grounded principles of religion," [89] he clearly served his purpose by showing the reader the awe-inspiring aspects of English law.

Following Pope's advice, Blackstone had "taught the world with Reason to admire." [90] Through the vocabulary of a rationalist aesthetic, the eighteenth-century student of law was being led to an unquestioning reverence. A sublime and incomprehensible natural grandeur was found in the disorder, complexity, and even in the obscurity of the law. Man was discouraged from any attempt to improve the law because the English system contained latent, undiscoverable perfections which he might unwittingly destroy. The aesthetic appeal of the laws of England, although to some extent rationally explained in the *Commentaries*, itself seemed a cause for limiting the scope of man's destructive reason. This latent anti-rationalism of the *Commentaries* was to be apparent in the very method of reason. And in the act of giving "reasons" for the rules of English law, Blackstone was to show his fear that reason might not lead him to his desired conclusion.

# II. REASON

## CHAPTER FIVE

# THE LIMITS OF
# REASON

## I. COMMON SENSE AND THE DISTRUST
## OF PHILOSOPHY

Blackstone had given reason the leading role in the discovery of the laws of nature and, through them, of the laws of England. It was clear, therefore, that whatever form anti-rationalism should take in the *Commentaries*, it could not be a frontal attack on reason. If it had been, Blackstone's praise of the rational virtues of English law would have come to nothing. Therefore the manner in which he expressed his anti-rationalism was oblique: he appealed from the "artificial" reasoning of philosophers to the natural good sense of mankind. And in doing this, Blackstone was expressing an attitude which by the middle of the eighteenth century in England had become popular.

The philosophy of Locke had in substance been a psychology; it had purported to discover the way men already thought, rather than to invent a framework for their thinking. Many of Locke's most ardent disciples thought that there was no higher praise for their mentor than to say that he had revealed men to themselves. As Laurence Sterne wrote in *Tristram Shandy* in 1759, "Pray, Sir, in all the reading which you have ever read, did you ever read such a book as Locke's 'Essay upon the Human Understanding?' . . . . I will tell you in three words what

the book is. — It is a history. — A history! of who?
what? where? when? Don't hurry yourself, — It is a
history-book, Sir, (which may possibly recommend it to
the world) of what passes in a man's own mind." [1]

But few men drew from Locke the individualistic, or
anarchistic, implication that every man should rely on his
private judgment. Instead, many men in eighteenth-
century England sought knowledge in the common consent of mankind, — in what had passed in most men's
minds. Locke himself had recognized that "there is nothing more commonly taken for granted, than that there are
certain principles . . . universally agreed upon by all mankind." [2] The consent of one's neighbour was the stamp of
truth. In his "Essay on Criticism," Pope advised:

> Trust not yourself; but your defects to know,
> Make use of ev'ry friend — and ev'ry foe. [3]

Since the new philosophy, rooting all ideas in experience,
had encouraged the study of history and urged all to profit
by the experience of their fellow men, men of letters distrusted metaphysics, fearing that it might lead them away
from natural standards of taste. Hume, writing in 1741
in his essay, "Of the Standard of Taste," explained:

> It is evident that none of the rules of composition are fixed
> by reasonings *a priori*, or can be esteemed abstract conclusions
> of the understanding, from comparing those habitudes and
> relations of ideas, which are eternal and immutable. Their
> foundation is the same with that of all the practical sciences,
> experience; nor are they any thing but general observations,
> concerning what has been universally found to please in all
> countries and in all ages. [4]

Dr. Johnson added that "few maxims are widely received
or long retained but for some conformity with truth and
nature," [5] and "what mankind have long possessed they
have often examined and compared; and if they persist to

value the possession, it is because frequent comparisons have confirmed opinion in its favour." [6] Common consent, the fullest stock of experience, was thus also the surest source of knowledge.

Although many people had found in Locke a justification of this appeal to common consent, many derived from the new philosophy a distrust of all philosophers. According to Matthew Prior:

> LOCK, wou'd the Human understanding show;
> In vain he squanders Thought & Time and Ink.
> People themselves most certainly must know,
> Better than he cou'd tell, how they can think? [7]

The bitterest epithets that Blackstone could use against Norman jurisprudence were "subtle" and "metaphysical," and many people shared the feelings he was thus expressing. Indeed, a whole school of philosophers grew up, whose purpose was to destroy the offensive distinctions of professional philosophy. [8] The "Common Sense Philosophers," by flattering the good sense of the layman, and providing reasons against the destructive arguments of scepticism, attained great popularity. The appeal to natural feeling, made earlier in various forms by Shaftesbury, Butler, and Hutcheson, had provided foundations for these new theories; and about the middle of the eighteenth century, when the subversive implications of scepticism had become apparent, "common sense" philosophies became numerous. Reid, Oswald, Beattie, and others, prospered by making philosophies to end philosophy. In his *Inquiry into the Human Mind*, in 1764, Reid declared:

> Admired Philosophy! daughter of light! parent of wisdom and knowledge! if thou art she! surely thou hast not yet arisen upon the human mind nor blessed us with more of thy rays, than are sufficient to shed a "darkness visible" upon the human faculties and to disturb that repose and security which mortals

enjoy, who never approached thine altar, nor felt thine influence! But if indeed thou hast not power to dispel those clouds and phantoms which thou hast discovered or created, withdraw this penurious ray: I despise philosophy and renounce its guidance; let my soul dwell with common sense.[9]

I am resolved to take my own existence, and the existence of other things, upon trust; and to believe that snow is cold, and honey sweet, whatever they may say to the contrary. He must either be a fool, or want to make a fool of me, that would reason me out of my senses.[10]

The belief of the material world is older and of more authority than any principles of philosophy. It declines the tribunal of reason, and laughs at all the artillery of logicians.[11]

The ordinary man, bewildered by the paradoxes of Berkeley and Hume, eagerly embraced these ideas. James Beattie's *Essay on Truth* was widely read, and secured for him the ultimate distinctions of a two-hundred-pound pension and an Oxford degree. George III always kept one copy of this work at Kew, and another in London,[12] and Dr. Johnson was glad to note that the book was "every day more liked."[13] In his work Beattie had defined "Common Sense" as "that power of the mind which perceived truth, or commands belief, not by progressive argumentation, but by an instantaneous, instinctive and irresistible impulse; derived neither from education nor from habit, but from Nature; acting independently on our will, whenever its object is presented, according to an established law, and therefore properly called *Sense*; and acting in a similar manner upon all or at least upon a great majority of mankind and therefore properly called *Common Sense*."[14] James Oswald in his *Appeal to Common Sense in Behalf of Religion* in 1766 complained of "that intemperate love of reasoning which may be called the epidemical distemper of the human mind."[15]

Too great reliance on one's own reason, with too little

attention to the common sense of mankind, was, however, more than a mere distemper. It was a vice; and in the eighteenth century was sometimes called the sin of pride. As Pope had written in his "Essay on Man":

> In pride, in reas'ning pride, our error lies;
> All quit their sphere, and rush into the skies. . . .
> The bliss of man (could pride that blessing find)
> Is not to act or think beyond mankind.[16]

Man must therefore restrain his reason, humbly confirming his private judgment by the opinions and experience of his neighbours.

From the nature of the English legal system it might have seemed unnecessary to test the common law by the common experience of mankind. For the common law was by definition the embodiment of the generally received and long accepted notions of Englishmen; the common law was, after all, "nothing else but custom, arising from the universal agreement of the whole community." [17] And what was custom but crystallized experience, the evidence of the agreement of many generations of men? Thus the executive power had been vested in a single person "by the general consent of the people, the evidence of which general consent is long and immemorial usage." [18] Custom, which was "the life of the common law," [19] in this way identified the English system with the lessons of everyday common sense.

## 2. THE WISDOM OF LEGAL MAXIMS

This natural identity of common law and common sense might seem to have made superfluous any evidence that particular rules were the product of experience. Nevertheless, Blackstone in his exposition of the law did use a device which indicated quickly that a particular rule was justified not by closet-philosophy, but by common sense.

This was the "maxim." Succinctly expressing what every-one already knew, the maxim summed up the proverbial wisdom of the past, and commended it to the future.

The maxim was, of course, not novel in the eighteenth century. From ancient times men had distilled their beliefs into proverbs to make them clearer, more self-evident and easier to remember; and lawyers long be-fore Blackstone's day had used the maxim as a way of stating a legal rule. When, in 1596, Francis Bacon wrote his *Elements of the Common Lawes of England*, he explained why he had described the law in the form of maxims:

Whereas I could have digested these rules into a certain method or order, which I know would have bin more admired, as that which would have made every particular rule through coherence and relation unto other rules seeme more cunning and deep, yet I have avoided so to do, because this delivering of knowledge in distinct and dis-joyned Aphorismes doth leave the wit of man more free to turne and tosse, and make use of that which is so delivered to more severall purposes and applications; for wee see that all the ancient wisdom and science was wont to be delivered in that forme.[20]

Although Bacon thought the maxim a device for "digest-ing" the law, he did not consider a maxim to be a reason for a rule, or even to be a part of a rule of law.

But Blackstone, unlike Bacon, was not eager to "leave the wit of man more free to turne and tosse." Therefore, he employed the maxim to indicate that all this turning and tossing of reason was unnecessary since the experience of the past had already been summarized into clear and succinct form. The *Commentaries*, by identifying the maxim with the law, invested the legal system with the validity of long usage and everyday common sense. Black-stone explained, "Some have divided the common law into two principal grounds of foundations: 1. Established cus-toms; such as that, where there are three brothers, the

eldest brother shall be heir to the second, in exclusion of
the youngest: and 2. Established rules and maxims; as
'that the king can do no wrong, that no man shall be
bound to accuse himself,' and the like. But I take these to
be one and the same thing. For the authority of these
maxims rests entirely upon general reception and usage:
and the only method of proving, that this or that maxim
is a rule of the common law, is by shewing that it hath
been always the custom to observe it." [21] Thus the *Commentaries* described "that collection of maxims and customs which is now known by the name of the common
law." [22]

The identification of maxim and law did not prevent
Blackstone from giving a maxim as the "reason" for a
legal rule. And this despite the fact that, in Blackstone's
own terms, this meant that he was giving one rule of law
as the reason for another. "First, the plea of *autrefoits
acquit*, or a former acquittal, is grounded on this universal
maxim of the common law of England, that no man is to
be brought into jeopardy of his life more than once for the
same offence. And hence it is allowed as a consequence,
that when a man is once fairly found not guilty upon any
indictment, or other prosecution, before any court having
competent jurisdiction of the offence, he may plead such
acquittal in bar of any subsequent accusation for the same
crime." [23] "It is a maxim, that *accessorius sequitur naturam
sui principalis*; and therefore an accessory cannot be
guilty of a higher crime than his principal; being only
punished as a partaker of his guilt." [24] Blackstone could
not present a better reason for a rule of law than that it
was the proverbial wisdom of the past.

Sometimes, of course, a maxim was used simply to sum-
marize neatly the discrete provisions of law, and was still
another way of revealing the orderly "beauty" of the legal
system. Thus, as to prosecutions for rape, "at present
there is no time of limitation fixed: for as it is usually now

punished by indictment at the suit of the king, the maxim of law takes place, that *nullum tempus occurrit regi.*" [25] But even in these instances the maxim was more than a mere label for a category of English laws. It was both a stamp of authority and a justification of the authority. In Blackstone's hands, the maxim became a method for making the rules of English law seem their own justification, at the same time that they were being justified by the general experience of mankind.

As the laws of nature confused the world as it was with the world as it ought to be, the maxims stating those natural rules inevitably showed a similar confusion. By using the maxim, the *Commentaries* could express a principle as a desired norm, imply disapproval of any deviations from the norm, and yet evade any too particular comparison of this ideal with the detailed rules of law. Maxims were such general statements that it was always easy to demonstrate, and hard to disprove, that they had been observed in particular legal rules. For example, "This maxim is ever invariably observed, that no fiction shall extend to work an injury; its proper operation being to prevent a mischief, or remedy an inconvenience, that might result from the general rule of law. So true it is, that *in fictione juris semper subsistit aequitas.*" [26] And as maxim and law were one, the law could be credited with the ideal simplicity of the maxim itself.

The maxim, moreover, identified the actual laws of England with the inevitable laws of human nature. "There is not a more necessary or more certain maxim in the frame and constitution of society, than that every individual must contribute his share . . . to the well-being of the community." [27] And the maxims of human nature were not clearly distinguished from the maxims of English law. Blackstone wrote, in his discussion of criminal capacity, "One lad of eleven years old may have as much cunning as another of fourteen; and in these cases our maxim is,

that, '*malitia supplet aetatem.*'" [28]  Because this maxim was
simply a commonplace about human nature, the English
rule described by the maxim was given all the inevitability
of the qualities of human nature.

It would be wrong, of course, to suggest that every
one of Blackstone's maxims carried all the implications
which we have described.  In many cases a maxim merely
restated a simple rule of law in a form which made it more
easily remembered or which endowed it with a solemn
Latinity.  "Land hath also, in its legal signification, an
indefinite extent, upwards as well as downwards.  *Cujus
est solum, ejus est usque ad caelum,* is the maxim of the law;
upwards, therefore no man may erect any building, or
the like, to overhang another's land." [29]  But even where
the maxim was merely making the law seem more orderly,
it was, by that very fact, making the law seem more
natural.

### 3. THE OBSCURANTIST APPEAL TO COMMON SENSE

This appeal to common experience, exemplified by
Blackstone's use of the maxim, served a purpose similar
to that of his Mystery of Law, and of all the concepts which
the *Commentaries* employed to discourage the corrosive ac-
tivity of man's reason.  By making the general approval of
mankind a criterion of law, Blackstone was disqualifying
man's individual reason from searching too critically into
the institutions around him.  In this sense, the mere fact
that they were "institutions" entitled them to acceptance.
But still, by the very appeal to experience, men might try
to justify their rash attempts to improve the law.  Might
not one appeal to the common consent of the great majority of people as a warrant for attacking institutions?
If the common sense philosophy were to become simple
empiricism, there might no longer be any theoretical safe-

guard against man's misguided efforts to improve. And there would have been no such safeguard if there had not been still another aspect to the common sense philosophy.

This aspect can perhaps best be described as a sort of mysticism. The conservatism of the common sense philosophy in the eighteenth century was derived from the fact that it was fundamentally not empirical, but rather obscurantist. When Dr. Johnson refuted Berkeley by "striking his foot with mighty force against a large stone," he was appealing to a philosophy of common sense. As Boswell remarked of the incident, "This was a stout exemplification of the . . . original principles of Reid and of Beattie; without admitting which we can no more argue in metaphysics, than we can argue in mathematics without axioms. To me it is not conceivable how Berkeley can be answered by pure reasoning." [30] Dr. Johnson, kicking the stone, was actually trying to refute philosophers by denying the validity of reasoning, and relying on the sanction of his intuition. As Beattie had said:

Except we believe many things without proof we never can believe any thing at all; for that all sound reasoning men ultimately rest on the principles of common sense, that is, on principles intuitively certain or intuitively probable; and, consequently that common sense is the ultimate judge of truth to which reason must continually act in subordination.[31]

Man's reliance on common sense was thus proportionate to his distrust of his rational faculties. A man of common sense was a man who relied on his intuitions; he distrusted reason partly because he could not predict where it would lead him. And he insisted on not being led to conclusions which violated his deepest feelings. Adam Ferguson, writing later in the century, went to the root of the matter when he said, "There is a mystery in thought, which none of the corporal images under which it has been expressed, can serve to illustrate." [32] Many of the eighteenth-century devotees of common sense clung to this philosophy because they felt they knew where they would be led by it, and had confidence in the conservatism of their own intuitions.

So it was that Blackstone, in the process of reasoning about institutions, was using a concept of reason which was only partly rational. While the appeal to experience and common consent was being employed to make the rules of English law intelligible, while the maxim was being used to give the legal system order, the *Commentaries* were also effecting an obscurantist purpose. The legal maxim, at the same time that it served the Science of Law by showing a rational simplicity, was serving the Mystery of Law by revealing intuitively imperative principles. And the appeal to common sense discouraged any perilous criticism of the law. Blackstone thus refused to press his search for "reasons" beyond bounds conveniently defined by the general experience of mankind.

The realm of reason was thus limited. But within that realm, how could reason operate? It would seem that the possibility of criticizing English law had been destroyed by the way the instrument of criticism had been blunted. But this did not prove to be the case. It was still possible to seek the "reasons" of English law. This Blackstone did by the use of a double method which itself was to have a conservative utility.

## CHAPTER SIX

# THE METHODS OF REASON

## I. NATURE AND THE DOUBLE MEANING OF REASON

THE LAWS OF NATURE, the object of Blackstone's quest, were themselves the perfection of reason. Yet they were at the same time the self-contained order of logic and the total facts of the sensory world. Blackstone could therefore hardly have been expected to use a method of reasoning which would distinguish clearly the vocabulary of self-consistent logic from the facts of physical experience. Like many men of the Enlightenment, he refused to believe that the physical world could not be identified with the world of rational order. Locke had said that "Reason" was "the discovery of the certainty or probability of such propositions or truths, which the mind arrives at by deductions made from such ideas which it has got by the use of its natural faculties, viz., by sensation or reflection."[1] Yet rational principles did not have to be "discovered" in nature, because reason was naturally immanent (Locke did not dare to say "innate") in man:

But God has not been so sparing to men to make them barely two-legged creatures, and left it to Aristotle to make them rational. God has been more bountiful to mankind than so. He has given them a mind that can reason, without being instructed in methods of syllogizing. The understanding is not taught to reason by these rules; it has a native faculty to perceive the coherence or incoherence of its ideas.[2]

Reason was, according to these notions, a self-existing system whose coherence was intuitively perceptible to man; yet somehow, rational principles were in accord with the physical world. Therefore the conclusions of reason could be derived from experience.

Now Blackstone, while proving the study of law to be a science, had shown that the laws of England, from their connections with the laws of nature, were themselves a system of reason; since this was the case, the legal system not only had a self-evident rationality, but also was in some sense derived from physical facts. And the *Commentaries* reveal that the method of reason for Blackstone was at the same time two techniques: first, reason was a way of testing the legal system by the self-evidence of its consistency; and secondly, reason was a way of verifying the legal system by its identity with physical facts. We do not mean to suggest that Blackstone was conscious of the duality of his concept of reason, or that the ambiguity was used with any deliberate deceptive purpose. These two techniques in some form or other have probably been used by lawyers of many ages, and are certainly in use today. Our concern is mainly to see how the *Commentaries* themselves revealed this duality which, to the eighteenth-century reader, probably increased their persuasive power. For treating the legal system as an isolated logic flattered man's reason by making the "reasons" for things mathematically demonstrable; in the self-completeness of the system were provided additional grounds for the acceptance of the laws and of the perfect God who made them. This was the effect of the first aspect of Blackstone's method of reason. And, to show the congruence of the legal system with immediate sensory facts was to make the rules appear more directly verifiable at the same time that they were being given the sanction of an obscurantist common sense.

## 2. THE LAW AS AN ISOLATED LOGIC

The first method of reason in the *Commentaries* was, then, to treat the law as an isolated system of logic. And according to this view the law was by its nature self-consistent. This consistency was to be tested not by any *a priori* criterion nor by accord with physical facts, but by an intuitive response. In discussing maxims we have already described something of this method of reasoning about the law. Locke, long before, had shown how the maxim was to be employed in the *Commentaries* when he had written, "There are a sort of propositions which, under the name of *maxims* and *axioms*, have passed for principles of science: and, because they are *self-evident*, have been supposed innate, without that anybody (that I know) ever went about to show the reason and foundation of their clearness or cogency." [3] But the maxim was merely one of the many devices for treating English law as a scheme of logic.

That the laws of nature, which were all derived from the same omniscient Creator, should not have fitted together into a cohering system was inconceivable. And, as the laws of England, insofar as they were valid, were in accord with this general design, the same might be said of them. The whole of the English law was a unified natural phenomenon like the rest of God's works. And to criticize the shape of the law would be like criticizing the shape of a tree. Was it not enough to say that roots were necessary, for without them there could be no leaves, and leaves were needed, for without them there could be no use for roots or trunk? What God had created man dared not judge. But, like the botanist, the lawyer might discover a latent harmony.

Thus, when Blackstone called law and equity "artificial systems, founded on the same principles of justice

and positive law," [4] he clearly did not mean to suggest
that men had made the reason in the law. On the contrary, judges and lawyers could simply try, in their feeble
way, to reveal at least part of the coherent rational system. "It is wisely therefore ordered, that the principles
and axioms of law, which are general propositions, flowing
from abstracted reason, and not accommodated to times
or to men, should be deposited in the breasts of the judges,
to be occasionally applied to such facts as come properly
ascertained before them. For here partiality can have
little scope: the law is well known, and is the same for all
ranks and degrees; it follows as a regular conclusion from
the premises of fact pre-established." [5] "The judgment,
though pronounced or awarded by the judges, is not their
determination or sentence, but the determination and
sentence of *the law*. It is the conclusion that naturally and
regularly follows from the premises of law and fact." [6] It
was therefore necessary to consider the law as a whole,
"for, without contemplating the whole fabric together, it
is impossible to form any clear idea of the meaning and
connection of those disjointed parts." [7] And, for Blackstone, contemplating the whole fabric together meant
considering the law as an independent realm of logic, and
treating it as a system of interdependent definitions.

Frequently those parts of the *Commentaries* which purported to be "reasoning" about the law, or to be critical
of it, were actually only demonstrating that in a closed
system there could be no inconsistency. The most general form of the argument was something like this: Rule A
is part of the legal system, and therefore necessary; Rule B
is a necessary consequence of Rule A; moreover, without
Rule A, one cannot have Rule B; therefore *both* Rule A and
Rule B are necessary. In this conclusive argument, Blackstone conveniently evaded the question whether either,
or both Rule A and Rule B had not better be abandoned for
Rule C. Similarly, one might defend the internal coherence

of baseball by arguing, "The pitcher is a necessary part of the game; since there is the pitcher there must. be the catcher; moreover, without the pitcher there could not be the catcher; therefore both the pitcher and the catcher are necessary. And thus, you see, baseball is a rational game." All the while, the baseball enthusiast would be avoiding the embarrassing question whether it might not be better to play football.

Such reasoning, of course, actually assumed the very thing it purported to be proving. Having accepted the desirability of the legal system as a whole, one needed, in order to prove the desirability of any particular rule, merely to show how it was dependent upon the rest of the system. This method avoided all consideration of consequences, except consequences for the symmetry of the law. For example, the legal relations of husband and wife were explained in just such fashion. Blackstone began by asserting that "by marriage, the husband and wife are one person in law: that is, the very being or legal existence of the woman is suspended during the marriage, or at least is incorporated and consolidated into that of the husband." [8] He then argued that "they are not allowed to be evidence for, or against, each other: partly because it is impossible their testimony should be indifferent, but principally because of the union of person; and therefore, if they were admitted to be witnesses *for* each other, they would contradict one maxim of law, '*nemo in propria causa testis esse debet*;' and if *against* each other, they would contradict another maxim '*nemo tenetur seipsum accusare.*'" [9] This reasoning was obviously circular: to say that husband and wife could not testify for or against each other because they were one in law was simply to say they could not because the law did not allow it. The statement that they were "one" in law was merely an inclusive description of such rules as this concerning their testimony. To use description as a "reason" was to attempt to justify the existing rule by saying that if it were not so it would be different. This technique of arguing from definition was sometimes used still more baldly. "The incapacity of a bastard consists principally in this, that he cannot be heir to anyone, neither can he have heirs but of his own body; for being *nullius filius,* he is therefore of kin to nobody, and has no ancestor from whom any inheritable blood can be derived." [10] This was merely a fancier way of saying that a bastard could not be an heir because the law did not permit it. Blackstone's way of stating the rule made the mere statement seem an argument.

Tautology was often concealed by the copiousness of the legal vocabulary. Thus, when the *Commentaries* argued that no man could be tenant at sufferance against the king because the king could not be guilty of *laches,* all that was being said was that it was convenient to have two ways of stating the same rule. [11] Once *laches* had been defined as something the king could not be guilty of and as something which was at the same time necessary to a tenancy at sufferance, the question had been foreclosed.

Moreover, "justifying" legal rules by defining them in terms of each other served the defence of the legal system as a whole. It was easy for Blackstone by this sort of reasoning to prove, for example, that in English law every possible injury was redressed. "It would be a great weakness and absurdity in any system of positive law to define any possible wrong, without any possible redress." [12] It was evident that the common law was not guilty of any such absurdity, "for wherever the common law gives a right or prohibits an injury, it also gives a remedy by action; and, therefore, wherever a new injury is done, a new method of remedy must be pursued." [13] Such a method of argument helped Blackstone in several difficult places. He thus explained that, because there could be no remedy against the king, the king could do no wrong. And he was able to show why in many cases where a person had suffered from a criminal act, the victim still had no civil action at law. Although "in all cases crime includes an injury; every public offence is also a private wrong, and somewhat more," the law of murder and robbery showed how "in these gross and atrocious injuries the private wrong is swallowed up in the public: we seldom hear any mention made of satisfaction to the individual; the satisfaction to the community being so very great." [14] But this did not mean that in these cases a wrong to an individual had gone unrequited. For, properly speaking, and in the legal sense, the individual had suffered no wrong. Why not? Simply because nothing was a wrong in the eye of the law unless the law had provided a remedy against it. Thus, "injury" having been defined as the kind of damage for which the common law gave redress, what seemed to be praise was really mere tautology. Since a wrong was by definition what was remedied, in English law no wrong could ever go unredressed.

To treat the law as a closed logical system, and to consider any legal rule primarily in its relation to other rules, had a further use for explaining the law as a whole. Thus the *Commentaries* could make one rule appear valuable simply because it negated another rule which was still more absurd or inconvenient. In seeking this sort of virtue it was imperative to consider the interdependence of rules. For example, Latin was declared to be preferable to English as the language of pleading. This was because, among other reasons, Latin was more economical of words. But why was such rigid economy of words necessary? And, especially, why should a lawyer raise such an argument? The answer was that the law itself, by imposing a stamp duty had limited the number of words on a sheet. [15] Similarly, in discussing benefit of clergy, Blackstone showed the great virtue of this institution in negating the large number of statutes which provided capital punishment.[16]  The legal system was being praised for overcoming obstacles of its own creation.

In all these cases, the *Commentaries* were reasoning about the laws of England by treating the law as a closed logical system.  For this kind of argument it was always important to emphasize the *legal* nature of the definitions and the reasoning used.  In the world of law, it would have been as absurd to say that the king could be guilty of *laches* or that an injury could go unremedied, as it would have been in the physical world to deny Newton's laws or to say that man was not born of woman.  Thus Blackstone was assuming that the world of law was something quite different from the world of fact; and that the legal world had its own iron rules.

## 3. THE LAW AS EVERYDAY EXPERIENCE

But in his use of reason, Blackstone did not follow only this method of treating the law as logic.  Alongside it, sometimes confused with it, he employed a much different technique.  In the *Commentaries*, reasoning about the law was also to be a way of appealing to experience.  The Lockean psychology and the concept of natural law required this.  There must be a method of reasoning about English law which would somehow compare legal rules directly with the experience of man's senses.  As Locke had written, "The child, when a part of his apple is taken away, knows it better in that particular instance, than by this general proposition, 'The whole is equal to all its parts.'" [17]  The "logical" method of reasoning on the law had consisted of the use of general propositions.  Blackstone was now to give his demonstration all the conclusiveness that the child must have felt when some of his apple was actually taken away.

Blackstone's first method of reason, which we have already described, advised the student entering the sanctum of the law, "Leave all memory of the physical world behind. The legal world is a law unto itself. Here whale and sturgeon are 'royal fish'; [18] here the king can do no wrong; here a bastard has no ancestors, — and all this regardless of how things happen in the layman's world." Blackstone's second method gave the student quite different, and apparently contrary, advice, telling the student of the law, "There is no distinction between the legal world and the world of nature. In the legal world the physical world is most clearly revealed; here the distinctions of the natural world are most sharply defined. The rules of law are nothing but descriptions of the physical world." It is easy to see how this latter method of reasoning, which we are about to consider, would have been congenial to the conception of natural law. For natural law was itself not clearly distinguished from the bare description of the world of experience. Here again, prescription, fact, and hope were not to be clearly separated.

The obvious feature of this second method of reason was its description of a legal rule as if it were merely a characteristic of the physical world. And in many cases the *Commentaries* stated a rule of law in such a manner as to make it appear that the law was merely recognizing a physical fact, rather than creating a rule by its own fiat. For example, because "from the instant of publication, the exclusive right of an author or his assigns to the sole communication of his ideas immediately vanishes and evaporates" this was "a right of too subtle and unsubstantial a nature to become the subject of property at the common law, and only capable of being guarded by positive statutes and special provisions of the magistrate." [19] Therefore copyright statutes had to be passed. Again, "the law looks upon goods and chattels as of too low and perishable a nature to be limited either to heirs, or such successors as are equivalent to heirs." [20] "A lease at will is not held to be such a particular estate as will support a remainder over. For an estate at will is of a nature so slender and precarious that it is not looked upon as a portion of the inheritance." [21] Blackstone's reader could thus see how the law recognized the natural qualities of the things with which it was dealing.

When Blackstone came to discuss the criminal law, the nature of his technique became still clearer. He treated the question of the age at which a person attained the capacity to commit a crime, as if the answer were as obvious and discoverable a physical fact as when a child began to walk or to talk.[22] Although the *Commentaries* explained that the precise age varied in different nations because of such factors as climate, still, "defect of will" was everywhere the characteristic of cases of incapacity to commit crime. The legal rule thus seemed to be defined by the simple description of man's physical nature. Crimes themselves were also described as if they were merely characteristics of the physical world. Blackstone's "grand criterion" for defining murder was "any evil design in general: the dictate of a wicked, depraved, and malignant heart." This notion would have made the definition of murder possible with reliance merely on everyday experience. Law and fact seemed to be one; and the legal rule had all the immediacy of the fact. Blackstone added, however, that in murder this "dictate of a wicked, depraved, and malignant heart . . . may be either *express* or *implied* in law." [23] By introducing the word "implied," he seemed to suggest that it would be difficult from the mere examination of the physical world to arrive at the correct definition of murder; to see when such malice was "implied in law" one would have to look to the law. Yet in characterizing murder, Blackstone still insisted on identifying law and fact. He distinguished manslaughter from murder by saying that the difference "principally consists in this, that manslaughter, when voluntary, arises from the sudden heat of the passions, murder from the wickedness of the heart." [24] One could understand the law of self-defence by seeing that the law "respects the passions of the human mind; and (when external violence is offered to a man himself, or those to whom he bears a near connection) makes it lawful in him to do himself that immediate justice, to which he is prompted by nature. . . . Self-defence, therefore, as it is justly called the primary law of nature, so it is not, neither can it be in fact, taken away by the law of society." [25] However seldom anyone might have seen a man with an implied wickedness of heart, Blackstone still seemed to be giving legal definition the character of physiological description.

Certain departments of law were peculiarly well suited to this method of reasoning. Thus the law of property in animals seemed to be treated almost as a branch of natural science. "First, then, of property in *possession absolute*, which is where a man hath, solely and exclusively, the right, and also the occupation, of any movable chattels; so that they cannot be transferred from him, or cease to be his, without his own act or default. Such may be all *inanimate* things, as goods, plate, money, jewels, implements of war, garments and the like: such also may be all *vegetable* productions, as the fruit or other parts of a plant, when severed from the body of it; or the whole plant itself, when severed from the ground; none of which can be moved out of the owner's possession without his own act or consent, or at least without doing him an injury, which it is the business of the law to prevent or remedy. . . . But with regard to *animals* which have in themselves a principle and power of motion, and (unless particularly confined) can convey themselves from one part of the world to another, there is a great difference made with respect to their several classes, not only in our law, but in the law of nature and of all civilized nations. They are distinguished into such as are *domitae*, and such as are *ferae naturae*: some being of a *tame* and others of a *wild* disposition." [26] The lesson in animal biology continued, "Our law apprehends the most obvious distinction to be, between such animals as we generally see tame, and are therefore seldom, if ever, found wandering at large, which it calls *domitae naturae*: and such creatures as are usually found at liberty, which are therefore supposed to be more emphatically *ferae naturae*, though it may happen that the latter shall be sometimes tamed and confined by the art and industry of man." [27] Animals like deer and rabbits "are no longer the property of a man, than while they continue in his keeping or actual possession: but if at any time they regain their natural liberty, his property instantly ceases; unless they have *animum revertendi*, which is only to be known by their usual custom of returning." [28] The *animum revertendi* is thus not defined as a technical concept used merely for convenience, but is rather described as if it were the same kind of observable physical fact as the bite of a dog or the scratch of a cat. Facts introduced to explain a legal rule were themselves confused with the rule.

The reader was encouraged to believe it as absurd that the English law of animals should be otherwise, as it would be for wild animals to be tame, and tame animals wild. Similar legal arguments were derived from all the rest of the physical world. Grants for free fishery were prohibited by Magna Charta because it seemed to be "unnatural to restrain the use of running water." [29] Fire, light, air, and water might be the objects of "qualified property." "A man can have no absolute permanent property in these, as he may in earth and land; since these are of a vague and fugitive nature, and therefore can admit only of a precarious and qualified ownership." [30] English law thus included the laws of physics no less than the laws of biology.

Moreover, it is often hard to tell from Blackstone's classifications whether his categories are primarily of legal, or of factual, significance. The *Commentaries* differentiated "two sorts" of poor: the "sick and impotent"; and the "idle and sturdy." [31] The four sorts of servants were also distinguished as if the "obvious" distinctions of fact fitted the inevitable distinctions of law.[32] One could then speak of the "precision" of the legal vocabulary, as if one were talking of the precision with which a tailor measured his patron, — as if in some sense the best legal system was the one in which the laws best "fitted" the facts. Thus, the English law "distinguishes with much accuracy" on the crime of arson; an expression in the law of real property showed a "precision peculiar to our own law"; and, in comparison with Roman law, the English phraseology of inheritance was sometimes "more accurate." [33] Here recurred the concept of the laws of nature as description. The law was considered simply "there," in the same sense in which a fact was there, with the job of the lawyer being to record what he saw.

If the law was just an aspect of the physical world, its rules must be as certain and as unalterable as the behaviour of matter itself. It was possible and even necessary that the law should accord with scientific truth. "And here also the first estate, and both the remainders, for life and in fee, are one estate only; being nothing but parts or portions of one entire inheritance; and if there were a hundred remainders, it would still be the same thing; upon a principle grounded in mathematical truth, that all the parts are equal, and no more than equal, to the whole." [34] Even within law "probability" and "possibility" must be considered. Rules of inheritance were explained by lawyer's terms like "common possibility" and "improbable possibility." [35] The notion of probability was also important if one was to understand the law of nuisance: "Indeed every continuance of a nuisance is held to be a fresh one; and therefore a fresh action will lie, and very exemplary damages will probably be given, if, after one verdict against him, the defendant has the hardiness to continue it. Yet the founders of the law of England did not rely upon probabilities merely, in order to give relief to the injured. They have therefore provided two other actions . . . which . . . strike at the root and remove the cause itself." [36] Physical and legal probability were thus made indistinguishable.

## 4. FACT, FICTION, AND THE USES OF REASON

Blackstone's combination of his two methods of reason is nowhere more apparent than in his use of the concept of "certainty" in the law. It was seldom clear whether by "certainty" he meant simply the clarity of definition which might be found in every logical system, or, on the other hand, a kind of physical predictability. This ambiguity appeared, for example, when he said that "experience will abundantly show, that above a hundred of our law-suits arise from disputed facts, for one where the law is doubted of." [37] Often, indeed, "certainty" meant merely the stability of an institution: it was important to adhere to the law in order that the people's "property may be as certain and fixed as the very constitution of their state." [38] Logical certainty in the law was demonstrated by considering it to be an isolated logical system; physical predictability was shown by considering the law as merely an aspect of the physical world. In both senses, however, the certainty was derived ultimately from a law of nature given by a beneficent God.

The use of the two methods of rationalizing the law sometimes led Blackstone into a difficulty greater than mere ambiguity. It was not easy always to justify the law as an isolated mathematic at the same time that one was explaining it as a part of everyday experience. The best example of this difficulty is in his discussion of legal fictions. The *Commentaries* often described "fictions" as devices essential to the logical symmetry of the law. Thus, they explained that "it is now usual in practice, to sue out the *capias* in the first instance upon the supposed return of the sheriff; especially if it be suspected that the defendant, upon notice to the action, will abscond; and afterwards a fictitious original is drawn up . . . with a proper return thereupon, in order to give the proceedings a colour of regularity." 39 Also, in consequence of changes in the feudal system, "it became a fundamental maxim and necessary principle (though in reality a mere fiction) of our English tenures 'that the king is the universal lord and original proprietor of all the lands in his kingdom.'" This was merely pretended, since "the fact was indeed far otherwise." 40 Legal logic dictated the form of a common recovery; "though these recoveries are in themselves fabulous and fictitious, yet it is necessary that there be *actores fabulae*, properly qualified." 41 If fictions were part of the logical order of the law, then there could be no objection to them and they could never defeat the purposes of law. "And these fictions of law, though at first they may startle the student, he will find upon farther consideration to be highly beneficial and useful; especially as this maxim is ever invariably observed, that no fiction shall extend to work an injury; its proper operation being to prevent a mischief, or remedy an inconvenience, that might result from the general rule of law." 42 Here clearly the *Commentaries* were explaining the fiction as part of the inner logic of the law.

But Blackstone was not satisfied with this explanation. His confusion of law and fact made him feel that there was something unreal about a legal fiction. Since the law necessarily harmonized with experience, he was careful to show that the law did not allow itself to be fooled by mere fiction. Thus, when the writ of *capias* became the fictitious first process, men ceased to be punished for disregard of the former original summons because "it was thought hard to

imprison a man for a contempt which was only supposed." [43] Similarly, "a writ of ejectment is not an adequate means to try the title of all estates; for on those
things whereon an entry cannot in fact be made, no entry
shall be supposed by any fiction of the parties." [44] Blackstone insisted that proceedings in the courts of criminal
jurisdiction "are plain, easy, and regular; the law not admitting any fictions, as in civil causes, to take place where
the life, the liberty, and the safety of the subject are more
immediately brought into jeopardy." [45] It was hardly a
virtue of the criminal law to refuse to use fictions if by
definition a fiction could produce nothing but justice. Yet
Blackstone's eagerness to prove the identity of law and
fact was as great as his eagerness to show that legal fictions
perfected the logical symmetry of the law.

It was not often, however, that the two methods of
reason, the logical and the experiential, appeared to conflict in the *Commentaries*. To us it may appear inconsistent
to say that the law is essentially a system of logic and at
the same time a description of experience; but to Blackstone such an inconsistency may have been less apparent.
For the law of nature, expressed in the laws of England,
was itself the perfection of reason at the same time that
it was all the fullness of experience. And Blackstone had
accepted the ambiguities of natural law as his principal
form for giving an appearance of order to the English legal
system. It might have been inconceivable to him that
any narrow distinction could or ought to be made between
the realm of logic and the realm of experience. Indeed, it
was the very coexistence of the prescriptive and the descriptive in the concept of natural law that had made it
feasible for him to rationalize, without criticizing, the law.
To consider the law as logic was at once rationally satisfying and emotionally pleasing; to identify law with fact
seemed to give the law the more immediate sanction of
intuitive common sense.

Here was just another example of the kind of coördination of apparently contrary ideas which Blackstone effected in his attempt to make a rational system of English law. At this point we must inevitably ask, What, apart from the concept of Nature, held together the English legal system? What provided the justification for Blackstone's effort of reason, and the foundation of his fear of being misled by reason? Without going into the question of Blackstone's motives, and, indeed, by continuing to focus our attention on the meaning of the *Commentaries*, it is still possible to find an underlying unity in the appeal and meaning of the document. This unity is found in the values which the *Commentaries* appeared to accept, and which they showed to be preëminently realized in English law.

# III. VALUES

CHAPTER   SEVEN

# HUMANITY

I.  THE  LAW'S  HUMANE  ACCORD  WITH  NATURE

WHEN WE ENTER the realm of values, we have left the realm of argument; statements of value are, by their very nature, propositions which a man accepts without the need of demonstration. He believes them and demonstration is superfluous or impossible. Therefore, in considering the values which the *Commentaries* took for granted, we will be discussing not how anything was proved, but rather what was believed to be good. We shall soon discover, however, that there was a kind of conflict even in this realm. This was not a conflict between methods of demonstrating the values to be good, but was rather a discord among the values themselves. The values that Blackstone professed were life, liberty, and property. In theory he could accept all of them and hold them at the same time. But when he came to show their practical bearing, they were seldom as compatible as they had been in theory. Indeed, the problem of applying the values to particular cases proved to be the problem of deciding which value was in each instance to be preferred. And by preferring one to another, Blackstone was demonstrating which of them was actually more fundamental in his scheme. For this reason, our attempt to define the system of values in the *Commentaries* becomes inevitably the attempt to describe a hierarchy, and to discover, in the crucial cases where preference had to be shown, which of the professed values was being allowed to prevail.

The first of these, the value of "life," as Blackstone often called it in the trichotomy of "life, liberty, and property," would be too narrowly defined if we accepted his word for our purposes. The *Commentaries* in many places showed that by the first of the three values was meant not simply respect for life, but rather the larger value of "humanity" in its eighteenth-century sense: what Dr. Johnson's *Dictionary* defined as "benevolence, tenderness." Blackstone's trust in human feeling has already been evident in his fear of subjecting the legal system to the cold scrutiny of reason. The history of English law showed, as he said, that "mankind will not be reasoned out of the feelings of humanity," [1] and the *Commentaries* clearly assumed that the manifold virtues of the law were not fully accessible to reason alone.

Yet in demonstrating the importance of "humanity" and individual human feeling, the Enlightenment had enlisted the aid of Reason herself. Shaftesbury, the philosopher of sentiment, believing in the natural goodness of man, had come to make the feelings of the individual the test not only of beauty, but also of virtue. As early as 1699 he had written:

To deserve the name of good or virtuous, a creature must have all his inclinations and affections, his dispositions of mind and temper, suitable, and agreeing with the good of his kind, or of that system in which he is included, and of which he constitutes a part. To stand thus well affected, and to have one's affections right and entire, not only in respect of oneself but of society and the public, this is rectitude, integrity, or virtue. [2]

The appeal to sentiment and affection led to the appeal to "humanity"; and this concern for the suffering of one's fellow-creatures was to be expressed in many ways. In 1726, James Thomson lamented:

Ah! little think the gay licentious proud,
Whom pleasure, power, and affluence surround —
They, who their thoughtless hours in giddy mirth,
And wanton, often cruel, riot waste —
Ah! little think they, while they dance along,
How many feel, this very moment, death
And all the sad variety of pain;
How many sink in the devouring flood,
Or more devouring flame; how many bleed,
By shameful variance betwixt man and man;
How many pine in want, and dungeon-glooms,
Shut from the common air and common use
Of their own limbs; how many drink the cup
Of baleful grief, or eat the bitter bread
Of misery. . . .
                    Thought fond man
Of these, and all the thousand nameless ills
That one incessant struggle render life,
One scene of toil, of suffering, and of fate,
Vice in his high career would stand appalled.[3]

Later in the century many were to follow Thomson's advice: Howard and the Quakers demanded prison-reform; Clarkson and his colleagues urged the abolition of the slave-trade. Already in 1758, Dr. Johnson was saying, "No sooner is a new species of misery brought to view, and the design of relieving it proposed than every hand is open to contribute something, every tongue is busied in solicitation and every art of pleasure is employed for a time in the interest of Virtue." [4]

A characteristic statement of this general belief in "humanity" and in the importance of its being realized in England is found in the work of the now little-remembered John Brown. His popular *Estimate of the Manners and Principles of the Times*, first published in 1757, went through seven editions in less than two years. In this work, Brown coupled the Spirit of Humanity with the Spirit of Liberty as the two remaining virtues in what he considered the effeminate England of his time: "By Humanity . . . is meant, 'that Pity for Distress, that Moderation in limiting Punishments by their proper Ends and Measures, by which this Nation hath always been distinguished.'" [5] It represented "Regard for *Individuals*, rather than the *Public* State." [6] "The Lenity of our Laws in capital Causes; our Compassion for convicted Criminals; even the general Humanity of our Highwaymen and Robbers, compared with those of other Countries: these are concurrent Proofs that the Spirit of Humanity is natural to our Nation." [7]

Now the *Commentaries* unmistakably assumed "humanity," in the form described by Brown, to be an important value; and, like Brown and others, Blackstone found its realization in English law. Of course, it would have been blasphemous to suggest that the laws of nature were not "humane." And it was impossible to deny that the laws of England, derived from the laws of nature, must be similarly filled with benevolence. Indeed, much of the time when the *Commentaries* appeared to be praising the "humanity" of English law, they were merely further demonstrating that the laws of England did accord with the laws of nature. When Blackstone addressed himself to the "humane legislator" who must hear "the dictates of conscience and humanity," [8] he was simply repeating his belief that the laws of nature were the only sure guide to the laws of England.

Many statements in the *Commentaries* which seemed at first to be extolling mercy, were actually only additional ways of saying that English law, in harmony with natural law, did take account of the minutiae and complexities of human nature. Thus, as we have seen, Blackstone had explained that in cases of self-defence the law "respects the passions of the human mind; and (when external violence is offered to a man himself, or those to whom he bears a near connection), makes it lawful in him to do

himself that immediate justice, to which he is prompted
by nature, and which no prudential motives are strong
enough to restrain." [9] "Such indulgence does the law
shew to the frailty of human nature, and the workings of
parental affection," that a father who had killed another's
child, because the child had beaten his son, was held guilty
only of manslaughter and not of murder. [10] The Roman law
declared that a common harlot could not suffer rape, but
English law accorded more closely with the rules of human
nature. "The law of England does not judge so hardly of
offenders, as to cut off all opportunity of retreat even from
common strumpets, and to treat them as never capable
of amendment. It therefore holds it to be felony to force
even a concubine or harlot; because the woman may have
forsaken that unlawful course of life." [11] By taking account of the motive of self-defence, of the strength of
parental affection, and of the possibility that a harlot
might have changed her way of living, English law demonstrated that it was fitted to the facts of human nature.

Even the limitations on capital punishment in English
law were not so much a merciful indulgence as an inevitable accord with the demands of nature. "This natural
life being . . . the immediate donation of the great Creator,
cannot legally be disposed of or destroyed by any individual, neither by the person himself, nor by any other of his
fellow-creatures, merely upon their own authority. Yet
nevertheless it may, by the divine permission, be frequently forfeited for the breach of those laws of society,
which are enforced by the sanction of capital punishments. . . . The statute law of England does therefore
very seldom, and the common law does never, inflict any
punishment extending to life or limb, unless upon the highest necessity; and the constitution is an utter stranger to
any arbitrary power of killing or maiming the subject
without the express warrant of law." [12] Describing the
English law of capital punishment was thus simply another

way of showing how the laws of England followed the laws of nature.

From these cases it is clear that often when Blackstone seemed to be praising the "humanity" of the law, he was merely reasserting his argument that the laws of England must and did follow the outlines of human nature. But this became still clearer when the *Commentaries* actually appealed to individual human feeling — the Spirit of Humanity, as Brown might have said — to justify the punishment of particular crimes. Never was it clearer that "humanity" to Blackstone did not always mean mercy. He insisted that a proper measure of punishment for crime was the "malignity," "heinousness," or "enormity" of an act committed.[13] Hatefulness and disregard for natural feelings, whenever such viciousness appeared in human action, had to be punished; "humanity" itself demanded it. Thus, the law knew no accessories in the case of treason; all were punished as principals "upon account of the heinousness of the crime." The penalties for the traitorous crime of *praemunire* were fittingly applied to "other heinous offences." [14] Murder demanded capital punishment because it was "a crime at which human nature starts, and which is, I believe, punished almost universally throughout the world with death." [15] The sexual "crime against nature" had to be similarly penalized because "this the voice of nature and of reason, and the express law of God, determined to be capital." [16] The feelings of humanity could alone explain why a mere intention or attempt was to be less severely punished than a completed crime. "For evil, the nearer we approach it, is the more disagreeable and shocking; so that it requires more obstinacy in wickedness to perpetrate an unlawful action, than barely to entertain the thought of it: and it is an encouragement to repentance and remorse, even to the last stage of any crime, that it never is too late to retract." [17] After all, "the dread of evil is a much more forci-

The Humanity of the Criminal Law: The Appropriateness of Punishments

ble principle of human actions than the prospect of good."[18]
Violations of "humanity" must not go unredressed. "Humanity," moreover, demanded that the law should not be
weak and vacillating, but strong and clear. The law of
crimes "should be founded upon principles that are permanent, uniform, and universal." [19] "One of the greatest
advantages of our English law is, that not only the crimes
themselves which it punishes, but also the penalties which
it inflicts, are ascertained and notorious; nothing is left
to arbitrary discretion: the king by his judges dispenses
what the law has previously ordained; but is not himself
the legislator." [20] The certainty, uniformity, and reasonableness which made law a science, also were guarantees of
its regard for the feelings of human nature.

Instead of justifying the law because it was humane,
Blackstone was, then, defining "humanity" as whatever
the laws of England, expressing the laws of nature, required. And by showing "humanity" in the English laws,
he was further confirming their derivation from natural
laws.

## 2. THE REMARKABLE MERCY OF THE
### CRIMINAL LAW

This use of the notion of "humanity," to praise the English legal system as a whole, becomes clearer when we consider the institutions which Blackstone singled out as the
principal safeguards of humanity. He boasted of "that
tenderness and humanity to prisoners for which our English laws are justly famous." [21] Yet he could not deny that
the English statute-book provided the same penalties for
destroying a fish-pond as for killing one's mother; so he
found it convenient not to look at the statute-book. It is
significant that Blackstone looked on this occasion where
he seldom had looked for the qualities of the legal system,
— namely, to actual everyday practice. And he seemed to

find no paradox in pointing out the theoretical severity of the criminal statutes as the very fact which had made possible the law's universal practical humanity. For what was humanity if not tenderness and the willingness to mitigate a rule to fit particular cases? Was not the spectacle of English criminal law in action, one of daily defiance of rigid and cruel laws where they violated the humane feelings of the English people? As the *Commentaries* remarked, the effect of the severity of English statutes was that "the injured, through compassion, will often forbear to prosecute; juries, through compassion, will sometimes forget their oaths, and either acquit the guilty or mitigate the nature of the offence; and judges, through compassion, will respite one half of the convicts, and recommend them to royal mercy." [22] Even the apparent severities of English law thus multiplied the occasions for mercy.

Everywhere in the criminal law, the *Commentaries* noted the English people seizing these opportunities for mercy which their legal system had so excellently provided. Thus, "the humanity of the English nation has authorized, by a tacit consent, an almost general mitigation of such parts of these judgments as savour of torture or cruelty: a sledge or hurdle being usually allowed to such traitors as are condemned to be drawn; and there being very few instances (and those accidental or by negligence) of any person's being emboweled or burned, till previously deprived of sensation by strangling." [23] The laws against gypsies indeed seemed hard on the books, and before 1660 had even been to some extent enforced, "but, to the honour of our national humanity, there are no instances more modern than this, of carrying these laws into practice." [24] The statutes against papists provided another example. "Of which the president Montesquieu observes, that they are so rigorous, though not professedly of the sanguinary kind, that they do all the hurt that can possibly be done in cold blood. But, in answer to this, it may be observed (what foreigners who only judge from our statute-book are not fully apprized of), that these laws are seldom exerted to their utmost rigour: and, indeed if they were, it would be very difficult to excuse them." [25] In theory, to be sure, the law made concealment of the death of a bastard almost conclusive evidence of the child's being murdered by the mother; but in practice, other evidence was required.[26] So fruitful was English law in creating occasions for mercy that some statutes seemed to have been designed with the certainty of this mitigation in mind. For example, the *"peine forte et dure"* was "a judgment, which was purposely ordained to be exquisitely severe, that by that very means it might rarely be put in execution." [27] The merciful nature of the English people was being dramatically evidenced by their refusal to adhere to the letter of the law.

Moreover, English law seemed to have a sort of institutionalized mercifulness. This was shown by the fact that one half of English criminal law consisted of devices for mitigating the severity of the other half. Recent research has confirmed Blackstone's observation that the severity of the criminal statutes was seldom realized in practice.[28] And, significantly, the *Commentaries* directed their praise of the humanity of the legal system to the arrangements by which the letter of the law was circumvented in order to make the practice of the law tolerable.

Perhaps the most prominent of these merciful arrangements was trial by jury. To the jury Blackstone gave some of his most eloquent praise; it was the "bulwark of northern liberty" and "the glory of the English law." [29] One can easily see why he would have felt this, since in the England of his day the merciful collusion of jurors was one of the principal causes of the humane non-enforcement of statutes. Fictitious verdicts were common: juries would declare a five-pound note to be under the value of five shillings in order to save the prisoner from the penalties of the Shop-lifting Act; they would declare it to be worth less than a shilling to keep him from the pains of grand larceny.[30] Blackstone, although sometimes showing a qualm about this "pious perjury," [31] still thought these verdicts to be examples of the excellence of the jury system, and hence of the excellence of English law as a whole. For instance, in the law of forfeitures, the rule theoretically was that flight from an accusation of treason, felony, or petit larceny involved forfeiture of goods and chattels; but "the jury very seldom find the flight; forfeiture being looked upon, since the vast increase of personal property of late years, as too large a penalty for an offence, to which a man is prompted by the natural love of liberty." [32] The jury was the Englishman's true safeguard against arbitrary injustice.[33] And, despite the fact that a function of the jury, according to Blackstone's own testimony, was to create merciful lies, he could still praise it as the institution best "adapted and framed for the investigation of truth." [34]

An even more dramatic example of the humanity of English law was the benefit of clergy. Because this institution was such a remarkably roundabout way of obstructing the severity of statutes, Blackstone found in it the more convincing evidence of the powers of compensation within the legal system. The extension of benefit of clergy by judges in the eighteenth century was preventing the imposition of the capital penalty in numberless cases.[35] So the *Commentaries* devoted a whole chapter to the institution, its history and uses, concluding that a "noble alchemy" had "converted, by gradual mutations, what was at first an unreasonable exemption of particular popish ecclesiastics, into a merciful mitigation of the general law, with respect to capital punishment." [36] The English legal system thus seemed to have an uncanny property of automatic adjustment to the needs of human nature.

Presiding over all the specific provisions of English law

was a universal certainty of mitigation founded in the king's power of pardon. Blackstone considered this of fundamental importance. "Law (says an able writer) cannot be framed on principles of compassion to guilt; yet justice, by the constitution of England, is bound to be administered in mercy; this is promised by the king in his coronation oath. . . . This is indeed one of the great advantages of monarchy in general, above any other form of government; that there is a magistrate who has it in his power to extend mercy, wherever he thinks it is deserved; holding a court of inquiry in his own breast, to soften the rigour of the general law, in such criminal cases as merit an exemption from punishment." [37] Wherever the letter of the law seemed to "border a little upon severity," as in the law punishing attempted suicide, one could rely on the power of alleviation in the sovereign to see that no injustice would be done.[38]

### 3. THE DUE REVERENCE FOR THE LAW

It is significant that the moral which Blackstone drew from his survey of the criminal law was actually not an insistence on the primary importance of mercy. He did not suggest that the ingenuity of the English people was securing them justice despite their laws; instead he delivered a panegyric on the English legal system. The intricacy of the devices by which the laws of England attained a rough sort of mercy was the focus of attention in the *Commentaries*. And, in place of remarking on the unreliability of perjurious jurors, metaphysical judges, and capricious sovereigns, he used the whole story as evidence that the legal system was itself the proper object of the Englishman's confidence. "Humanity" was actually being used to explain away apparent deformities in the legal system, and was being subordinated to some other value which was embodied in that system and which in all cases had to be preserved. The appeal to "humanity" had in the first place demonstrated how indissolubly the English law was bound up with the law of nature, and had thereby forestalled criticism of English institutions. Now Blackstone pointed to fictitious verdicts, benefit of clergy, royal pardon, and other legal devices, to prove that English law contained within itself a mitigating principle, and that the legal system as a whole was therefore entitled to respect and preservation.

Nowhere in the *Commentaries* was the subordinate position of the value of "humanity" more evident than in the argument for reform of the criminal law. Here Blackstone made more adverse criticism of the legal system than anywhere else. He did not like the "sanguinary" statutes: "It is a melancholy truth, that among the variety of actions which men are daily liable to commit, no less than a hundred and sixty have been declared by act of parliament to be felonies without benefit of clergy; or, in other words, to be worthy of instant death." [39] He wanted to see these statutes changed, and he seems, superficially at least, to have been urging "reform" of the criminal law. It is important, however, to see that this criticism fitted into his acceptance of the English legal system, and not to be misled by his general remarks or by the reputation of his reformist mentor in criminology. The theory of criminal law suggested by Montesquieu, and developed by Beccaria, was wholeheartedly adopted by Blackstone.[40] And, although Beccaria's *Essay on Crimes and Punishments* did not appear until 1764, Blackstone referred to it several times and made extensive use of the ideas in it. Beccaria in his Introduction had called himself the student of Montesquieu, and had explained, "I shall be happy, if, with him, I can obtain the secret thanks of the obscure, and peaceful disciples of reason, and philosophy, and excite that tender emotion, in which sensible minds sympathize with him, who pleads the cause of humanity." [41] The gist of Beccaria's program was that punishments should be reduced, made more certain and "proportionate" to the various crimes, and more suitable to the conditions of particular countries. Throughout his *Essay*, Beccaria attempted to show that the aims of humanity and expedience were inseparable, and that criminal laws could never be really effective until the principle of proportion in punishment had been adopted. It is easy to see how excellently this theory suited the purpose of the *Commentaries*. Since the beneficent God of Nature had identified the "humanity" of laws with their effectiveness, Blackstone was provided with still another argument in favour of the existing English legal system, which was already the most humane in Europe,[42] and which contained within itself intricate mitigating devices.

But, if this was the case, how could Blackstone favour reform in the English criminal law? The answer to this is found in the kind of arguments which he gave for reform and in the end he hoped to see it attain. Blackstone actually did not complain that the law required reforming because it was inhumane. He had given too much evidence of the humanity of English law to permit himself such an argument; the English laws were already as humane as possible in a polite, commercial country. The *Commentaries* did, however, — and this is significant — complain that "sanguinary statutes" must be abolished because they were ineffective, and had bred general irreverence for law. The very humanity of English criminal laws in operation had made the convict consider himself "peculiarly unfortunate, in falling at last a sacrifice to those laws, which long impunity has taught him to contemn."[43] Blackstone believed in law and order, and he was disturbed to see the widespread contempt for law which had sprung from the existence of so many unenforceable statutes.

It was therefore expedience, much more than "humanity" that had encouraged Blackstone to favour Beccaria's merciful penology. For "sanguinary laws are a bad symptom of the distemper of any state, or at least of its weak constitution. . . . It is a kind of quackery in government, and argues a want of solid skill, to apply the same universal remedy, the *ultimum supplicium*, to every case of difficulty." [44] The criminal laws that were the most effective, and that encouraged the greatest respect for laws in general, were those built on preventive principles. [45] The *Commentaries* devoted a whole chapter to "Means of Preventing Offences," which explained, "Really it is an honour, and almost a singular one, to our English laws, that they furnish a title of this sort; since *preventive* justice is, upon every principle of reason, of humanity, and of sound policy, preferable in all respects to *punishing* justice; the execution of which, though necessary, and in its consequences a species of mercy to the commonwealth, is always attended with many harsh and disagreeable circumstances." [46] The principles of preventive justice were now clear since Beccaria had shown that "crimes are more effectually prevented by the *certainty*, than by the *severity*, of punishment. For the excessive severity of laws (says Montesquieu) hinders their execution: when the punishment surpasses all measure, the public will frequently out of humanity prefer impunity to it." [47] On every side, in the history of attainting juries, in the growth of constructive treasons, in the evasion of the provisions against smuggling, were examples of laws which because of their over-violence were not being enforced. [48]

Blackstone's interest in legal "reform" had thus grown out of concern about the general disrespect for law, and not primarily out of humanitarian zeal. Laws which invited evasion and spread disregard for the letter of the statutes were themselves subversive of civil society. The very course of Blackstone's argument for the repeal of criminal statutes was in this way evidence of the subordinate position which he gave to "humanity" in the law. Indeed, the reform that he was suggesting would, according to his own statement, have been likely to make the law less merciful rather than more so. The criminal law, in the form described by the *Commentaries*, was already in its haphazard way providing more opportunities of mitigation than would have been the case under any rigid system of proportioned, universally-enforced punishments. But Blackstone was still the advocate of "reform," since by that advocacy he could urge the importance of preserving the legal system as a whole, and of encouraging due reverence for law.

The examination of Blackstone's concept of "humanity" must lead us to the conclusion that it was in his scheme a subordinate value.[49] "Humanity" was a concept to which the *Commentaries* could appeal in order to invest the legal system with a certain desirability, by showing it to be closely in harmony with the laws of nature, and richly endowed with powers of self-mitigation. Moreover, the *Commentaries* showed that not only must an expedient law be humane; a law could not be expedient unless it was humane. Where English law was humane, it could not help being effective, and where it might seem inhumane, a guiding Providence prevented it from being enforced. Any apparent lack of humanity in theory could thus not become an inhumanity in practice. The upshot of all this was that "humanity" was simply a means toward the effectiveness of English law. But if "humanity" was a subordinate value in the scheme of the *Commentaries*, what were the superior values which themselves justified the existence of the legal system? In order to answer this question we must now turn to the second of the terms in Blackstone's trinity.

# LIBERTY

## I. THE ENGLISH GODDESS OF LIBERTY

E ASY THOUGH IT WAS for Blackstone to profess an equal belief in humanity, in liberty, and in property, the application of his credo, we have already seen, revealed certain preferences. Therefore, when we attempt to define Blackstone's meaning of "liberty," we are in quest not only of the precise eulogistic sense of the word, but of a definition of its place in his hierarchy of values. When Blackstone asserted the value of liberty, he was, to be sure, simply expressing a popular enthusiasm. Since the Revolution of 1688, political theory and polite literature had been praising the Noble Goddess. And, at least till the time of Wilkes and the French Revolution, liberty was in England a shibboleth of conservatives, who liked to believe that the last revolution had attained the ultimate in free constitutions. In 1710, Addison devoted a number of *The Tatler* to a description of his vision of the goddess of liberty:

Every glance of her eye cast a track of light where it fell, that revived the spring, and made all things smile about her. My heart grew cheerful at the sight of her, and as she looked upon me, I found a certain confidence grow in me, and such an inward resolution as I never felt before that time.[1]

Poets joined in singing her praises; and Pope said through the mouth of his peasant:

> "Give me again my hollow Tree,
> A Crust of Bread, and Liberty!"[2]

Many thought that to praise liberty was to praise England. James Thomson's long poem, "Liberty," was published in the seventeen-thirties; it was an "attempt to trace Liberty from the first ages down to her excellent establishment in Great Britain." [3] "The Goddess of Liberty, who is supposed to speak through the whole, appears, characterized as British Liberty." [4] He, too, could not restrain his impassioned praise:

> "Hail! independence, hail! heaven's next best gift
> To that of life and an immortal soul!
> The life of life! that to the banquet high
> And sober meal gives taste; to the bowed roof
> Fair-dreamed repose, and to the cottage charms. " [5]

Who could resist the eloquence of poets? Who could fail to throb at the very name of liberty? Again John Brown described the general sentiment when he said, in his *Estimate of the Manners and Principles of the Times* in 1757, that with the Spirit of Humanity, the Spirit of Liberty was one of the great remaining virtues of England. Of liberty he wrote, "This great Spirit hath produced more full and compleat Effects in our own Country, than in any known Nation that ever was upon Earth. It appears, indeed, from a Concurrence of Facts too large to be produced here, that whereas it hath been ingrafted by the Arts of Policy in other Countries, it shoots up here as from its natural Climate, Stock, and Soil." [6] "Liberty is the first necessary Ingredient in the Composition of *English* Happiness." [7]

Foreigners had joined Englishmen in their praise of liberty, and helped confirm the belief that England was her natural home. Montesquieu, writing in his *Spirit of Laws* in 1748, showed that although all governments had peace as their end, "one nation there is also in the world that has for the direct end of its constitution political liberty." That country was, of course, England, where "liberty will appear in its highest perfection." [8]  Blackstone, following Montesquieu, was easily persuaded that to honour English laws was a way of honouring the desirable goddess. Anyone who had read and believed Montesquieu might have found it difficult to say whether he was praising the English constitution because he loved liberty, or praising liberty because he loved the English constitution. They seemed by nature inseparable.

Yet the *Commentaries* were more subtle; they were not satisfied with such an obvious definition. And Blackstone, in the course of his work, showed that liberty represented two things: first, the free expression of the *will* of the individual; and, second, the full assertion of the *rights* of the individual. A legal system which left free the will of each man without thereby infringing the rights of other men would perfectly realize the value of liberty.

## 2. LIBERTY AS THE EXPRESSION OF FREE WILL

The individual's freedom of will had, of course, been the very foundation of society. Since "the only true and natural foundations of society are the wants and the fears of individuals," civil society had come into existence when men freely exercised their wills in an original contract.[9] Thus the criminal law derived its authority from the supposed free decision of all men, including even criminals, to obey it. "Whatever power, therefore, individuals had of punishing offences against the law of nature, that is now vested in the magistrate alone; who bears the sword of justice by the consent of the whole community. . . . As to offences merely against the laws of society . . . punishing such criminals is founded upon this principle, that the law by which they suffer was made by their own consent." [10] Laws themselves were in this sense the emblems of freedom.

Since laws expressed the freedom of the individual's will, the laws punished only those misdeeds which had been the product of an individual's free will. "All the

several pleas and excuses, which protect the committer of
a forbidden act from the punishment which is otherwise
annexed thereto, may be reduced to this single consideration, the want or defect of *will*. An involuntary act, as
it has no claim to merit, so neither can it induce any guilt:
the concurrence of the will, when it has its choice either to
do or to avoid the fact in question, being the only thing
that renders human action either praiseworthy or culpa-
ble." [11] All instances of exemption from punishment were
then classified under the various "species of defect in
will." [12] It would indeed have been a strange deviation
from the law of nature if English law had been otherwise;
because the freedom of the will had been the precious gift
of a beneficent God to the most favoured of his creatures.
"Punishments are therefore only inflicted for the abuse of
that free will which God has given to man." [13] To have
denied expression to this God-given faculty would have
been not merely tyranny, but sacrilege as well.

The laws of England, as Blackstone showed, made no
such denial. This was a "free constitution," used "in a
land of liberty," and he found everywhere in England
"proof of that genuine freedom, which is the boast of this
age and country." [14] Numerous examples in the *Commentaries* showed that the English constitution was one, if not
the only one, "where political or civil liberty is the direct
end of its constitution." [15] This fact was assured by the
unique customary nature of English law: "our common
law depends upon custom; which carries this internal
evidence of freedom along with it, that it probably was
introduced by the voluntary consent of the people." [16]
Blackstone's appeal to common agreement and his use of
the maxim, which we have already discussed, demonstrated how important he considered this general consent
in validating the legal system. All this meant that the
British subject, by simple obedience to the laws, and adherence to custom, was loudly declaring the desires of his

own will and showing his power actually to create law. This theory made the freedom of will of every Englishman automatic, and even compulsory.

The *Commentaries*, moreover, went on and proved that in England not only was the individual free to make laws; he was actually in a sense free to disobey them. Municipal laws were rules "commanding what is right and prohibiting what is wrong." [17] As these rules derived their compulsive force from the laws of nature, it was important to recognize that where an individual saw an ostensible law to be a violation of God's prescriptions, he was obliged to disobey it. A good man could not be bound in justice to obey unnatural laws. To have accepted this principle in unqualified form would, however, have left the peace of society to the perverse discretion of the criminal. Yet, on the other hand, if the laws of society were so peremptory as to force a man to do what the man knew to be natural evil, they could not retain their virtuous identity with the laws of nature. Blackstone found for this dilemma a logical solution which, though tortuous, was not unconvincing. Every man surely was in conscience bound to obey the natural law; but Blackstone painstakingly explained that, in the case of merely positive laws, "conscience is no farther concerned, than by directing a submission to the penalty, in case of our breach of those laws: for otherwise the multitude of penal laws in a state would not only be looked upon as an impolitic, but would also be a very wicked thing; if every such law were a snare for the conscience of the subject. But in these cases the alternative is offered to every man; 'either abstain from this, or submit to such a penalty:' and his conscience will be clear, which ever side of the alternative he thinks proper to embrace." [18] In this way Blackstone fitted together a jurisprudence of liberty.

In addition to these general principles, there were many specific provisions in the English constitution to assure the identity of the free wills of the subjects with the determinations of the law. The jury, "the voice of the people," in which Blackstone found the virtue of humanity, also helped Englishmen secure their liberty. It was an institution which obviously made legal decisions, at least in important cases, conform to the desires of the individuals in the society.[19] Another safeguard of the freedom of individuals was the system of checks and balances: such a nice equilibrium had been established by the separation of executive, judicial, and legislative powers that no one of them could oppress the British subject. In the English constitution "all the parts of it form a mutual check upon each other."[20] The general principles, which might themselves have seemed sufficient surety for the free will of Englishmen, were improved by these practical arrangements.

The *Commentaries* thus clearly made the expression of the free will of the individual a desirable end of the laws of England. Blackstone's theology declared that in the beginning God had endowed mankind with this freedom. "The absolute rights of man, considered as a free agent, endowed with discernment to know good from evil, and with power of choosing those measures which appear to him to be most desirable, are usually summed up in one general appellation, and denominated the natural liberty of mankind. This natural liberty consists properly in a power of acting as one thinks fit, without any restraint or control, unless by the law of nature; being a right inherent in us by birth, and one of the gifts of God to man at his creation, when He imbued him with the faculty of free will."[21] But surely not all men, now, had this power of acting "without any restraint or control."

Blackstone was careful to show that the laws of England discriminated with great nicety to be sure that only men who were really capable of this freedom had their wills embodied in law. And he descended to particulars in order to show how the decisive power to make laws resided in the hands of only the truly free. Just as infants and lunatics had a defect of will which entitled them to freedom from punishment by the criminal law, so some men had a defect of will which deprived their warped desires of any title to expression in the laws of the community. "In a free state every man, who is supposed a free agent, ought to be in some measure his own governor; and therefore a branch at least of the legislative power should reside in the whole body of the people." [22] Who were the men who were qualified by their independence of spirit to exercise this power for the whole people? Obviously, only men of property. In a revealing passage, Blackstone showed, at length, how necessary was this answer to the question. "The true reason of requiring any qualification, with regard to property, in voters," the *Commentaries* explained, "is to exclude such persons as are in so mean a situation that they are esteemed to have no will of their own. If these persons had votes, they would be tempted to dispose of them under some undue influence or other. This would give a great, an artful, or a wealthy man, a larger share in elections than is consistent with general liberty. If it were probable that every man would give his vote freely and without influence of any kind, then, upon the true theory and genuine principles of liberty, every member of the community, however poor, should have a vote in electing those delegates, to whose charge is committed the disposal of his property, his liberty, and his life. But, since that can hardly be expected in persons of indigent fortunes, or such as are under the immediate dominion of others, all popular states have been obliged to establish certain qualifications; whereby some, who are suspected to have no will of their own, are excluded from voting, in order to set other individuals, whose wills may be supposed independent, more thoroughly upon a level with each other." [23] The apparent limitation of the franchise

The Free Englishman at Election Time

was thus, in truth, no limitation at all; it assured the unfettered expression of all wills that were truly free.

Even though the possession of property was made the necessary prerequisite of freedom, there was still latent, in this notion of liberty as expression of free will, a potentially dangerous individualism. If free will and not protection of property was the final objective, might it not be open to misguided persons to attempt to show that some kind of free will could be attained by persons without property? Or, worse, would it not be possible to argue that since free will was the desired end, and the possession of property the only means, the state should undertake to give every subject sufficient property so that he could be truly free? Surely this reasoning was possible; and Blackstone was careful to forestall these subversive arguments.

## 3. LIBERTY AS THE PROTECTION OF RIGHTS

By a remarkable irony Blackstone used the very notion which, before the end of the eighteenth century, Paine and Jefferson and Robespierre were to use to make the name of liberty odious to conservative ears.[24] This conception was "The Rights of Man." Blackstone employed it in order to disconcert any who might argue from the desirability of freedom of will to the importance of spreading property to give all such a freedom. "The Rights of Man" provided the salutary check which, according to Blackstone, could alone make liberty feasible. So he made the second element in his conception of liberty the protection of the rights of the individual. Indeed, the expressions "rights of Englishmen" and "liberties of Englishmen" were used in the *Commentaries* interchangeably. "For civil liberty, rightly understood, consists in protecting the rights of individuals by the united force of society." [25] "The absolute rights of man ... are usually summed up in one general appellation, and denominated the natural liberty of mankind." [26] Moreover, "the absolute rights of every Englishman (which, taken in a political and extensive sense, are usually called their liberties,) as they are founded on nature and reason, so they are coeval with our form of government." [27] The primary place that Blackstone sometimes seemed to give to the protection of "liberty" was thus due to the fact that on these occasions he had equated "liberty" with the protection of rights, and had made the protection of rights the primary end of government.

The whole structure of the *Commentaries* was built around the concept of rights. The first chapter of the first book was entitled "Of the Absolute Rights of Individuals," and Blackstone never forgot the fundamental importance of the notion from which he had started in this opening chapter. In every discussion, rights were considered primary, while duties were treated as secondary or merely negative. Thus, the first and second books of the *Commentaries* dealt with rights; the third and fourth, with wrongs. The law of property, by a dubious jurisprudence, was described under the "Rights of Things." And Blackstone justified the primary position of rights since "wrongs [he discreetly forbore saying 'duties'] . . . for the most part convey to us an idea merely negative, as being nothing else but a privation of right. For which reason it was necessary, that before we entered at all into the discussion of wrongs, we should entertain a clear and distinct notion of rights." [28] The legal philosophy of the *Commentaries* may not seem so confused if we remember that for Blackstone rights always held the center of the stage.[29] He chose to consider even duties as a kind of rights: "Now the rights of persons that are commanded to be observed by the municipal laws are of two sorts: first, such as are due *from* every citizen, which are usually called civil *duties*; and, secondly, such as belong *to* him, which is the more popular acceptation of *rights* or *jura*.

Both may indeed be comprised in this latter division." [30]
The law, moreover, was partial to rights, and, although it
would not enforce all absolute duties, it did enforce all
absolute rights.[31] Blackstone sometimes founded the
whole of law, — indeed the whole of society — on the
need for protecting the rights of man. "For the principal
aim of society is to protect individuals in the enjoyment
of those absolute rights which were vested in them by the
immutable laws of nature; but which could not be preserved in peace without that mutual assistance and intercourse which is gained by the institution of friendly and
social communities. Hence it follows, that the first and
primary end of human laws is to maintain and regulate
these *absolute* rights of individuals." [32]

But what were these "absolute rights of individuals"
which signified man's liberty? Blackstone answered clearly
and concisely: they were life or security, liberty, and
property.[33] Thus, in order to understand what the *Commentaries* meant by liberty we must consider in turn each
of these "absolute rights." The right of life, which, as we
saw in the last chapter, was often equated with "humanity," was in the discussion of liberty often subsumed under
the right to security: "The right of personal security consists in a person's legal and uninterrupted enjoyment of his
life, his limbs, his body, his health, and his reputation." [34]
Yet Blackstone's insistence here was not so much on the
absolute inviolability of the individual, as on the need to
respect the individual's rights, if society was to be maintained as a going concern.

It is obvious from his definition of the right of personal
security that Blackstone did not consider this to be an
absolute value; rather for him it seemed a means toward
preserving everything else valuable in society. The section on crimes that dealt with homicide opened with the
explanation, "Were these injuries [to individuals] indeed
confined to individuals only, and did they affect none but

their immediate objects, they would fall absolutely under the notion of private wrongs; for which a satisfaction would be due only to the party injured. . . . But the wrongs, which we are now to treat of, are of a much more extensive consequence: 1. Because it is impossible they can be committed without a violation of the laws of nature. . . . 2. Because they include in them almost always a breach of the public peace. 3. Because by their example and evil tendency they threaten and endanger the subversion of all civil society." [35] The maintenance of the right of personal security was, thus, subordinate to the preservation of the public peace. This was further evidenced by the fact that, in the case of treason, murder, and robbery which were the most "gross and atrocious" attacks on personal security, the private wrong was "swallowed up" in the public, and the wronged individual actually received no satisfaction at all.[36] It is significant that the right of life or personal security filled only a small place in the *Commentaries* as a whole: one short chapter dealt specifically with the remedies which the individual had for protecting this security of his person.[37] All other mention of this right was included under general discussions either of liberty or of property. The right of life and personal security, whether considered in its aspect of "humanity" or of "security," was, according to the *Commentaries*, properly inferior to other values in the legal system. It appears, then, that the first of the "absolute" rights contained in the notion of liberty, was really not absolute at all, but was merely a means toward protecting the legally constituted society in which Blackstone believed.

The second of the absolute rights of which Blackstone's "liberty" consisted was (by an impeccable logic) the "right of liberty." This might seem like mere tautology; but in fact it was not. For when he defined the "right of liberty," Blackstone omitted the notion of the freedom of the individual will. The reason for this is obvious, since

a right to a free will would have given every man a right
to enough property to make him truly free.

Even apart from this crucial omission of the notion of
freedom of the will, the description of the right to liberty
was not entirely redundant. For now, to his definition of
liberty, Blackstone added the right of freedom from imprisonment. "This personal liberty consists in the power
of locomotion, of changing situation, or moving one's person to whatsoever place one's own inclination may direct,
without imprisonment or restraint, unless by due course
of law." [38] However significant was this right, and however potent was secret imprisonment as the instrument of
tyranny, still the right of freedom from imprisonment was
not absolute. As the *Commentaries* declared, "sometimes,
when the state is in real danger, even this [deprivation of
liberty] may be a necessary measure." [39] The description
of legal devices for preventing infringement of this personal liberty did not loom large in Blackstone's discussion of the laws of England,[40] for the right to be protected
from the rare threat of false imprisonment could not in that
polite and enlightened age have seemed of much practical
importance. The real importance of the "absolute" right
of liberty in the *Commentaries* was, rather, in its identity
with all of man's rights, in its equivalence with the rights
of security, liberty, and property.

But the rights of security and of liberty were, as Blackstone said, properly abridgeable by law. In other words,
these were actually rights for the definition of which one
could look only to the law of England. For example, "the
liberty of the press is indeed essential to the nature of a
free state; but this consists in laying no *previous* restraints
upon publications, and not in freedom from censure for
criminal matter when published. . . . To punish (as the
law does at present) any dangerous or offensive writings,
which, when published, shall on a fair and impartial trial
be adjudged of a pernicious tendency, is necessary for the

preservation of peace and good order, of government and religion, the only solid foundations of civil liberty. Thus the will of individuals is still left free; the abuse only of that free-will is the object of legal punishment. Neither is any restraint hereby laid upon freedom of thought or enquiry: liberty of private sentiment is still left; the disseminating, or making public, of bad sentiments, destructive of the ends of society, is the crime which society corrects.... To censure the licentiousness, is to maintain the liberty, of the press." [41] Thus freedom of expression itself helped conserve the existing social order.

The general definition of legal rights in the *Commentaries* stated that they were only those rights for the infringement of which there was a legal remedy.[42] Therefore a man's liberty, — if it was the expression of his legal rights — meant nothing more than his freedom to do whatever the law allowed him to do. Was not the argument then circular? And if this was the case, Blackstone, when he called the right of security and the right of liberty "natural rights," was simply using an epithet which made the existing limitations on the legal rights of Englishmen seem inevitable. Both "life" and "liberty" were really being subordinated to some other value.

At this stage it might seem that the only absolute value which was to appear was the legal system itself. But Blackstone did insist that there was some right which was not merely the possession of a legal permission. This he found in the third of the "absolute" rights which he had subsumed under the concept of liberty. Here Blackstone was to discover a liberty which was truly absolute, a right subordinate to none, and inviolable. When we consider property, we are, then, approaching the high altar of Blackstone's legal theology.

# CHAPTER NINE

# PROPERTY

## I. THE ELEMENTS OF OBSCURITY

SOME OF THE MOST OBSCURE — one might say mystical — passages in the *Commentaries* are the descriptions of the right of property. And this must be at least partly explained by the position that this right held in Blackstone's system of values. Subordinate values, like humanity and liberty, could be defined without too much difficulty; but here the Mystery of Law protected the primary value of the whole system from the gaze of the vulgar and the attack of the ill-intentioned.

Another explanation of the obscurity of Blackstone's creed of property is found in the fact that "property" actually corresponded to a rapidly-changing set of social circumstances. By the middle of the eighteenth century in England, the changes that were to be the Industrial Revolution were under way. Even before 1765, the growth in population, changes in agriculture, enclosures, innovations of steam power and machinery, and the expansion of commerce had begun to transform English life. The mercantilist system was disintegrating. Forces were at work which would eventually take the country away from the landowners and give it to the shopkeepers and their masters, the manufacturers. Yet, in spite of the fact that, between 1688 and 1776, property as a social fact was undergoing striking metamorphosis, the popular theory of property was hardly changing at all. The England of Adam Smith was surely not the England of John Locke; yet the theory of property of the *Wealth of Nations* was substantially the theory of the *Civil Government*. Indeed, Locke's formulation of the nature of property was the accepted theoretical statement throughout the eighteenth century; and his theory could be used to justify the changing social fact, partly because of its many-sidedness. In the course of the century it was many things to many men, and "Locke" became the pseudonym for everyman's theory of property.

The opportunity for this ambiguity and for the use of his doctrine by both radicals and conservatives had been created by Locke himself in the double nature of his doctrine. This ambivalence was due to the part played in his theory by the two figures, Nature and Civil Government. The famous fifth chapter of his Second Essay of Civil Government explained that ownership of a thing was rooted in the fact that a man had mixed his labour, and therefore his personality, with that thing; the title thus originated in nature, and even before there had been any government. If this appeal to nature had been the only element in his theory, it might not have been easy for English conservatives in the eighteenth century, and all conservatives since then, to find his theory useful for their purposes. But Nature was only one figure in his story. And as Nature played a prominent role as the founder of property, the institution of property, according to Locke, was in turn given a crucial role in the foundation of Civil Government. By this explanation the theoretical justification of the state was strengthened; Civil Government became the bulwark of an institution of property that had been created by Nature's laws and God's own prescriptions. The fact that civil society had not created property, but had merely recognized it, gave the state itself a high purpose which none of the petty needs of men could have given. The

state as the protector of property seemed thus to be the
protector of natural values. This theory which had made
Civil Government seem so much more important than if
men had set it up for their own purposes, clearly had conservative uses. The state, property, nature, and God
could all become confused into the single value of keeping society as it was. "Locke's Theory of Property," even
according to Locke, thus contained contrary elements.
For radicals could, and did, appeal to the concept of nature
as the real foundation of private property, and as the
justification for revising the existing property-structure;
while conservatives could appeal to the state-protected
status of property as giving all existing property the approval and sanctions of Nature herself.[1]

Now in Blackstone's theory of property we will be able
to find the contrary elements of Locke's theory. "Nature"
and "Civil Government" are the foundations of his explanation, and, at the same time, the elements of his
obscurity. We will discover that the *Commentaries* defined the right of property as an absolute value, which
should not be abridged under any circumstances. Yet the
foundation of property was laid both in nature and in the
state. We will see that some of the apparent confusion in
Blackstone's theory derived from the fact that he was so
careful to provide a definition of property which would
include all the forms of property that were found in his
society. Many of these forms, as even Blackstone admitted, had not been created in nature. Thus, to justify
the whole institution of property as it existed in eighteenth-
century England, it was necessary to assert that property
had been created not only by Nature but also by Civil
Government. Blackstone, of course, insisted that which-
ever was given the more prominent original role, property
was always inviolable. Whatever the effect of the duality
of his theory in making his doctrine appear confused, this
doubleness actually strengthened his assertion of the

inviolability of property. And, we shall see that, while the institution of property was being invested with the ambiguous and numerous virtues of natural law, it was at the same time being made identical with the peace and progress of society.

## 2. THE ORIGIN OF PROPERTY IN NATURE

The *Commentaries* explained, in the first place, that property was ultimately founded in the law of nature, which God had in this case clearly proclaimed in the Bible. "In the beginning of the world, we are informed by holy writ, the all-bountiful Creator gave to man 'dominion over all the earth; and over the fish of the sea, and over the fowl of the air, and over every living thing that moveth upon the earth.' This is the only true and solid foundation of man's dominion over external things, whatever airy metaphysical notions may have been started by fanciful writers upon this subject. The earth, therefore, and all things therein, are the general property of all mankind, exclusive of other beings, from the immediate gift of the Creator." [2] Of course, this primitive communism had not lasted. Men, following God's order, first established a sort of property in the mere use of things, before finally establishing what Blackstone called property in the very substance of things. Individual property had been first appropriated "by the bodily labour of the occupant, which bodily labour, bestowed upon any subject which before lay in common to all men, is universally allowed to give the fairest and most reasonable title to an exclusive property therein." [3] To be sure, certain things, like light, air, water, and wild animals, were by nature capable of only a limited form of ownership. [4] Still, changes in the form of property, ultimately dictated by the law of nature, were brought about when men, following their self-interest, had given the institution the new shapes which their increasingly complex life demanded. And in this way, even the more modern forms of property had the sanction of nature. Within these changing limits prescribed by nature, property was, according to Blackstone, always inviolable. "So great moreover is the regard of the law for private property, that it will not authorize the least violation of it; no, not even for the general good of the whole community." [5] There were many cases therefore "in which the law of the land has postponed even public necessity to the sacred and inviolable rights of private property." [6] The law of nature dictated that "every man has, or ought to have, by the laws of society, a power over his own property." [7] Property was thus an absolute right because it existed even independently of society. [8]

Yet when Blackstone attempted to define the natural limits of property, there seemed at first to be an incompatibility between property and civil government. The right of property was "that sole and despotic dominion which one man claims and exercises over the external things of the world, in total exclusion of the right of any other individual in the universe." [9] But was not the aim of civil government to limit that dominion when it conflicted with the right of other individuals? If the right of ownership was founded in the right of a man to retain what he could occupy, [10] was not society daily inhibiting man's exercise of this right by prescribing the rules of occupancy? As Blackstone himself said, "There is no foundation in nature or in natural law, why a set of words upon parchment should convey the dominion of land; why the son shall have the right to exclude his fellow creatures from a determinate spot of ground, because his father had done so before him: or why the occupier of a particular field or of a jewel, when lying on his death-bed, and no longer able to maintain possession, should be entitled to tell the rest of the world which of them should enjoy it after him." [11] This was all very curious, particularly in view of the fact that the *Commentaries* had not explained that man had given up any of his natural right of property on entering society.[12] For Blackstone, however, the natural demands of property and the needs of civil society were not in conflict. Government, at least in England, had not abridged man's natural right in property; on the contrary, this natural right had actually been enlarged and given fuller expression. Every case which at first seemed to be an abridgement was revealed, as one looked deeper, to be necessary to the fullest realization of the natural right.

## 3. THE FULFILLMENT OF PROPERTY IN ENGLISH LAW

The English constitution, according to Blackstone, had fulfilled and enlarged the right of property in many ways. English law had, for example, found an owner for everything that was by its nature capable of ownership, even where nature had neglected to make an assignment. Forests, waste grounds, wrecks, estrays, game, and all the things that had not been "appropriated in the general distribution" had been distributed by the laws of England according to the natural canons.[13]

Moreover, the *Commentaries* showed that the apparent restrictions on property imposed by the laws were really merely the accurate expression of the natural rules of the creation of property. Thus, there was no injustice in the restrictions of the game laws, because they did not abridge a present right of property in man, but simply prevented the acquisition of future property.[14] Infringement on the "ownership" of tame animals was not felony "if they are only kept for pleasure, curiosity, or whim, as dogs, bears, cats, apes, parrots, and singing-birds; because their value is not intrinsic, but depending only upon the caprice of the owner."[15] Copyright was founded in the natural claim of a man to the product of his labour.[16] The right of eminent

domain was in no way an invasion of property. "If a
new road, for instance, were to be made through the
grounds of a private person, it might, perhaps, be exten-
sively beneficial to the public; but the law permits no
man, or set of men, to do this without consent of the owner
of the land. . . . Besides the public good is in nothing
more essentially interested than in the protection of every
individual's private rights, as modelled by the municipal
law. In this and similar cases the legislature alone can,
and indeed frequently does, interpose, and compel the
individual to acquiesce. But how does it interpose and
compel? Not by absolutely stripping the subject of his
property in an arbitrary manner; but by giving him a full
indemnification and equivalent for the injury thereby
sustained. The public is now considered as an individual,
treating with another individual for an exchange. All
that the legislature does is to oblige the owner to alienate
his possessions for a reasonable price." [17] But what of
taxation? Was this not a compulsive acquisition of private property by society? Surely not. "For no subject
of England can be constrained to pay any aids or taxes,
even for the defence of the realm or the support of government, but such as are imposed by his own consent, or that
of his representatives in parliament." [18] Nowhere did
English law allow the invasion of property.

It was easy for Blackstone to find evidence that the law
had enlarged the right of property even beyond the form
which it had in nature. The right to transfer property was
a "social advantage" for which man had to thank the
laws of England.[19] The right to make a will and the right
of inheritance were both the creations of positive law.
"For, naturally speaking, the instant a man ceases to be,
he ceases to have any dominion: else if he had a right to
dispose of his acquisitions one moment beyond his life,
he would also have a right to direct their disposal for a
million of ages after him: which would be highly absurd

and inconvenient. All property must therefore cease upon death, considering men as absolute individuals, and unconnected with civil society: for, then, by the principles before established, the next immediate occupant would acquire a right in all that the deceased possessed. But . . . the universal law of almost every nation (which is a kind of secondary law of nature) has either given the dying person a power of continuing his property, by disposing of his possessions by will; or, in case he neglects to dispose of it, or is not permitted to make any disposition at all, the municipal law of the country then steps in, and declares who shall be the successor, representatives, or heir of the deceased." [20] Some of the most valuable of the perquisites of property thus derived directly from the law of civil society.

Of course, the fact that the laws of England were themselves derived from the laws of nature meant that, to Blackstone, the distinction between the natural and the civil origins of property might not have seemed important. But the *Commentaries* sometimes clearly declared that the laws of civil society had been primarily responsible for the creation of property. And, for all that Blackstone had said of the origin of property in nature, he now said that all property was founded in the civil law. Thus, the forfeiture of goods and lands under English law was justified, because "all property is derived from society, being one of those civil rights which are conferred upon individuals, in exchange for that degree of natural freedom which every man must sacrifice when he enters into social communities. If therefore a member of any national community violates the fundamental contract of his association, by transgressing the municipal law, he forfeits his right to such privileges as he claims by that contract; and the state may very justly resume that portion of property, or any part of it, which the laws have before assigned him." [21] Not only did all property owe its existence ulti-

mately to the state, but the state was continually creating
new forms of property, to meet the needs of men. Blackstone showed how the law had created a new form of
property in establishing the right of presenting a clerk
to a benefice.[22] English law had recently given all personal
property a greater importance than it had had in feudal
times.[23] The recently-introduced system of raising the
public revenue by borrowing, and then taxing merely to
pay the interest on the debt, had resulted in "converting
the principal debts into a new species of property, trans-
ferable from one man to another at any time and in any
quantity."[24] More than once Blackstone clearly demonstrated how new forms of property were continually
being created by civil society.

One of the most striking evidences of the importance
which the *Commentaries* attached to the power of the
state to create property was in the finality of the law's
specific creations. Once the state had brought a form of
property into existence, it was indestructible, and not even
the state itself could deprive a subject of his right. This
was illustrated by the respect shown to the informer's
claim to his legal reward. Blackstone explained that the
king could not pardon an offence against a penal statute
after the informer had brought his information, "for
thereby the informer hath acquired a private property in
his part of the penalty."[25] The law was so jealous of the
right of property that after a man had acquired it, even
through the indulgence of the law, his right was not to be
taken away.

Civil society had, in still a different sense, been the
principal creator of property. Without the intervention of
positive law the natural principles of property would have
been self-destructive. Some discreet restraint was necessary in order to give the precepts of natural law any practical meaning, and the state had provided such restraint.
"And, first, a property in goods and chattels may be ac-

quired by *occupancy*: which, we have more than once remarked, was the original and only primitive method of
acquiring any property at all; but which has since been
restrained and abridged, by the positive laws of society, in
order to maintain peace and harmony among mankind." [26]
A fight for occupancy, if it should be allowed to go on in
eighteenth-century England would surely be bitter and
disruptive; all property rights might in consequence of
such disorders become illusory. But the laws of England
were careful to prevent this misfortune, and by the apparently restrictive rules made certain that the natural
rule of occupancy would be peacefully realized in modern
practice. In this way the English constitution was not
simply preserving existing social arrangements. It was,
in addition, protecting the weak and helpless from the
strong and ruthless, because, "if an acquisition of goods
by either force or fraud were allowed to be a sufficient title,
all property would soon be confined to the most strong, or
the most cunning; and the weak and simple-minded part
of mankind (which is by far the most numerous division)
could never be secure of their possessions." [27] The laws of
England had in this manner protected all property at the
same time that the weak were protected in their meagre
possessions.

## 4. THE DEFINITION OF PROPERTY

Moreover, the *Commentaries* insisted that, for the definition of all property, the subject must look only to the
laws of England. The lawyer might be concerned with
philosophical inquiries into origins, but "these inquiries,
it must be owned, would be useless and even troublesome
in the common life. It is well if the mass of mankind will
obey the laws when made, without scrutinizing too nicely
into the reasons of making them." [28] Therefore, the ordinary Englishman was urged to limit his investigation of

the nature of property to an understanding of his rights under the laws of England. And when the subject looked to English laws, he found property defined as follows: wherever a man has in a thing a right which the law protects, there he has a property right and that right is inviolable. However tautological this statement might at first seem, Blackstone did not have difficulty in using it to explain why persons had rights in some cases and not in others. Thus, the master could sue anyone who illegally deprived him of the labour of his servant, because of "the property which the master has by his contract acquired in the labor of the servant." [29] In many cases the law gave no remedy to the inferior of the parties in a relationship: the child had no action for injury to the parent, and the wife had no action for injury to the husband, because "the inferior hath no kind of property in the company, care, or assistance of the superior, as the superior is held to have in those of the inferior; and therefore the inferior can suffer no loss or injury." [30] The protection of the law thus became the only test of the existence of a right of property.

The very redundancy of this definition showed, according to the *Commentaries*, how solicitous was English law of the right of property. For it clearly revealed that in England the right of property was something which by definition was always protected. The line of reasoning was something like this:

Since, 1. "Property" is that in which a person has a right by the laws of England,

And, 2. A "right" is by definition that which is protected by the laws of England, [31]

Therefore, 3. All property is protected by the laws of England.

Obviously, the last term, if it was true, was contained in the first alone, but the introduction of the middle term somehow made the right of property seem more absolute and appeared to amplify the demonstration. Blackstone seemed unaware that the apparent persuasiveness of his argument was due to his ambiguous use of the word "property" and to the fact that he was employing it in the last stage of his reasoning in a different and much more extensive sense than that with which he had begun. Indeed, if Blackstone had been aware of the ambiguity, it probably would not have disturbed him, since the ambiguous identity of the laws of England and the laws of nature made it impossible to describe the laws of England as they were, without suggesting the laws of nature as they ought to be.

By this kind of reasoning, the absolute right of property was shown to be perfectly realized in the existing legal arrangements of society. And the slightest alteration of the distribution of rights would be an attack on property. The *Commentaries*, however, actually went further than this, and showed that the existing distribution of rights was itself essential to the maintenance of any property at all. It was the qualitative difference in property-rights that had made possible the system of balanced government — the safeguard of the whole institution of property. For the different elements in the British constitution represented different kinds of property, and the landed interest was balanced against the trading interest to facilitate a system of checks and balances that assured the meanest artisan that his property was safe.[32] Similarly, existing quantitative differences in wealth were a safeguard of the very existence of property. The fact that some men had more property than others was the surest guarantee of the property of all. "Due subordination of rank" and a "gradual scale of authority" were the only foundations of stable government.[33] These differences had made possible in England a House of Lords, consisting of the only class of men who were qualified and desirous of

protecting the entire institution of property.[34] Any Englishman, therefore, even if he had less property than his
fellows, or if his economic interest appeared to conflict
with theirs, need not be disturbed; he should be confident
that the very qualitative and quantitative differences in
property-relations were helping him to keep what he
already had.

Since all these arrangements of English law were themselves the products of natural law, it was hard to say
whether the protection of property was due primarily to
nature or to the positive establishments of civil society. To
Blackstone such a question would quite properly have
seemed meaningless. The laws of England and the laws of
nature were so identified that it was really impossible to
separate them, or to assign to either system the whole
credit for the protection of property. In his discussion of
property, Blackstone called on both aspects of the law
of nature: the prescriptions of nature were the ideal form
for property; but the description of eighteenth-century
England was the surest guide to the real nature of the
inviolable institution. And in his definition of property,
he significantly emphasized the descriptive aspect of
natural law; the natural property arrangements were
those found in England at the time.

But these property relationships were the command of
Nature, because, as the *Commentaries* showed, they were,
in a sense, the assurance of that peace without which
there could be no civil society at all. A beneficent God had
prescribed peace as the "very end and foundation of civil
society." [35] This peace had been originally obtained by the
creation of property, which had terminated the bitter
struggle for occupancy. Only when the law had assigned
to every thing capable of ownership its proper owner, had
tranquillity been secured; the law had thus "wisely cut
up the root of dissension." [36] English law, obeying Nature,
had brought peace by recognizing property. It was in-

conceivable that society could have come into existence
in any other way. Peace and property had been born
together.

All this seemed quite obvious; but it had important
implications. Peace clearly was the demand of a kind
Providence; and once property had created peace, property became the guardian of peace. Therefore, any attack
on the existing arrangements of property was a defiance
of the orders of Nature herself. This was so clearly recognized by the laws of England that "the law always
couples the idea of force with that of intrusion upon the
property of another." [37] Even apparently minor violations of property, like picking someone's pocket or stealing food to keep oneself alive, deserved the capital penalty,
because they were inevitably blows at the peace of
society.[38]

Thus, whatever confusion there may at first seem to
have been in saying at once that property had been commanded by Nature and had been created by the state,
Blackstone actually made the two ideas complementary.
The law of nature had made property possible and necessary, but the laws of England had fulfilled the possibility,
and had shown new aspects of ownership which Nature
herself had not dreamed of. By attributing property to
this double source, the *Commentaries* had strengthened its
sanctions. Every right of property which was protected
by the law of England in Blackstone's day thus had ultimately the protection of Nature and of Nature's God.

## 5. COMMERCIAL PROPERTY: THE QUINTESSENCE
### OF VALUES

And yet, as the science of human nature had demonstrated, and as the *Commentaries* were quick to admit,
property had not been a static institution; its improvements had made progress possible.[39] It would, therefore,
have been absurd to expect property always and every-

The INDUSTRIOUS 'PRENTICE grown rich,& Sheriff of London.

Proverbs Ch:IV. Ver:7, 8.
With all thy getting get understanding.
Exalt her & she shall promote thee: she
shall bring thee to honour, when
thou dost embrace her.

Plate 8.

Design'd & Engrav'd by W.ᵐ Hogarth.

Publish'd according to Act of Parliam.ᵗ Sep.ᵗ 30 1747.

THE REWARDS OF COMMERCE: THE INDUSTRIOUS MERCHANT

where to be the same, or to think that a polite and commercial age could be satisfied with the arrangements of primitive and barbarous peoples. But Blackstone was to show, by his description of property, that further changes in the institution now were undesirable or unnecessary. For he found in the institution of property in the middle of the eighteenth century in England the fullest possible realization of the ideal form of property, and the quintessence of humanity, liberty, and property.

For property, in the form in which it was most dramatically appealing in Blackstone's day, was commercial property. Although England was still, to be sure, predominantly an agricultural society, the striking, exciting, and developing form of property had already come to be the property of a commercial society. When the *Commentaries* were being written, commerce had become the symbol of England's present wealth and its future prosperity. The rise to power of the commerical middle class, already foreshadowed in the Revolution of 1688,[40] was well under way by mid-century. Until the end of the seventeenth century, England had been a second-rate commercial power, but now life had begun to quicken and every year were to be seen new signs of the commercial expansion that lay ahead. The Bank of England had been founded in 1694, and the reëstablishment of the East India Company in 1708 marked the extension of English business interests to the ends of the earth. By Blackstone's time, Adam Smith was demonstrating the crucial importance of the mercantile class and of free commerce to the happiness of the community.

The growing enthusiasm had been expressed by Addison when in *The Spectator* in 1711, he showed that commerce had become a thing of glamour, to fire the imagination of loyal Englishmen:

There is no place in the town which I so much love to frequent as the Royal Exchange. . . . I have often been pleased to hear disputes adjusted between an inhabitant of Japan, and an alderman of London, or to see a subject of the Great Mogul entering into a league with one of the Czar of Muscovy. . . . This grand scene of business gives me an infinite variety of solid and substantial entertainments. As I am a great lover of mankind, my heart naturally overflows with pleasure at the sight of a prosperous and happy multitude, insomuch that at many public solemnities I cannot forbear expressing my joy with tears that have stolen down my cheeks. For this reason I am wonderfully delighted to see such a body of men thriving in their own private fortunes, and at the same time promoting the public stock. . . . If we consider our own country in its natural prospect, without any of the benefits and advantages of commerce, what a barren uncomfortable spot of earth falls to our share! . . . Nature indeed furnishes us with the bare necessaries of life, but traffic gives us a great variety of what is useful, and at the same time supplies us with every thing that is convenient and ornamental. . . . For these reasons there are not more useful members in a commonwealth than merchants. They knit mankind together in a mutual intercourse of good offices, distribute the gifts of nature, find work for the poor, add wealth to the rich, and magnificence to the great. Our English merchant converts the tin of his own country into gold, and exchanges its wool for rubies. The Mahometans are clothed in our British manufacture, and the inhabitants of the frozen zone warmed with the fleeces of our English sheep. . . . Trade, without enlarging the British territories, has given us a kind of additional empire.[41]

Writing in his *Plan of the English Commerce*, Defoe found in commerce in 1728 more substantial benefits, as he asked, "Are we a rich, a populous, a powerful Nation, and in some Respects the greatest in all those particulars in the World, and do we not boast of being so? 'Tis evident it was all deriv'd from Trade. . . . There is not a Nation in the known World, but have tasted the Benefit, and owe their Prosperity to the useful Improvements of Commerce." [42]

The enthusiasm of Addison and Defoe, and the later, more calculated opinion of Adam Smith, were embodied in Blackstone's attitude toward the place of commerce in English society.

The *Commentaries* displayed proudly the spirit of English society, where dwelt a "great commerical people," well fitted for the demands of "this commercial age." Commerce had produced wealth, and the increase of wealth had made possible the improvement of civil society. But the growth of commerce, if it had meant the increase of property, had also meant its transformation. Blackstone called attention to this transformation, — simply another example of the organic development of which English law was capable. The most important change had been the "vast increase of personal property of late years." [43] In earlier times men had "entertained a very low and contemptuous opinion of all personal estate, which they regarded as only a transient commodity. The amount of it indeed was comparatively very trifling, during the scarcity of money and the ignorance of luxurious refinements, which prevailed in the feudal ages. . . . But of later years, since the introduction and extension of trade and commerce, which are entirely occupied in this species of property, and have greatly augmented its quantity, and, of course, its value, we have learned to conceive different ideas of it." [44] Commerce had also given to the law of contract an enlarged place in the creation of property.[45]

Now this unfolding of the commercial forms of property enabled Blackstone to make property the quintessence of all man's natural rights, — inclusive even of liberty. For one of the most prominent characteristics of property in a commercial age was the freedom, on which Adam Smith was to insist, and which Blackstone had demonstrated already to exist under the laws of England. "Experience hath shown, that property best answers the purposes of civil life, especially in commercial countries, when its transfer and circulation are totally free and unrestrained." [46]

The history of property in England showed how the growth of commerce had inevitably increased the freedom of men to deal with their property as they pleased. "It is an object, indeed, of the utmost importance in this free and commercial country, to lay as few restraints as possible upon the transfer of possessions from hand to hand, or their various designations marked out by the prudence, convenience, necessities, or even by the caprice, of their owners." [47] Trade always meant exchange, and by every act of exchange a man was demonstrating his liberty to do as he wished with his own.

In accord with these requirements of commerce, English law actually forced property to be free. The free exchange of property was enforced, for instance, by the rules against perpetuities; and the provisions against the creation of future property in personal goods, since "the exigencies of trade requiring also a frequent circulation thereof, it would occasion perpetual suits and quarrels, and put a stop to the freedom of commerce, if such limitations in remainder were *generally* tolerated and allowed." [48] The very right to transfer property had, of course, been a creation of the state; and indeed, every exercise of the freedom of trade served the public interest, whether or not the individual knew it or so intended.[49] "Neither is it a nuisance to set up any trade, or a school, in neighbourhood or rivalship with another: for by such emulation the public are like to be gainers." [50] Many legal rules which, at first sight, appeared to be restrictions on trade, were really needed to protect that general freedom of property which consisted in commerce. Thus the rule of market overt protected the purchaser even where the seller had no property in the goods, because "otherwise all commerce between man and man must soon be at an end." [51] The act which prevented a merchant from shipping his goods as he pleased was surely necessary as "the most beneficial statute for the trade and commerce of these

kingdoms." [52] The regulation of apprenticeship was useful in saving commerce from the damages of unskillful
workmen, and in the "employing of youth, and learning
them to be early industrious." [53] Laws against engrossing
were needed to prevent monopoly. Apparent exceptions
like patent and copyright were themselves provisions made
to enlarge the genuine freedom of property by a more
thriving commerce. [54]

As commerce was the product of increasing wealth, the
English constitution guarded against any unwarranted
destruction of goods. It discouraged the waste of estates,
and had a special writ of estrepement for waste, "so odious
in the sight of the law is waste and destruction." [55] The
laws of England always fertilized the roots of commerce
by their manifold ways of encouraging the industry of the
people. For finally no wealth could be produced without
labour. While the laws against vagabonds were proving
the English contempt for "idleness," the apprentice laws
were training the lower classes to a life of industry. [56]
English law refused to require a parent to maintain his
issue, "for the policy of our laws, which are ever watchful
to promote industry, did not mean to compel a father to
maintain his idle and lazy children in ease and indolence." [57]
The rule of primogeniture was justified because without it
there would be a danger of "inducing younger sons to take
up with the business and idleness of a country life, instead
of being serviceable to themselves and the public." [58] The
laws concerning the poor showed Englishmen to be aware
that "there is not a more necessary or more certain maxim
in the frame and constitution of society, than that every
individual must contribute his share in order to the well-
being of the community: and surely they must be very
deficient in sound policy, who suffer one-half of a parish to
continue idle, dissolute, and unemployed." [59] The laws of
commerce, at the same time that they were protecting
every man in his freedom to deal with his property, were

thus insuring that the community would increase the quantity of property for all its uses.

It is not then difficult to see why the value of property was for Blackstone most fully realized in commerce. Commerce was the assertion of the right of property and the promise of the increase of property. But commerce was still more. It was the integration of all man's natural rights: humanity, liberty, and property all were achieved by the activities of commerce. The means of mercy and charity, and the opportunity for personal security were the by-products of trade. Liberty in its most important form was the freedom to do what one wanted with one's own. Property, the twin of peace, and the great end of civil society, was obtained and enlarged by the arts of commerce. Trade was at once the cause and the effect of all that man could value on this earth. Some years after the *Commentaries* were published, Voltaire wrote, "'Liberty and property' is the great national cry of the English. It is certainly better than 'St. George and my right,' or 'St. Denis and Mont joie'; it is the cry of nature." [60] Blackstone's cry would have been, "Liberty *of* property!" And that liberty was the fruit of commerce. Although Blackstone's system of values comprised humanity, liberty, and property, the greatest of these was property — natural in origin, legal in its expression, and English in its essence.

# CONCLUSION:

## THE ADVANTAGE OF BEING
## A REASONABLE CREATURE

AT THE BEGINNING of this book I said it was my purpose to see how Blackstone was able to make a
rational and apparently coherent statement of the legal
system of his day. And yet the greater part of this study
has demonstrated that the *Commentaries* had implicit in
them many contrary ways of thinking. The law was made
to seem a science and at the same time a mystery. The
concept of nature endowed the legal system with the reality of the existing world and the desirability of the ideal
world, with the simple virtue of primitive man and the
sophisticated subtlety of civilization, with the beauty of
order and the sublimity of obscurity. In the very process
of reasoning there was a simultaneous appeal to the discordant authorities of isolated logic and of everyday
experience.

Where, then, is the "unity" of the document? What is
the element which gave it coherence and which prevented
the reader from being uncomfortably aware that the work
was pervaded with inconsistency? An answer emerges
clearly and incontrovertibly from the evidence that has
been presented. What held the document together was no
abstract system of philosopher's logic; indeed, Blackstone's work is not understandable in terms of closet-
philosophy. The *Commentaries* were, rather, the product
of a man who believed in certain moral and social values,
and who employed all the ideas he found around him, to

convince himself and to persuade his readers that English law, embodying these values, was entitled to reverence and support.

In the Introduction I insisted that there is nothing diabolical or unfair in Blackstone's, or anyone's, enlisting the processes of reason to encourage general acceptance of what he considers ultimate values. I insist on that proposition once again. Indeed, I might say that any student of society who felt profoundly the importance of certain values, and yet failed to enlist his critical faculties in support of those values, would be failing in his duty as a reasonable creature and as a moral man.

Still, as our study of the *Commentaries* has amply illustrated, the line between reason and faith is always difficult and sometimes almost impossible to define. Whether Blackstone was proving an institution to be rationally defensible because he believed it to be morally good, or whether he believed it to be morally good because it was rationally defensible, is seldom to be discovered from the document itself. We have been able to discover, however, that the rational tools which Blackstone employed, and which he found at hand in his society, were capable of many, and opposite, uses. The vocabulary of natural law and of the rights of man, which Blackstone was using to demonstrate the validity of the English legal system, was, almost before Blackstone's death, to be used for attacking those very values in which he believed. "Reason" itself, with Blackstone, was so full of ambiguity that it would have been impossible to predict what results were likely to come from its application to the legal system. But Blackstone, like other intelligent men, must have been constantly employing reason to help him understand the consequences of his scheme of values — to help him decide whether he really believed in the values which would lead him to those consequences, and in the end to help him redefine for himself the values which he truly accepted.

From this point of view, then, we are justified in judging the document by the values embodied in it, and by the social meaning of those values in Blackstone's time. And we shall not be unfair if, in determining the stature of the man and the validity of the document, while admitting its logical limitations we judge it mainly by the moral acceptability and social desirability of the values of Humanity, Liberty, and Property, as they were described in the *Commentaries*.

Some students of the social sciences — and among these are lawyers and sociologists — would insist that there is another way of estimating the worth of any document which "rationally" analyzes institutions. These people are the victims of the rationalist fallacy. They believe that man in his attempt to analyze his institutions is a perfectly free agent, neither guided in his reasoning by what he already believes to be good, nor limited in his perspective by the values of his society. They seem to believe that it is somehow possible or desirable for the social scientist to stand outside society and let "science" have its way though morality and all human values should thereby be dissolved. In the terms of the lawyer, this attitude might be expressed in an emended maxim, *fiat lex ruat caelum*. These people exalt the scientifically "precise" above the morally good, and consider logic and rigour the highest qualities of human thought. Judged by these standards the *Commentaries* are of course of small significance.

Blackstone was not a rigorous thinker, and his work does not rank with the great books which demonstrate the nicest intricacies of the mind of man. Moreover, the mere fact that a book supports a good or a widely accepted system of values is not enough to give it greatness or influence. But it is interesting to see how the victims of the rationalist fallacy have gone about criticizing Blackstone's work; their criticisms are good examples of the hyper-scientific approach to institutions. Jeremy Bentham is the prototype of the critics of Blackstone, and certainly the least charitable of them all. His well-known attack on the *Commentaries* took the form principally of an attack on Blackstone's "reasoning"; he called the concept of natural law "nonsense on stilts," and demonstrated to his own and his disciples' satisfaction that the *Commentaries* were worthless because they were not clearly reasoned. Now Bentham himself was what might be called a "clear reasoner." He narrowed the qualities of human nature into endless subdivisions, sharpened his distinctions, and defined his terms, until much of the rich complexity and nearly all the meaning of life had been destroyed. Bentham was, to be sure, a rigorous thinker. But despite all his rigorousness, and despite all his criticism of the *Commentaries*, he presupposed a scheme of social values and a concept of property which were hardly distinguishable from Blackstone's. While life was being wrung from the framework-knitters, while the dispossessed English peasant lacked bread, Bentham went on with his arrogant science, making distinctions and creating "incentives." Bentham's excuse for any untoward consequences of his principles could always be that his "science" demanded it; Blackstone, whatever his method, insisted that society had a moral purpose, and that man should not let science lead him by the nose.

And surely, Blackstone seldom showed he thought that mere logical demonstration could ever make social values irrelevant. His work had a unity which must have seemed to his readers to be due not to any cold consistency of its logic, but rather to the meaning of its values for society. The *Commentaries* sometimes lacked a philosopher's consistency, but they had a sort of social consistency. It is this kind of consistency, certainly, by which the work attained its vast significance in America, and by which it ought finally to be judged.

For in every document which attempts to subject institutions to rational analysis, the function of reason is
in a sense subordinate. Reason must be used to show man
the consequences of his system of values and to persuade
others to accept that system. But man must know his
values; and he should be unafraid to assert them, if he is
not to be confused by the very pretence of rigorousness
in his method. As Franklin said, in the words from his
*Autobiography* taken as the motto of this book, "So convenient a thing it is to be a reasonable creature, since it
enables one to find or make a reason for everything one
has a mind to do." The all-important factor in this process
of reason, then, is what one has a mind to do. If man is to
be self-conscious, to know the limits and understand the
purposes of his critical faculty, he must therefore be aware
that his reason is serving a preconceived and desired purpose. Only in this way can man be sure he has given his
reason a function which justifies its use. Only in this way
can the student of institutions, instead of resting in a specious sense of freedom, be certain that his reasoning about
society will subserve some moral end.

# NOTES

# NOTES

In the following notes, where no title is given, Roman numerals followed by Arabic numerals refer to volume and page (standard pagination) of the *Commentaries*.

## INTRODUCTION

1. Quoted in Charles Warren, *History of the American Bar* (Boston, 1911), p. 187. For a general discussion of the importance of Blackstone in the education of the early American lawyer, *ibid.*, pp. 177 ff.

2. *Brothers Karamazov*, translated by Constance Garnett, Bk. I, Chap. 5.

## CHAPTER I

1. Translated by Thomas Nugent (New York, 1899).

2. "An Appeal from the New to the Old Whigs," *Works* (London, 1903), III, 114.

3. For an excellent discussion of the popularity of Newton's philosophy in eighteenth-century England, see Carl Becker, *The Declaration of Independence* (New York, 1933), Chapter II, especially pp. 40 ff.

4. *Complete Poetical Works*, edited by H. W. Boynton (Boston, 1903), p. 135. This epitaph was probably written about 1731.

5. Edmund Malone's note to James Boswell's *Life of Samuel Johnson*, quoted in the edition by Roger Ingpen (Boston, 1925), p. 374, note 1. Boswell himself reported, "I heard him maintain the superiority of Sir Isaac Newton, over all foreign philosophers." *Ibid.*, p. 374.

6. For a discussion of the influence of Locke in this period, see Kenneth Mac-Lean, *John Locke and English Literature of the Eighteenth Century* (New Haven, 1936). References for most of the facts in this paragraph will be found in his Introduction.

7. *Poetical Works*, edited by C. C. Clarke (Edinburgh, 1868), p. 291. This poem first appeared in the *Gentleman's Magazine* for October, 1739.

8. Abridged and edited by A. S. Pringle-Pattison (Oxford, 1924), p. 271.

9. *Ibid.*, p. 272.

10. Lines 1 ff.

11. "Ninth Night," lines 1851 ff.

12. London, 1748, p. 3.

13. Quoted from the fourth edition (London, 1734), pp. 345 ff.

14. *Works* (London, 1903), II, 350.

15. Although Blackstone began lecturing on the common law at Oxford in November, 1753, the first volume of the *Commentaries* did not come out until 1765. The remaining volumes followed in successive years.

16. I, 4. The fact that Blackstone was writing an "elementary disquisition" for beginners in the subject probably had something to do with this emphasis

on first principles. It is difficult, however, to believe that this was the only or even the principal reason for his emphasis on the conception of law as a science. The word "science" certainly had in the eighteenth century a more general sense than that which we attach to it. Thus, Dr. Johnson's *Dictionary* defined "science":

1. Knowledge.
2. Certainty grounded on demonstration.
3. Art attained by precepts, or built on principles.
4. Any art or species of knowledge.
5. One of the seven liberal arts, grammar, rhetorick, logick, arithmetick, musick, geometry, astronomy.

Most of the time, Blackstone appeared to be using the word in senses "2" and "3." It is clear, moreover, from the context in which the word is used in the *Commentaries,* and from the work as a whole that Blackstone started from the assumption that there was a demonstrable certainty in the law, and that the effort of the student should be to define the "principles" of the subject. Other examples of the description of law as a "science" reducible to principles: equity called a science by analogy with law, III, 55; judgments of law spoken of as "flowing" from reasons or premises, III, 379 f.; "general definitions," IV, 127. For discussion of "principles" found even in the minutiae of the law, see: definition of "day," II, 140 f.; marine insurance, II, 460.

17. I, 34; II, 2.
18. IV, 5.
19. I, 425.
20. III, 200.
21. III, 271.
22. II, 383.
23. I, 32, 35.
24. II, 172.
25. III, 266.
26. III, 320 f.
27. I, 412 f.
28. I, 69 f. For a detailed discussion of Blackstone's theory of precedent, see C. K. Allen, *Law in the Making* (2d ed., Oxford, 1930), pp. 147 ff. In his third edition, Dr. Allen revises his interpretation and now comes to the conclusion that Blackstone, when he said that decisions "contrary to reason" were not law, was really referring to the "cases as reported," and was simply attacking the inaccuracy of the law reports of his day. According to Dr. Allen, the *Commentaries* were making a plea for accurate reporting "rather than any theory (which would have been quite contrary to well-recognized judicial principles) that the 'reason' or 'convenience' of each case was a matter for the individual discretion of the Judge." Going still further, he explains that when Blackstone asserted that precedents were only the best "evidence of the law" and not the law itself, he was merely pronouncing the same principle which is "true today," namely, that every case is valuable to the lawyer merely for the principle contained in it. *Law in the Making* (3d ed., Oxford, 1939), pp. 219 f. It appears to me that the description found in the second edition of Dr. Allen's work comes nearer to an accurate statement of Blackstone's attitude to precedent. See, for

example, the statement quoted in the text, that "if it be found that the former decision is manifestly absurd or unjust, it is declared, not that such a sentence was *bad law*, but that it was *not law*; that is, that it is not the established custom of the realm, as has been erroneously determined." I, 70. The reference to "former decisions" rather than to reports of former decisions clearly shows that Blackstone was thinking of the case itself, rather than the record of it. Moreover, if Blackstone had meant to attack the inaccuracy of reporters it is hard to see why, in his elementary textbook, he would have done it so obliquely. There is no place in the *Commentaries*, to my knowledge, where the student is cautioned against the mistakes of the reporters.

29. IV, 336. Thus, the exceptions to the rule that "no man can recover possession by mere entry on lands, which another hath by descent" are explained simply as cases "wherein those reasons cease, upon which the general doctrine is grounded." III, 177.

30. III, 219.

31. IV, 336 f.

32. Blackstone wrote, "These are the external, immutable laws of good and evil, to which the Creator himself, in all his dispensations, conforms; and which he has enabled human reason to discover, so far as they are necessary for the conduct of human actions." I, 40.

33. One of the factors influencing Blackstone's attitude may have been that part of his audience was to consist of beginners in the study of law, who should be urged to understand and appreciate the law before they dared criticize it.

34. Quoted from the commentary by Voltaire appended to the English translation of Beccaria's *Essay on Crimes and Punishments* (3d ed., London, 1770), pp. lxxviii f. Yet, starting from this point of view, Voltaire found reason to approve English law.

35. *The Philosophy of History* (London, 1767), pp. 314 f.

36. *Reflections on the Revolution in France, Works* (London, 1903), II, 311 f., 323.

37. *Ibid.*, p. 359.

38. I, 212.

39. I, 241.

40. I, 42.

41. I, 41.

42. III, 145.

43. I, 70. "Law" here appears strikingly similar to primitive taboo. See Bronislaw Malinowski, *Crime and Custom in Savage Society* (London, 1926), and, for an older view, James George Frazer, *The Golden Bough*, abridged edition (London, 1933).

44. I, 70.

45. *Ibid.* Blackstone's logic was hardly impeccable here. He was speaking of the law as presuming the law to be well-founded.

46. III, 190; II, 376.

47. IV, 371.

48. III, 327 f.

49. I, 71.

50. IV, 441.

51. III, 328.

52. III, 431.
53. IV, 287, 350. Dr. Johnson's *Dictionary* defined "genius" as follows:

1. The protecting or ruling power of men, places, or things.
2. A man endowed with superior faculties.
3. Mental power or faculties.
4. Disposition of nature by which any one is qualified for some peculiar employment.
5. Nature; disposition.

Most of the time Blackstone was using the word in senses "1," "4," or "5." Always he gave it a connotation of a "ruling spirit" which was to be seen only in its expression in the law and the people themselves. Thus, it was only a reflection of the genius which man could see; the genius itself was a sort of mystical essence which could not be approached directly. Some additional examples: "genius of the English nation," I, 17; "genius of a free nation," I, 306; The power of impressing seamen must, "from the spirit of our constitution" reside in the crown alone, I, 420; Exercise of a criminal jurisdiction by the court of admiralty would have been "contrary to the genius of the law of England," IV, 268. For further illustrations, see below, Chap. II, Sec. 5, and also Chap. II, n. 111.

54. I, 212.
55. IV, 287.
56. III, 100.
57. The American "Realist" school of jurisprudence, represented by men like Jerome Frank and Karl Llewellyn, would seem to be in revolt against this kind of notion. But many common lawyers in America, and even more in England, probably still believe in what Holmes called the "brooding omnipresence" of the law. Some future historian of law in America may find beneath the Restatements of the American Law Institute an assumption of the mysterious clarity of law.
58. Article, "Law (Natural)" (2d ed., London, 1824), IV, 303 f.

## CHAPTER II

1. *Letters on the Study and Use of History* (London, 1752), I, 15.
2. *Ibid.*, p. 13.
3. *Ibid.*, p. 147.
4. *Essays: Moral, Political, and Literary.* Edited by T. H. Green and T. H. Grose (London, 1898), II, 11.
5. *Treatise of Human Nature.* Edited by L. A. Selby-Bigge (Oxford, 1896), p. xx.
6. *Essays: Moral, Political, and Literary.* Edited by T. H. Green and T. H. Grose (London, 1898), II, 68.
7. It is easy to show, for example, that Gibbon, in his *Decline and Fall of the Roman Empire*, used as his principle of relevance the importance of a fact for the science of human nature. Thus, he gave considerable space to the indecent adventures of the Empress Theodora, and described the personal characteristics of Attila the Hun; but devoted less attention to facts which were to affect more

crucially the later course of history. For an excellent discussion of the New History in the eighteenth century, see Carl Becker, *The Heavenly City of the Eighteenth Century Philosophers* (New Haven, 1932), Chap. III.

8. The full title of Adam Smith's work was *An Enquiry into the Nature and Causes of the Wealth of Nations.* The chapter here referred to treated "Of the Expence of the Institutions for the Instruction of People of all Ages." Modern Library edition (New York, 1937), pp. 740 ff.

9. *Works* (London, 1901), II, 333. His *Philosophical Enquiry into the Origin of our Ideas of the Sublime and Beautiful,* first published in 1756, was a study of aesthetics considered as a branch of the science of human nature. And this interest later appeared repeatedly throughout the *Reflections on the Revolution in France.*

10. *Discourses,* Edited by Roger Fry (London, 1905), pp. 83, 99. See also his statement that "the works . . . which are built upon general nature live forever." *Ibid.,* p. 105.

11. Bk. III, Chap. I.

12. Bk. I, Chap. I. Italics are Fielding's.

13. "The Vanity of Human Wishes," lines 1 f. First published, 1749. See *Rasselas,* Chap. X. Dr. Johnson had set his story in Abyssinia. Similar examples of the cosmopolitan tendency of the eighteenth century are found in Oliver Goldsmith's *Citizen of the World* and Montesquieu's *Persian Letters.* But Dr. Johnson insisted on the moral view, and said that the intrinsic significance of the science was not enough. Man must search for Higher Truths. Thus, he wrote, "Whether we provide for action or conversation, whether we wish to be useful or pleasing, the first requisite is the religious and moral knowledge of right and wrong; the next is an acquaintance with the history of mankind, and with those examples which may be said to embody truth, and prove by events the reasonableness of opinions." From *Lives of the Poets,* "Milton," *Works* (London, 1810), IX, 97 f.

14. Before the *Commentaries,* nearly all general works on the common law had been called "Institutes" or "Abridgements." For a list of these earlier works, see P. H. Winfield, *The Chief Sources of English Legal History* (Cambridge, Massachusetts; 1925). He discusses abridgements, pp. 238 ff.; textbooks and treatises, pp. 252 ff. It is significant, however, that there was a sudden increase in the production of abridgements in the eighteenth century.

15. Author's Preface to the *Commentaries.*

16. *Collected Papers* (Cambridge, England; 1911), III, 453. For a discussion of legal scholarship in this period, see Sir William Holdsworth, *Sources and Literature of English Law* (Oxford, 1925), pp. 140 ff., and *History of English Law* (London, 1924), V, 378 ff.

17. Hale's *History of the Pleas of the Crown* was also a notable contribution to legal scholarship. Although ordered printed in 1680, it was not actually printed until 1736. See Holdsworth, *Sources and Literature,* pp. 152 f. and *History,* VI, 585 ff.

18. Sir William Blackstone, *Analysis of the Laws of England* (Oxford, 1756), p. vii.

19. In the Preface to the first edition of his work, Reeves said he had been inspired by the closing chapter of the *Commentaries*; he wished " to fill up with

some minuteness the outline there drawn." See Holdsworth, *History*, XII, 412 ff.

20. Of course, Blackstone himself published other works besides the *Commentaries* dealing with legal history. The most notable of these were: "An Essay on Collateral Consanguinity," "Considerations on Copyholders," "The Law of Descents in Fee Simple," and "The Great Charter and Charter of the Forest, with other Authentic Instruments: to Which is Prefixed an Introductory Discourse, Containing the History of the Charters." These were collected and published in his *Law Tracts*, 2 vols. (Oxford, 1762). For a general discussion of these works, see Holdsworth, *History*, XII, 709 ff.

21. II, 44. Compare this justification of the study of the past with that by Edward Gibbon in his *Autobiography* (Oxford, 1907), pp. 156 ff., esp. p. 160.

22. I, 254 f., 357 f., 396 ff.

23. Bk. II, Chap. IV. Historical explanations: the conditional fee, II, 110; powers of a tenant for life or in tail to grant leases, II, 318 ff.

24. IV, 64 f.

25. Book II of the *Commentaries* contains his excellent exposition of the land law. Blackstone's deficiencies in dealing with the law of commerce are illustrated by his loose statement of the law of bills of exchange. II, 466 f. Of course his difficulties here may have been partly due to the unsettled state of the law of commerce compared with that of the land law. See C. H. S. Fifoot, *Lord Mansfield* (Oxford, 1936), p. 26. Sir William Holdsworth has called the *Commentaries* "the best history of English law which had yet appeared." *History*, XII, 725.

26. III, 196.

27. II, 268. Some other examples of the interest in earlier forms of legal rules: study of the ancient ways of rating taxes "will greatly assist us in understanding our ancient laws and history," I, 308; the various "revolutions in the doctrine of dower," II, 133 f.; history of law of abduction, III, 139; history of trial by battle, III, 337 f.

28. I, 220, 275 f., 283 f., 288, 324 f.

29. Bk. II, Chap. V.

30. III, 35, 68, 73.

31. II, 306; III, 337 ff.

32. III, 53 ff.

33. III, 148 n. "v."

34. III, 408 n. "d." Blackstone's significant reference for this fact was, among others, "*Encyclopédie*, tit. Horloge."

35. IV, 110.

36. IV, 113 f.

37. IV, 165 f.

38. *Letters on the Study and Use of History* (London, 1752), I, 170.

39. The edition which I have used purports to be the second authorized edition, and to have been published at London in 1747. Blackstone was himself a subscriber. See p. xcix.

40. *Miscellaneous Works* (London, 1814), I, 41.

41. "General Preface," *An Universal History from the Earliest Account of Time*, I, iii. Note that this is the second p. "iii" in the second edition.

42. *Ibid.*, I, xxxv ff.

43. *Ibid.*, I, 219 f., and plate opposite p. 219.

44. "Speeches in the Impeachment of Warren Hastings," Fourth day, *Speeches* (London, 1857), I, 118. It is significant that Burke was here not speaking merely of moral questions: he talked, for instance, of such details of local law as the rules governing accepting presents, and he referred to English statutes.

45. I, 266 f.

46. I, 370.

47. II, 10 f. Other examples of general uniformities in law: "In all well-governed nations some notoriety of this kind [investiture] has been ever held requisite," II, 311 f. Jury trial, as one can see from an example of the time of Emperor Conrad, "was ever esteemed, in all countries, a privilege of the highest and most beneficial nature," III, 350. Again, "all over the world, actions transitory follow the person of the defendant, territorial suits must be discussed in the territorial tribunal," III, 384. It hardly required evidence to show that "the criminal law is in every country of Europe more rude and imperfect than the civil," IV, 3; "through our own, and all other laws" there is "the one uniform principle . . . that where a crime, in itself capital, is endeavoured to be committed by force, it is lawful to repel that force by the death of the party attempting," IV, 181 f. The objections of those opposed to the Church of England were bad because they were "encroaching on those rights which reason and the original contract of every free state in the universe have vested in the sovereign power," IV, 104. "Wilful murder" was, to be sure, "a crime at which human nature starts, and which is, I believe, punished almost universally throughout the world with death," IV, 194.

48. II, 210.

49. III, 31 ff.

50. Some references to borrowings in English rules: generally, I, 35 f.; royal fish, I, 280; marriage, I, 434, 436; accession and Roman Law, II, 404.

51. I, 221.

52. I, 260.

53. I, 413 n. "x."

54. I, 431 n. "m."

55. I, 443 n. "w."

56. II, 51 n. "y."

57. II, 83.

58. II, 428.

59. II, 482 n. "u."

60. IV, 246. Other examples of foreign analogies: In discussing the mitigation of the rule that all shipwrecks go to the king, one should note that "in like manner" Constantine the Great altered the law of Rome, I, 291, n. "d." Notice the "great resemblance" between the English relation of lord and vassal and the Roman relation of patron and client, II, 64. Just as the Druids among the ancient Britons, had their *omnium rerum immunitatem*, so the tenants in frankalmoign "were discharged of all other services, except the *trinoda necessitas*," II, 102. The security required of the plaintiff for prosecuting his claim is "in like manner, as by the Gothic constitutions no person was permitted to lay a complaint against another, '*nisi sub scriptura aut specificatione trium testium, quod actionem vellet persequi*;' and as by the laws of Sancho I, king of Portugal,

damages were given against a plaintiff who prosecuted a groundless action," III, 275. In the case of murder of bastard infants, this law which made "the concealment of the death almost conclusive evidence of the child's being murdered by the mother, is . . . to be also met with in the criminal codes of many other nations of Europe; as the Danes, the Swedes, and the French," IV, 198.

A few more random examples chosen from the myriad references to analogies of particular institutions of English law to those of other legal systems: Romans also regarded custom, I, 73; Nestor's account in *Iliad* of reprisals, I, 259 n. "m"; civil law of shipwreck, I, 294 n. "s"; Swedish analogues to churchwardens, I, 394 n. "d"; 40-day knight service in Poland, I, 410 n. "e"; master's liability for servant, I, 431; Spartan and Danish counterparts to English villeins, II, 92; rules of descent and French similarity, II, 222; Emperor Frederick and university courts, III, 84; attachment in Roman and English law, III, 280 f.; oral and open testimony in Roman and English law, III, 374; laws of Florence and other states of Italy also made mere knowledge of plot against the state a crime, IV, 120; laws of Solon also made crime of going armed, IV, 149; Emperor Zeno against monopolies, IV, 160; homicide by misadventure in "Mosaical law," laws of Greece, of Saxony, and of France, IV, 187, also example from *Iliad*, IV, 188 n. "e"; Athenian law of suicide, IV, 189; Roman law of perjury, IV, 196 f.; Jewish law and civil law on kidnapping, IV, 219; civil law on stealing from ships in distress, IV, 235; Athenian law and wager of law (by oaths), IV, 347 f.; decrees of Nebuchadnezzar and Cyrus on destroying property of felons, IV, 385.

61. III, 49.
62. III, 49 n. "e."
63. III, 441.
64. *Ibid.*
65. III, 432. Foreign analogies of "characteristically English" legal institutions:

The treatment of equity is interesting in this connection: chancellor's function in "modern kingdoms of Europe," III, 46 f.; "Truth and justice are always uniform," III, 429; Injunction granted in equity is "in the nature of an interdictum by the civil law," III, 442; depositions "according to the manner of the civil law," III, 449. For a discussion of the actual similarities and differences between English equity and the similar institutions of Roman law, generally, see W. W. Buckland, *Equity in Roman Law* (London, 1911). For particular discussion of English equity compared to Roman *jus praetorium*, W. W. Buckland and A. D. McNair, *Roman Law and Common Law* (Cambridge, England; 1936), pp. 4 ff. It would be interesting to speculate on how important this desire to find similarities to other legal systems was in impelling Blackstone to his theory of the relations between law and equity; see Sir William Holdsworth, *History*, XII, 583 ff. for detailed study of Blackstone's views and comparison with Lord Mansfield's.

In the law of contracts everywhere comparisons are to be found. "The use of seals, as a mark of authenticity to letters and other instruments in writing, is extremely ancient. We read of it among the Jews and Persians in the earliest and most sacred records of history. . . . In the civil law, also, seals were the evidence of truth," II, 305 f. The doctrine of consideration was explained by understanding that "our law has adopted the maxim of the civil law, that *ex nudo pacto non oritur actio*," II, 445. Here, similarly, one might speculate on how much his desire to assimilate Roman and English law influenced his exposition of the doctrine of consideration.

Some random examples of peculiarly English legal rules for which foreign counterparts were found: treasure trove in Germany, France, Spain and Denmark, I, 296; deodand, in "Mosaical law," and law of "the Athenians and the ancient Goths," I, 301 n. "d"; repair of "bridges" in *"trinoda necessitas"* understood to include "roads" also in similar Roman rule, I, 357; Roman counterpart of earl, I, 398; and of knight, I, 403 f.; and of gentleman, I, 406; ages of consent for marriage in Rome, France, and Holland, I, 437; English guardian equalled Roman guardian and curator, I, 460; penalties for corporations in England and Rome, I, 476 f., and 476 n. "i"; Roman law of mortmain, I, 479 n. "y"; non-liability of members of corporation for debts in Roman law, I, 484; villein services and English copyhold tenure, Scottish custom of lord providing piper for diversion of villeins, "as in the kingdom of Whidah, on the slave coast of Africa, the people are bound to cut and carry in the king's corn from off his demesne lands, and are attended by music during all the time of their labour," II, 96 n. "h"; compelling partition of joint-tenancy in Rome, II, 185 n. "c"; Roman law of copyright, II, 406 f.; implied warranty of title in sale, also in civil law, II, 451; Roman analogy to English rule of incapacity of wife to make will of her own of personal property, II, 498; civil law and distinction between vested and contingent legacies, II, 513; *donatio mortis causa* among the Greeks, II, 514 n. "m"; statute of distributions and Roman law of succession *ab intestato*, II, 516; English hotchpotch rule and the *"collatio bonorum"* of imperial Roman law, II, 516 f.

Also, honorarium for lawyers in Rome, III, 28; Philip the Fair, Maximilian I, and the settling of king's courts in one central place, III, 39; use of fiction of foreign contract being made in England to give jurisdiction to court of common law, compared with Roman fictions of *postliminium* and the *lex Cornelia*, III, 107; action against unskillful physician also in Roman law, III, 122; Roman counterpart of writ of *cessavit*, III, 232; imparlance, gospel precept, and rule of XII Tables in Rome, III, 299; prohibition of use of abbreviations in legal proceedings also in Rome, by precept of Justinian, III, 323; trial by battle among Burgundi, ancient Goths, and Swedes, III, 337; wager of law and Mosaic law, III, 342; best evidence rule and evidentiary value of account books in Roman law, III, 368; costs as "necessary appendage" to judgment also in civil law, III, 399; "feigned issue" in court of equity, and *sponsio judicalis* of Roman law (borrowed), III, 452; age of capacity to commit crime in Rome, IV, 231; maxim *"ignorantia juris . . . neminem excusat,"* also in Rome, IV, 27; receiving stolen goods in French and Gothic systems, IV, 39; Roman law analogies to forestalling, regrating, and engrossing, IV, 159; homicide by misadventure in Athenian and Roman law, IV, 183; indictment for theft of goods of person unknown compared to Roman *lex Hostilia de furtis*, IV, 236; "hue and cry" in "many of the eastern countries" and the Mogul empire, IV, 294; bail for capital crimes in Athens earlier, IV, 297; wergeld systems among ancient Germans in "Irish Brehon law," Saxon law, and law of Turkey, IV, 316.

Detailed comparisons of arbitrary numerical definitions: "Reasonable day's journey" is "twenty miles: as indeed it is usually understood not only in our own law, but also in the civil, from which we probably borrowed it," III, 218. Twelve is the number of jurors, "in which patriarchal and apostolical number Sir Edward Coke hath discovered abundance of mystery." "Pausanias relates that at the trial of Mars, for murder, in the court denominated *Areopagus* from that incident, he was acquitted by a jury composed of *twelve* pagan deities. And Dr. Hickes, who attributes the introduction of this number to the Normans, tells us that among the inhabitants of Norway, from whom the Normans as well as the Danes were descended, a great veneration was paid to the number *twelve*," III, 365, and n. "l." A note was in the first edition comparing the English rule that "every cartway must be made eight feet wide at least" with a rule of the XII Tables at Rome, I, 347 (1st ed.), n. "i."

66. III, 116 f.

67. See, generally, Bk. III, Chap. XIX. And particularly: summons equals *in jus vocando*, III, 279; taking of issues from absconding defendant equals "*mittitur adversarius in possessionem bonorum ejus*," III, 280 f.; a man's house his castle, civil law counterpart, III, 288; Bail "answers in some measure to the *stipulatio* or *satisdatio* of the Roman laws," III, 291.

68. III, 366. Resemblance of jury to Greek counterpart, III, 366 n. "n"; Roman counterpart to challenges to jury, III, 365; "method of accelerating unanimity" also used in Rome, III, 375; but note, unanimity perhaps unique to England, III, 376; uniform consequences when jury system or its analogue decays, III, 379.

69. *An Essay on the Law of Bailments*, first published, 1781. The quotation is from an American edition (Boston, 1796), p. 173. Jones said it was among his purposes "to illustrate our laws by a comparison of them with those of other nations, together with an investigation of their true spirit and reason," *ibid.*, p. 5. Of Blackstone he said, "His commentaries are the most correct and beautiful outline, that ever was exhibited of any human science," *ibid.*, p. 6. He thought this was true although he admitted that Blackstone's treatment of the law of bailments had been deficient.

70. I, 461, 462 n. "n."

71. II, 234 f.

72. III, 296 f.

73. III, 310. Some additional examples of Roman counterparts for English rules: Uses and trusts were institutions "answering more to the *fidei-commissum* than the *usus fructus* of the civil law," II, 327 f. In England, "these king's counsel answer in some measure to the advocates of the revenue, *advocati fisci*, among the Romans," III, 27. Drawing and quartering for treason "is warranted by divers examples in Scripture; for Joab was drawn, Bithian was hanged, Judas was embowelled, and so of the rest," IV, 93 n. "k." One should not be diverted by mere difference in terminology from noticing the foreign rule, that "warrants" or "answers to" the English: Note, for instance, "the offence of *embezzling the public money*, called among the Romans *peculatus*." Or in the case of larceny, "This taking and carrying away, must also be *felonious*; that is, done *animo furandi*: or, as the civil law expresses it, *lucri causa*," IV, 232.

74. I, 446. This is an important example, as it refers to what might seem to be a rule of positive law.

Some general examples of use of foreign rules as "warranting" English rule, and of the assumption that the natural rule was being narrowed, or extended: English institution of surveyors of highways "exactly answers that of the *curatores viarum* of the Romans" according to Mr. Dalton, though Blackstone qualified this, I, 358 n. "i"; punishing desertion in English and Roman law, I, 415; Roman nuncupative wills for soldiers, but "our law does not indeed extend this privilege so far as the civil law; which carried it to an extreme that borders upon the ridiculous," I, 417; English tenure by knight-service "answering to the *fief d'haubert* of the Normans," II, 62; Mortgaged property when taken into mortgagee's own hands was "in the nature of a pledge, or the *pignus* of the Roman law; whereas, while it remains in the hands of the mortgagor, it more resembles their *hypotheca*," II, 159; "attorning" also in Bretagne, II, 288, n. "f"; English ecclesiastical custom of "mortuary" or sort of "ecclesiastical heriot," and "pursuance of the same principle, by the laws of Venice" and "a similar policy, in France," II, 425; rights of personal property in great measure depend on contract, also in civil law, II, 443; bankruptcy in English and Roman law, II, 472 f.; Doctrine of "relation back" for defining property available to creditors, in France, is "carried to a very great length," II, 486; computing relationship for assigning administration in Germany and England, II, 504 n. "o."

Also, attorneys allowed in Roman and English law "upon the same principle of convenience," III, 26; In battery neither English nor Roman law distinguished between degrees of violence, both are "upon a similar principle," III, 120; no remedy for "slander" if allegations true "agreeable to the reasoning of the civil law," III, 125; After entry disseisee may have action for act done after disseisin, "by a kind of *jus postliminii*," III, 210; limitation of power of arrest because a man's house was his castle, "which principle is carried so far in the civil law that," III, 288; Bail "answers in some measure to the *stipulatio* or *satisdatio* of the Roman laws," III, 291 f.; French rule as to money paid into court, on similar principle, III, 304 f.; In statutes of limitation, Athenian laws acted "upon the same principle," III, 307 f.; challenges to the polls also in Roman law, III, 361; *subpoena ad testificandum*, action "upon the same principle, in the Athenian courts," III, 369; High treason in English law is "equivalent to" *crimen laesae majestatis* of Roman law, IV, 75; same rule as to clipping coins in Rome, IV, 90; perjury in Roman law, IV, 139; punishment of false prophecies on "same principle" among ancient Gauls, IV, 149; kidnapping also capital by Jewish law, comparison of Roman law, IV, 219; in Athens also no bail in felonies and other capital crimes, IV, 297.

75. III, 58.
76. III, 145.
77. IV, 316.
78. I, 453.
79. II, 9.
80. III, 209. Further examples of laws of nature explained as underlying the rules of English law: reprisals, I, 259; *Bona vacantia* belong to first occupant, I, 298 f.; Law gives by implication what is necessary to enjoy something already given, II, 36; "Monster" has no inheritable blood, II, 246 f.; every man's right to animals *ferae naturae*, II, 411; *lex talionis*, IV, 12 ff.; "the crime against

nature," IV, 216; burglary, IV, 223; picking pockets, IV, 241 ff.; mercy dictated by law of nature *in favorem prolis* in case of pregnant woman condemned to death, IV, 394 f. These examples could be multiplied, but, as suggested above, it is not merely where specific reference is made to the law of nature, that Blackstone is dependent on it for his explanation. Often he merely adduces examples from other legal systems, and then, by implication suggests that the rule is so universally accepted and so well founded in reason as necessarily to be a law of nature. For example, idleness was an offence in China, Athens, and elsewhere, IV, 169.

81. II, 96 n. "h."

82. David G. Ritchie, *Natural Rights* (3d ed., London, 1894), pp. 20 ff.

83. *Ibid.*, Chap. II. See also, H. F. Jolowicz, *Historical Introduction to the Study of Roman Law* (Cambridge, England; 1932), pp. 103 ff.

84. Ritchie, *op. cit.*, p. 41.

85. It would not be difficult to find a place in the tradition of natural law for some of Blackstone's bitterest critics, for example, Bentham and the utilitarians. See Crane Brinton, art. "Utilitarianism," *Encyclopaedia of the Social Sciences* (New York, 1937).

86. Otto Gierke, *Natural Law and the Theory of Society*, translated by Ernest Barker (Cambridge, England; 1934), I, 35 f. See Georges Gurvitch, art. "Natural Law," in *Encyclopaedia of the Social Sciences* (New York, 1937).

87. I, 39 f.

88. I, 41. For a discussion of the religious aspects of natural law, see the address by Ernst Troeltsch, "The Ideas of Natural Law and Humanity in World Politics," quoted in full as an appendix to Volume I of Gierke, *Natural Law*. Troeltsch points out some significant relations between the tradition of natural law and the tradition of Christianity.

89. Several other writers on natural law were, of course, used by Blackstone and often referred to in the *Commentaries*. The most important of these others were Burlamaqui and Grotius. It seems clear, however, that Blackstone relied most on Puffendorf, both from the fact that he referred to him most often, and that he followed so closely the form of his argument. Even if Puffendorf was not the main "source," the argument made here is not affected, inasmuch as most of the other writers on natural law, at least after Puffendorf, made the points which were useful for Blackstone's purposes, — in any case many of these ideas were in the air in the eighteenth century.

90. See Gierke, *Natural Law*, I, 95–105. He says that "the guiding thread of all speculation in the area of Natural Law was always, from first to last, individualism — an individualism steadily carried to its logical conclusions. Every attempt to oppose this tendency was necessarily a revolt, on this point or on that, against the idea of Natural Law itself," *ibid.*, I, 96. I do not mean to suggest that natural law has seldom been useful to conservatives; it has, for example, often been used as an argument in favor of existing property relations.

91. I, 42; compare 54 f.

92. I, 70.

93. I, 54 f.

94. I, 40.

95. A good summary discussion of some of the solutions of the problem of theodicy in eighteenth-century England, is found in Leslie Stephen, *History of English Thought in the Eighteenth Century* (2d ed., London, 1881), II, 25 ff. For a more general treatment see W. Windelband, *History of Philosophy*, translated by James H. Tufts (2d ed., New York, 1931), 490 ff.

96. First published, 1714. Mandeville was a master of paradox, and even while refuting Shaftesbury's optimism, provided substantial, though hardly moral, grounds for belief that all would turn out for the best. See Leslie Stephen, *op. cit.*, II, 33 ff., and Elie Halévy, *The Growth of Philosophic Radicalism*, translated by Mary Morris (London, 1928), pp. 15 f.

97. I, 40.

98. I, 40 f. Blackstone went on, "For he has so intimately connected, so inseparably interwoven the laws of eternal justice with the happiness of each individual, that the latter cannot be attained but by observing the former; and, if the former be punctually obeyed, it cannot but induce the latter. In consequence of which mutual connection of justice and human felicity, he has not perplexed the law of nature with a multitude of abstracted rules and precepts, referring merely to the fitness or unfitness of things, as some have vainly surmised, but has graciously reduced the rule of obedience to this one paternal precept, 'that man should pursue his own true and substantial happiness.' This is the foundation of what we call ethics or natural law," *ibid.* Puffendorf had said, "According to our Judgment, there seems no way so directly leading to the Discovery of the Law of Nature, as is the accurate Contemplation of our Natural Condition and Propensions. . . . Man hath this in Common with all other Creatures endued with a Sense of their own Being, that he loves himself as highly as is possible, that he endeavours by all Ways and Means to secure his own Preservation." *Law of Nature and Nations*, translated by Basil Kennet (3d ed., London, 1717), I, 135. Puffendorf used this self-love and man's "wonderful impotency," to prove that man was by nature sociable, since society was necessary to preserve men's interests, *ibid.*, pp. 135 ff.

99. I, 41.

100. II, 489 f.

101. IV, 169. Other examples of explanation of a rule as developed to meet particular, but uniform needs of human nature: legitimacy of child born after father's death, I, 457; symbolic entry on land, II, 312 f.; legality of devise preventing too great accumulation of wealth, II, 374; *"partus sequitur ventrem,"* and reasons for exception in case of swans, II, 390 f.; sale, "a method of exchange introduced for the convenience of mankind," II, 466 f.; law-Latin, III, 320; burglary, IV, 224; more serious offence to steal certain kinds of things, IV, 239; seriousness of offence of picking pockets, even in state of nature, IV, 241 f.

102. I, 70.

103. Blackstone often showed how particular rules had been "invented" to meet particular difficulties: expenses of sheriffs, I, 346; Romans invented corporations, I, 468; Churches invented common recoveries, II, 271; invention of way of alienating property, II, 293 f.; invention of money, II, 454 f.; purpose of distress for rent, III, 9; invention of action on implied contract for judgment

debt, III, 159; purpose of "*ac etiam*" clause in action of trespass, III, 287 f.; "convenience" served by new rule as to section of country from which jurors might come, III, 359.

104. III, 325 ff. Some examples of Blackstone's describing relation between law and climate or other elements of environment: jury system among northern nations, III, 350; drunkenness and climate, IV, 26; "Baron Montesquieu lays it down, that luxury is necessary to monarchies, as in France; but ruinous to democracies, as in Holland. With regard therefore to England, whose government is compounded of both species, it may still be a dubious question how far private luxury is a public evil," IV, 170; polygamy and climate, IV, 164. Compare Kohler's conception of a law of nature with a changing content, as discussed in Roscoe Pound, *Interpretations of Legal History* (Cambridge, England; 1930), pp. 141 ff.

105. Because of the very uniformity of man's nature, one could expect that when man's environment changed his nature would have to be expressed in new institutions. Montesquieu, in his *Spirit of Laws*, one of the books most often cited in the *Commentaries*, had provided a sort of morphology to ascertain what institutions were natural to their time and place. But Montesquieu was careful to explain in his Preface, "I write not to censure anything established in any country whatsoever. Every nation will here find the reasons on which its maxims are founded. . . . Could I but succeed so as to afford new reasons to every man to love his prince, his country, his laws; new reasons to render him more sensible in every nation and government of the blessings he enjoys, I should think myself the most happy of mortals." Translated by Thomas Nugent (New York, 1899), I, xxxii.

106. IV, 139.

107. I, 261.

108. III, 83.

109. III, 100; IV, 287.

110. I, 420.

111. For additional examples, see above, Chap. I, Sec. 3, and, also Chap. I, n. 53. But here note these examples: "spirit of liberty" in constitution and English law of slavery, I, 127; "Spirit of nation" prevented slavery in England, I, 424; contrary to "genius and spirit of English law" to allow man to be tried twice for same offence, IV, 259; inroads upon jury system, "fundamentally opposite to spirit of our constitution," IV, 350.

112. I, 41.

113. IV, 346.

114. IV, 417.

115. *Op. cit.*, I, 127.

116. *Ibid.*, p. 131. Compare Blackstone's statement in the *Commentaries*, I, 54 f.

117. *Ibid.*, pp. 135 ff.

118. Although, sometimes, as in the clear assertion that wills and succession were the creations of positive law (II, 489 ff.), Blackstone appeared to be demonstrating that the institution was not the product of nature, yet even here, the fact that the state itself was the creature of nature, and that all existing property was sanctioned by nature, confused his position. Indeed, it is hard to find a

single English rule which Blackstone unequivocally classified as due exclusively to positive law. For a discussion of this problem in relation to the law of property, see below, Chap. IX.

119. II, 390 f. Still, it must be admitted that Blackstone did a few times present the local variations of a natural rule in such a way as to suggest that the local rule might be simply the fiat of the state, and yet be "law." Thus the English rule of coming of age was compared with the Greek and the Roman: "By the constitutions of different kingdoms, this period, which is merely arbitrary, and *juris positivi*, is fixed at different times. Scotland agrees with England in this point; both probably copying from the old Saxon constitutions on the continent . . . ; but in Naples they are of full age at *eighteen*; in France, with regard to marriage, not till *thirty*; and in Holland at *twenty-five*," I, 463 f. According to Blackstone's system, this should have been a case where the rule was dictated by climate and nature and not merely arbitrarily made by civil society.

CHAPTER III

1. A. O. Lovejoy and George Boas, *Documentary History of Primitivism and Related Ideas*, Vol. I, *Primitivism and Related Ideas in Antiquity* (Baltimore, 1935).

2. The word "primitive" in modern usage is also ambiguous, meaning either "extremely ancient" or merely "crude and uncivilized"; and primitivism in modern art takes its models both from the works of the most ancient period of art, and from the works of the modern savage.

3. Nathanael Culverwel, *An Elegant and Learned Discourse of the Light of Nature, with Several Other Treatises* (London, 1654), pp. 72 f. Quoted by Lois Whitney, *Primitivism and the Idea of Progress in English Popular Literature of the Eighteenth Century* (Baltimore, 1934), at p. 19.

4. Anthony, third Earl of Shaftesbury, "The Moralists," first published 1709, quoted from *Characteristics of Men, Manners, Opinions, Times, etc.*, edited by John M. Robertson (London, 1900), II, 137. I am not interested here in the problem of consistency in Shaftesbury's philosophy. This is well discussed by Lois Whitney, *op. cit.*, pp. 27 ff., esp. 35 ff.

5. A. Wolf, *History of Science, Technology, and Philosophy in the Eighteenth Century* (New York, 1939), pp. 410 ff. See also, J. N. L. Baker, *History of Geographical Discovery and Exploration* (London, 1931), pp. 145 ff., 159 ff.

6. Quoted from *Hypochondriack* in Chauncey Brewster Tinker, *Nature's Simple Plan* (Princeton, 1922), p. 1.

7. References for the above incidents will be found in Tinker, *op. cit.*, Chap. I.

8. See Benjamin Bissell, *The American Indian in English Literature of the Eighteenth Century*, Yale Studies in English, Number 68 (New Haven, 1925); and Hoxie Neale Fairchild, *The Noble Savage, a Study in Romantic Naturalism* (New York, 1928).

9. An excellent summary of this popular literature is to be found in Lois Whitney, *op. cit.*, Chaps. II, III, and IV.

10. Letter from Gray to Brown, February 8, 1763, quoted in Tinker, *op. cit.*, at p. 66.

11. I, 10.

12. II, 44.
13. II, 334.
14. IV, 414.
15. III, 325 f.
16. III, 60.
17. IV, 418.
18. II, 52.
19. III, 381.
20. IV, 443.
21. II, 58.
22. III, 184. Other references to the primitive form of law as the ideal type: "But who, that is acquainted with the difficulty of new-modelling any branch of our statute laws (though relating but to roads or to parish settlements), will conceive it ever feasible to alter any fundamental point of the common law, with all its appendages and consequents, and set up another rule in its stead?" III, 267. "For, though I thought it necessary to throw out a few observations on the nature of real actions, however at present disused, in order to demonstrate the coherence and uniformity of our legal constitution, and that there was no injury so obstinate and inveterate, but which might in the end be eradicated by some or other of those remedial writs," III, 271. The crime of treason consisted "originally, in grossly counteracting that allegiance which is due from the subject by either birth or residence; though, in some instances, the zeal of our legislators to stop the progress of some highly pernicious practices has occasioned them a little to depart from this its primitive idea," IV, 92. Since Charles II most changes in private law have been "the cutting off, by the statute for the amendment of the law, a vast number of excrescences, that in the process of time had sprung out of the practical part of it," IV, 441.
23. III, 190.
24. I, 70.
25. I, 365.
26. III, 59.
27. III, 278.
28. III, 328. Some instances of demonstration that there was a good reason for every rule of the ancient common law: "those ends, of social commerce, and providing for the sudden contingencies of private life, for which property was first established," II, 174; wisdom of ancestors in limiting jurisdiction of justices of the peace, IV, 282; As to the opposition of the original common law to the *peine forte et dure*, "the uncertainty of its original, the doubts that were conceived of its legality, and the repugnance of its theory, (for it was rarely carried into practice) to the humanity of the laws of England, all concurred to require a legislative abolition of this cruel process, and a restitution of the ancient common law," IV, 328; Normans corrupted a system which the Saxons "originally intended as a law of liberty," IV, 413.
29. III, 305 f.
30. III, 423.
31. III, 433 f. Some other examples of attributing defects in the law to the mistakes of men, and thus maintaining that the law was itself free of those defects: "The law rarely hesitates in declaring its own meaning; but the judges are

frequently puzzled to find out the meaning of others," III, 329; "The dubious points, which are usually agitated in our courts, arise chiefly from the difficulty there is of ascertaining the intentions of individuals, in their solemn dispositions of property; in their contracts, conveyances, and testaments," III, 329. "Formerly, if a lord of parliament had a cause to be tried, and no knight was returned upon the jury, it was a cause of challenge to the array: but an unexpected use having been made of this dormant privilege by a spiritual lord, it was abolished by statute 24 Geo. II, c. 18," III, 359; "Our laws against gaming are not so deficient, as ourselves and our magistrates in putting those laws in execution," IV, 173; defects in administration of revenue law, IV, 281.

32. I, 5.
33. III, 268.
34. III, 436.
35. II, 150, cf. 95.
36. III, 99. There was a significant, and, for Blackstone, a useful ambiguity in the word "ancient." This appeared in the definition of the word in Dr. Johnson's *Dictionary*:

1. Old; that happened long since; of old time; not modern. . . .
2. Old; that has been of long duration.
3. Past; former.

Most of the time the *Commentaries* seem to be employing the word simultaneously in senses "1" and "2." The very ambiguity made it possible to invest "old" institutions with the virtues of primitivism and the profits of progress. The word could help make the institution seem both to have the pristine simplicity of the early age of its origin, and the advantages of the long experience since. For examples of this ambiguity in Blackstone, see: "understanding our ancient laws and history," I, 308; Coke's opinion on a point in land law seemed "founded upon solid principles of the ancient law," II, 250, cf. 345; "The wisdom of our ancient law determined nothing in vain," III, 190; Remedial rules of English law had been "refined by the experience of more than a century," III, 268; Elizabeth's poor law was a model for all subsequent laws on the subject, and "the farther any subsequent plans for maintaining the poor have departed from this institution, the more impracticable and even pernicious their visionary attempts have proved," IV, 432. Yet surely Elizabeth's law was not early enough to have had the virtues of "pristine vigour."

37. A. O. Lovejoy and George Boas, *op. cit.*, in Vol. I, Introduction on "Primitivistic Reformers."
38. J. B. Bury, *The Idea of Progress* (New York, 1932), p. 219.
39. Quoted in J. B. Bury, *op. cit.*, pp. 221 ff.
40. *Decline and Fall of the Roman Empire*, edited by J. B. Bury (2d edition, London, 1925), IV, 180.
41. *Ibid.*, IV, 181. Although the first volume of Gibbon's work was not published until 1776, he had been preparing it for many years. Cf. William Robertson, "A View of the Progress of Society in Europe," first published as a part of the *History of Charles V* in 1769, in *Works* (London, 1826), Vol. III, on the fortunate effects of the "Roman desolation" in Europe, p. 10, and on society advancing "towards the full splendour of day," p. 40. Cf. p. 103.

42. *Wealth of Nations*, edited by Edwin Cannan (New York, 1937), p. 81.
43. W. C. Lehmann, *Adam Ferguson and the Beginnings of Modern Sociology* (New York, 1930), pp. 148 ff.
44. *Ibid.*, pp. 193 ff.
45. *An Essay on the History of Civil Society* (3d ed., London, 1768), p. 48.
46. *Ibid.*, pp. 278 f.
47. *Ibid.*, p. 283.
48. Lois Whitney, *op. cit.*, Chap. VII. See also, Elie Halévy, *op. cit.*, pp. 193, 220, and *passim*; and A. O. Lovejoy, *The Great Chain of Being* (Cambridge, Massachusetts; 1936), Chaps. VI, VII, VIII, and X.
49. Most revolutionary philosophies of history, like those of Rousseau, Marx, and Lenin, seem to show faith in progress in some form or other.
50. I, 21.
51. I, 72.
52. I, 201.
53. I, 267; II, 228.
54. II, 455.
55. III, 58.
56. III, 99.
57. IV, 49.
58. IV, 345. Some further examples of condescending reference to the past as inferior times: "A more open and generous way of thinking begins now universally to prevail," I, 26 f.; ancient laws of wrecks at sea, "those savage laws, which formerly prevailed in most northerly regions of Europe," I, 293; "those early days," I, 345; "feudal law was introduced here in all its rigour," I, 410; "the feudal rigour was apace wearing out," II, 108; the severity of the feudal law, II, 318; superstitition of ancient times, II, 375; oppressive tenures, III, 258; quaintness of Coke's writing "in the pithy dialect of that age," III, 311; "the military spirit of our ancestors joined to a superstitious frame of mind," III, 337; "barbarous and unchristian custom of duelling," III, 351; "horrid doctrines" of the end of the last century, IV, 44; "those days of blind zeal and pious cruelty," when heretics were mistreated, IV, 45; "Our ancestors were mistaken in their plans of compulsion and intolerance," IV, 52; Queen Mary's, "that sanguinary reign," IV, 143; "superstition" of ancestors and ancient modes of trial, IV, 342; trial by ordeal "universal in the times of superstitious barbarity," IV, 343 f.; "those days of ignorance and her sister superstition," IV, 367; "From the whole of this detail we may collect, that however in times of ignorance and superstition that monster in true policy may for a while subsist, of a body of men, residing in the bowels of a state, and yet independent of its laws; yet, when learning and rational religion have a little enlightened men's minds, society can no longer endure an absurdity so gross, as must destroy its very fundamentals," and though benefit of clergy formerly was such an institution, it no longer is, IV, 371; "at this distance from those turbulent times," IV, 406; The days of Elizabeth were "not those golden days of genuine liberty that we were taught to believe," IV, 433.
59. I, 30.
60. I, 469.
61. IV, 370.

62. III, 347.
63. III, 159.
64. II, 271.
65. I, 245. Further examples of improvements in the law in response to
needs: Foundation of the state itself had been in response to the need to take
man out of state of nature, I, 48; "How impossible it is, in any practical system
of laws, to point out beforehand those eccentrical remedies, which the sudden
emergence of national distress may dictate, and which that alone can justify,"
I, 251; post office, I, 321; limiting expenses of sheriff, I, 346; improvements on
feudal law of emblements, II, 123; changes in law of dower, II, 133 f.; "That a
man shall not stultify himself hath been handed down as settled law: though
later opinions, feeling the inconvenience of the rule, have in many points endeavoured to restrain it," II, 292; "Those mischiefs and contentions would
ensue, which property was introduced to prevent," II, 293 f.; "Our modern
deeds are in reality nothing more than an improvement or amplification of the
*brevia testata*," II, 307; "Conveyances in writing were the last and most refined
improvement," II, 313 f.; means invented "to get the better of that stubborn
statute *de donis*," II, 360; transfer of property allowed "in order to maintain
peace and harmony to mankind," II, 400 f.; heriot, II, 423 f.; improvement of
law of usury, II, 454 f.; improvement of law of marine insurance, II, 460;
testaments, II, 489 f. Also, Finch's system of equity was affected by "the reason
and necessities of mankind, arising from the great change in property by the
extension of trade and the abolition of military tenures," III, 55; Rules of equity
"have all been extended and improved by many great men," III, 55; court of
chivalry, III, 104; habeas corpus, III, 135; law of abduction, III, 139; replevin,
III, 149 f.; assizes, III, 184; action of ejectment, III, 201 ff.; *Information* device supplants *quo warranto* writ, III, 263; The "more simple and commercial
mode of property" demands speedier devices, but instead of a "great legislative
revolution" our ancestors "endeavoured, by a series of minute contrivances, to
accommodate such personal actions as were then in use to all the most useful purposes of remedial justice," III, 268; "new expedients" of civil remedies, III,
268; "niceties" of defense gradually and "deservedly discountenanced," III,
297 ff.; adding "*ac etiam*" clause to writ of trespass, III, 288; residence of
jurors, III, 359; improvement in system of attaints, III, 389 f.; punishments,
III, 404; idiots and lunatics, III, 427; general improvement of equity, III,
433 f.; criminal law, IV, 3; punishment of heresy, IV, 46 ff.; liberation of lands,
bodies, minds, IV, 49; witchcraft, IV, 61 f.; convicted traitor no longer dragged
to gallows, IV, 92; popery, IV, 105; sanctuary, IV, 129; liberty of the press,
IV, 152; *peine forte et dure*, IV, 329; jurors no longer punished for contrary
verdict, IV, 361; Bracton's improvement on old rules of pleading, IV, 425.
66. IV, 409.
67. IV, 428 f.
68. IV, 425.
69. IV, 427.
70. IV, 4. See below, Chap. VII.
71. IV, 371.
72. III, 390.
73. IV, 442.

74. III, 9.
75. IV, 187.
76. II, 298.
77. I, 64.
78. IV, 409.

## Chapter IV

1. Pt. I, lines 68 ff.
2. Lines 88 ff.
3. New edition (London, 1810), p. viii. This edition has the pagination of the first.
4. *Ibid.*, p. 71.
5. B. Sprague Allen, *Tides in English Taste* (Cambridge, Massachusetts; 1937), I, 160 f.
6. Quoted in B. Sprague Allen, *op. cit.*, I, 160.
7. *Ibid.*, I, 159 f.
8. *Oxford English Dictionary*, *s.v.* "aesthetics."
9. Quoted from Thomas Sheridan, *A Course of Lectures on Elocution* (new ed., London, 1787), p. v.
10. *Works* (London, 1902), I, 141 f.
11. "Illustrations on Sublimity," in *Dissertations, Moral and Critical* (London, 1783), p. 605.
12. Quoted from second edition (London, 1785), I, 100 f. See also, I, 72 f.
13. B. Sprague Allen, *op. cit.*, I, 156 ff.
14. Longinus, *On the Sublime*, translated by W. Rhys Roberts (New York, 1930), section viii. See also, Samuel H. Monk, *The Sublime, a Study of Critical Theories in Eighteenth Century England* (New York, 1935), pp. 10 ff.
15. Quoted in Lane Cooper, *Theories of Style with Special Reference to Prose Composition, Essays, Excerpts and Translations* (New York, 1930), p. 178.
16. *Op. cit.*, I, 59.
17. The beautiful: Burke, *Works*, I, 141 f.; Lord Kames, *Elements of Criticism*, first published 1761, (2d ed., Edinburgh, 1763), I, 251 ff., esp. pp. 257, 259, 263; Blair, *op. cit.*, I, 100 f. The sublime: Burke, *op. cit.*, pp. 88 ff.; Lord Kames, *op. cit.*, I, 275 ff.; Blair, *op. cit.*, I, 58 ff.
18. For the effect of these changing theories on the conception of poetry, see Dr. Johnson's *Lives of the Poets, passim.* For changes in painting which accompanied the increasing popularity of the sublime, see Monk, *op. cit.*, pp. 164 ff. Changes in landscaping and architecture are discussed by B. Sprague Allen, *op. cit.*, II, 43 ff., 115 ff. Irving Babbitt, in *The New Laokoön* (Boston, 1910), dealt with some of these changes as part of what he called "the pseudo-classic confusion of the arts."
19. I, 40 f.
20. *Analysis of the Laws of England* (Oxford, 1756), p. v. But Blackstone acknowledged the debt of students to Wood and Finch "for their happy Progress in reducing the Elements of Law from their former Chaos to a regular methodical Science," *ibid.*, p. vi.
21. There were hardly more than fifty pages difference between any two of the "natural" divisions of the *Commentaries.*

22. I, 122.

23. Blackstone wrote, "I shall follow the same method that was pursued with regard to the distribution of rights: for as these are nothing but an infringement or breach of those rights, which we have before laid down and explained, it will follow that this negative system of *wrongs* must correspond and tally with the former positive system of *rights.* ... And the absolute rights of each individual were defined to be the right of personal security, the right of personal liberty, and the right of private property, so that the wrongs or injuries affecting them must consequently be of a corresponding nature," III, 119. But see below, Chap. VIII.

24. "Rights are, however, liable to another subdivision; being either, first, those which concern and are annexed to the persons of men, and are then called *jura personarum*, or the *rights of persons*; or they are, secondly, such as a man may acquire over external objects, or things unconnected with his person, which are styled *jura rerum*, or the *rights of things*. Wrongs also are divisible into, first, *private wrongs*, which, being an infringement merely of particular rights, concern individuals only, and are called civil injuries; and secondly, *public wrongs*, which, being a breach of general and public rights, affect the whole community, and are called crimes and misdemeanors. The objects of the laws of England falling into this fourfold division, the present commentaries will therefore consist of the four following parts," I, 122.

25. IV, 5.

26. I, 446.

27. I, 376.

28. I, 218.

29. I, 422.

30. IV, 162.

31. IV, 161 ff.

32. III, 174. Some other examples of numerical symmetry: statutes classified into general or special, public or private, I, 85 f.; "prerogatives are either direct or incidental," I, 239; revenue is either "ordinary or extraordinary," I, 281; "two sorts" of poor, I, 360; "Constables are of two sorts, high constables, and petty constables," I, 355; allegiance of "two sorts of species," I, 369; three "states," I, 396; four sorts of gentlemen, I, 406; sorts of servants, I, 423; sorts of guardians, I, 461; sorts of corporations, I, 469; advowsons classified, II, 22; kinds of "common," II, 32 ff.; "three manner of rents," II, 41; two species of lay tenures, II, 101; "For an office, either public or private, may be forfeited by *misuser* or *non-user*," II, 153; "Considered in this view, estates in any quantity or length of duration, and whether they be in actual possession or expectancy, may be held in four different ways," II, 179; classification of escheats, II, 254 f.; classification of conveyances by common law into "original or primary" and "derivative or secondary," II, 309, 324; kinds of injury to right of personal property in possession, III, 144; the "four heads" of challenges to the polls of the jury, III, 361 ff.; kinds of judgments, III, 395 ff.; causes extrinsic or intrinsic to record, III, 387, 393; kinds of writ of habeas corpus, III, 129.

Some additional examples of more or less forced classifications: classification of remedies for private wrongs, III, 3; "All civil injuries are of two kinds, the one *without force* or violence," III, 118; contracts either express or implied, III,

153; five methods of working disseisin of freehold rent, III, 170; injury to real property is either "with amotion from possession or without amotion from possession," III, 208; "preventive and corrective" the two kinds of redress for waste, III, 225; "absolute" and "relative" duties, IV, 41 f.; miscellaneous offences under "felonies, injuries to the king's prerogative," IV, 94 ff.; misprision either "negative" or "positive," IV, 120; offences against public justice "divided into such a number of inferior and subordinate classes," IV, 127; offences against church, either "positive" or "negative," IV, 150; Homicide is of three kinds, IV, 177 f.; stealing an heiress included under offences against the person, IV, 208; criminal courts classified, IV, 258; contempts, "direct" or "consequential," IV, 283 f.; "Clergy" is number eight in the "twelve heads" of "ordinary methods of proceeding in courts of criminal jurisdiction," IV, 289; two ways of reversing judgment, IV, 390; heads and objects of criminal laws, IV, 406.

See especially for charm of numbers: twelve as number of jurors, "patriarchal and apostolical number" in which Coke "hath discovered abundance of mystery"; trial of Mars by Areopagus; Normans and Danes venerate number twelve, III, 365 n. "l."

33. II, 125.

34. II, 388.

35. A similar device was to treat one rule as a "qualification" of another: Thus estates upon condition were qualifications of other estates, II, 152; there was a similar explanation of the nature of chattels real, II, 386.

36. II, 444 f.

37. II, 391. Moreover, the contracts whereby chattels personal were acquired were classified, following the Roman order, into sale or exchange, bailment, hiring and borrowing, and debt, II, 446 ff. Roman law actions were personal, real, or mixed, and "under these three heads may every species of remedy by suit or action in the courts of common law be comprised," III, 118.

38. For a discussion of the significance of hierarchical arrangement of ideas in eighteenth-century thought generally, see, A. O. Lovejoy, *The Great Chain of Being* (Cambridge, Massachusetts; 1936), esp. Chaps. VI and VII.

39. IV, 258 f.

40. III, 179.

41. II, 326.

42. IV, 36. Some additional examples of the hierarchical arrangement of legal rules and rights: Allodium is "property in its highest degree," II, 105; "Escheat therefore operates in subordination to this more ancient and superior law of forfeiture," II, 252; "Having thus distinguished the different *degree* or *quantity* of *dominion* or *property* to which things personal are subject, we may add a word or two concerning the *time* of their *enjoyment*, and the *number* of their *owners*: in conformity to the method before observed in treating of the property of things real," II, 398; debts ranked according to the forcefulness, debt of record being "of the highest nature," II, 464 f.; priority of right to wrong, III, 2; the Statute of Frauds justified as dealing with agreements of "so important a nature," III, 157; action of formedon "highest action that tenant in tail can have," III, 190; "*juris et seisinae conjunctionem*," the highest of all titles, III, 190; "the great and final remedy of a writ of right," III, 191; "The writ of *capias ad satisfaciendum* is execution of the highest nature," III, 415;

"Seizing of lands by *elegit* is of so high a nature, that after it the body of the defendant cannot be taken," III, 419; "A record or enrolment is a monument of so high a nature," III, 331.

43. IV, 375.

44. II, 267.

45. IV, 14.

46. II, 271. Some other examples of the fitness of law to various ranks in the community: uses of legal knowledge according to rank of student, I, 7 f., 13; fines for swearing and cursing adapted to rank of offender, IV, 59 f.; effects of gambling laws on various ranks, IV, 170 f.

47. For an analysis of this method of reasoning about the law, see below, Chap. VI. And for a discussion of the notion of proportion applied to the existing property distribution, see below, Chap. IX.

48. I, 390.

49. I, 430.

50. Stanley Pargellis, "The Theory of Balanced Government," in *The Constitution Reconsidered*, edited by Conyers Read (New York, 1938), p. 46.

51. *The Spirit of Laws*, Bk. XI, Sec. 6.

52. I, 155.

53. IV, 349.

54. III, 60.

55. II, 473.

56. I, 154 f. Additional examples of the use of the notion of balance or equilibrium: "It is highly necessary for preserving the balance of the constitution, that the executive power should be a branch, though not the whole, of the legislative," I, 154; Franchise "steers between the two extremes," I, 172; Property requirement for election to parliament "somewhat balances the ascendant which the boroughs have gained over the counties by obliging the trading interest to make choice of landed men," I, 176; dangers of overturning the "balance of the constitution," I, 244; "balance of power," I, 246; "The balance is inclined pretty strongly to the popular scale," I, 334; "The distribution of common justice between man and man was thrown into so provident an order, that the great judicial officers were made to form a check upon each other," III, 39 f.

Use of equivalents: "As wager of law is equivalent to a verdict in the defendant's favour, it ought to be established by the same or equal testimony, namely, by the oath of *twelve* men," III, 343; where infant is plaintiff defendant shall not wage his law, since infant cannot wage his law, III, 345.

57. IV, 309.

58. III, 438.

59. II, 128.

60. III, 269. Blackstone continued, "And, besides, I should have done great injustice to the founders of our legal constitution, had I led the student to imagine that the remedial instruments of our law were originally contrived in so complicated a form as we now present them to his view," III, 269. He later thought it "necessary to throw out a few observations on the nature of real actions, however at present disused, in order to demonstrate the coherence and uniformity of our legal constitution," III, 271.

61. III, 429 ff.

62. I, 217. Italics mine.

63. II, 376.

64. IV, 417 f.

65. I, 10.

66. Some additional examples of the dangers of destroying the beautiful simplicity and symmetry of the law: feudalism originally a "plan of simplicity and liberty," II, 58; objection to considering the case of Clere and Brooke as a precedent for the law of inheritance because it destroyed "the otherwise entire and regular symmetry of our legal course of descents," II, 238 ff.; English courts a great pattern of reason and wisdom, III, 59 f.; great perfection of ancient forms of writs, III, 183 f.; Alfred's task, "out of its old, discordant materials, which were heaped upon each other in a vast and rude irregularity, to form one uniform and well-connected whole," IV, 411; "proportion" of the whole of the English legal system, IV, 443.

67. Quoted from second edition (Edinburgh, 1763), I, 312.

68. Quoted from second edition (London, 1785), I, 65 f.

69. III, 86.

70. III, 422.

71. III, 265 f.

72. I, 245.

73. III, 440.

74. I, 251.

75. III, 268. Additional examples of the inevitability of variety and disorder in adapting the law to changing needs:

*Equity.* "From this method of interpreting laws, by the reason of them, arises what we call *equity*, which is thus defined by Grotius: 'the correction of that wherein the law (by reason of its universality) is deficient.' For, since in laws all cases cannot be foreseen or expressed, it is necessary that, when the general decrees of the law come to be applied to particular cases, there should be somewhere a power vested of defining these circumstances, which (had they been foreseen) the legislator himself would have expressed. And these are the cases which, according to Grotius, '*lex non exacte definit, sed arbitrio boni viri permittit.*' Equity thus depending, essentially, upon the particular circumstances of each individual case, there can be no established rules and fixed precepts of equity laid down, without destroying its very essence, and reducing it to a positive law. And, on the other hand, the liberty of considering all cases in an equitable light must not be indulged too far, lest thereby we destroy all law, and leave the decision of every question entirely in the breast of the judge." I, 61 f.

*Forgery.* "So that, I believe, through the number of these general and special provisions, there is now hardly a case possible to be conceived, wherein forgery, that tends to defraud, whether in the name of a real or fictitious person, is not made a capital crime," IV, 250.

*Miscellaneous.* Age of consent, I, 463 f.; municipal laws "which various accidents conspire to render different in almost every country in Europe," III, 87. For the natural adaptation of rules to circumstances of time and place, see above, Chap. II.

76. III, 297 f.

77. III, 410.

78. IV, 417.

79. IV, 418. Blackstone sometimes objected to the rigid application of a legal rule since the rigid application might itself justify radical change: "New-modelling" of charters of corporation-towns under Charles II; "this exertion of power, though perhaps *in summo jure* it was for the most part strictly legal, gave a great and just alarm; the new-modelling of all corporations being a very large stride toward establishing arbitrary power," III, 264.

80. III, 266.

81. III, 267, 423 f. Blackstone was here summarizing Montesquieu. See *The Spirit of Laws*, Bk. XI. Yet the *Commentaries* made it clear that the inconvenience of this necessary complexity had, in England, been reduced to a minimum.

82. III, 325 f. This complexity was also a necessary protection to the institution of property. See, below, Chap. IX.

83. *Op. cit.*, I, 63 ff.

84. *The Sublime and Beautiful, Works* (London, 1902), I, 91.

85. I, 67. The law and custom of parliament were "not defined and ascertained by any particular stated laws." But, "the dignity and independence of the two houses are therefore in great measure preserved by keeping their privileges undefined," I, 163 f.

86. IV, 409. Blackstone added two more causes of uncertainty: thirdly, the means whereby Christianity was propagated; and, fourthly, the subdivision of the kingdom into a heptarchy. See also, the "doubt" as to whether it was a civil injury in the eighteenth century to take away from a father a child who was not an heir. This doubt was made to rest on a point of history, III, 140 f.

87. Some illustrations of the "Gothic" as a type of "sublimity" and "grandeur": Gothic church, Lord Kames, *op. cit.*, I, 312; Hugh Blair explained, "A Gothic cathedral raises ideas of grandeur in our minds, by its size, its height, its awful obscurity, its strength, its antiquity, and its durability," *op. cit.*, I, 66.

88. III, 268.

89. I, 34.

90. "Essay on Criticism," Pt. I, line 101.

## CHAPTER V

1. Bk. II, Chap. II.

2. *Essay Concerning Human Understanding*, abridged and edited by A. S. Pringle-Pattison (Oxford, 1924), p. 17.

3. Pt. II, lines 13 f.

4. *Essays, Moral, Political, and Literary*, edited by T. H. Green and T. H. Grose (New York, 1898), I, 209.

5. Number 2, *The Rambler*, first published, 1750. Quoted from *Works*, edited by Arthur Murphy (London, 1810), IV, 9.

6. "Preface to Shakespeare," *Works*, II, 134. Dr. Johnson went on, "The reverence due to writings that have long subsisted arises therefore not from any credulous confidence in the superiour wisdom of past ages, or gloomy persuasion of the degeneracy of mankind, but is the consequence of acknowledged and indubitable positions, that what has been longest known has been most considered, and what is most considered is best understood." *Ibid.*, p. 135.

7. From "Verses Intended for Lock and Montaigne," *Dialogues of the Dead and other Works in Prose and Verse*, edited by A. R. Waller (Cambridge, England; 1907), p. 323. Quoted in Kenneth MacLean, *John Locke and English Literature of the Eighteenth Century* (New Haven, 1936), p. 10. Matthew Prior lived from 1664 to 1721; he did most of his writing after 1713.

8. Leslie Stephen, *English Thought in the Eighteenth Century* (2d ed., London, 1881), I, 60 ff.; II, 46 ff. See also, W. R. Sorley, *History of English Philosophy* (New York, 1921), Chap. X.

9. *Works* (New York, 1822), I, 141 f. The *Inquiry* was first published in 1764.

10. *Ibid.*, p. 147.

11. *Ibid.*, p. 188.

12. Leslie Stephen, *op. cit.*, I, 381.

13. James Boswell, *Life of Johnson*, edited by Roger Ingpen (Boston, 1925), p. 422. Beattie was a great friend of Dr. Johnson and much respected by him.

14. *An Essay on the Nature and Immutability of Truth in Opposition to Sophistry and Scepticism* (3d ed., Dublin, 1773), p. 27. This work was first published in 1770.

15. Quoted from second edition (London, 1768), pp. 58 f. This work was first published in 1766. See Leslie Stephen, *op. cit.*, I, 383 ff.

16. Epistle I, lines 123 f., 189 f.

17. I, 472. This notion had important implications for the conception of liberty. See below, Chap. VIII, Sec. 2.

18. I, 190.

19. II, 150.

20. Preface (London, 1636), p. [10]. This work was written in 1596, and was published posthumously. For a general discussion of its significance, see Sir William Holdsworth, *History*, V, 398.

Bacon continued, "Whereas I might have made more flourish and ostentation of reading, to have vouched the authorities, and sometimes to have enforced or noted upon them, yet I have abstained from that also, and the reason is, because I judged it a matter undue and preposterous to prove rules and maximes; wherein I had the example of Mr. Littleton and Mr. Fitzherbert. . . . Well will it appear to those who are learned in the lawes, that many of the cases are judged cases, either within the bookes or of fresh report, and most of them fortified by judged cases, and similitude of reason, though in some few cases I did intend expressly to weigh downe the authority by evidence of reason, and therein rather to correct the law, than either to sooth a received error, or by unprofitable subtlety, which corrupteth the sense of law, to reconcile contrarieties: for these reasons I resolved not to derogate from the authority of the rules, by vouching of any of the authority of the cases, though in mine owne copy I had them quoted. . . ." *Ibid.*, p. [12].

William Noy, an Attorney-General under Charles I, wrote a book of *Maxims*, first published in 1641, which was widely read in the eighteenth century, both in England and America. New American editions of this work were issued even in the nineteenth century. The most popular of books of common law maxims today is probably Broom's *Legal Maxims*, first published in 1854, which had reached a tenth edition by 1939.

It is significant that in 1728, Richard Francis published the first edition of his influential *Maxims of Equity*, which Professor Pound calls "the immediate point of origin" of the modern maxims of equity. See his interesting article, "On Certain Maxims of Equity," *Cambridge Legal Essays* (Cambridge, England; 1926), where he shows that Francis' maxims were "for the most part independent attempts to state principles derived from study of the cases," pp. 261 f. For a discussion of the importance of this type of book in the development of equity, see also, Sir William Holdsworth, *History*, XII, 188 ff.

21. I, 68.

22. I, 67. Blackstone also wrote of "that admirable system of maxims and unwritten customs which is now known by the name of the *common* law," IV, 412.

23. IV, 335.

24. IV, 36.

25. IV, 36. Other examples where the maxim seemed to be nothing more than a device for neat summary: "For it is a settled rule and maxim that nothing shall be averred against a record, nor shall any plea, or even proof, be admitted to the contrary," III, 24; "For, at the common law, *nemo tenebatur prodere seipsum*," IV, 296; "*nam qui libet potest renunciare juri pro se introducto*," IV, 317.

26. III, 43.

27. I, 365.

28. IV, 23. He continued, "Under seven years of age indeed an infant cannot be guilty of felony; for then a felonious discretion is almost an impossibility in nature: but at eight years old he may be guilty of felony." For a further discussion of the method of reasoning by identifying law with fact, see below, Chap. VI, Sec. 3.

29. II, 18.

30. *Life of Johnson*, edited by Roger Ingpen (Boston, 1925), p. 286. Boswell significantly explained the circumstances under which the incident occurred: "After we came out of the church, we stood talking for some time together of Bishop Berkeley's ingenious sophistry to prove the non-existence of matter, and that every thing in the universe is merely ideal. I observed, that though we are satisfied his doctrine is not true, it is impossible to refute it. I never shall forget the alacrity with which Johnson answered, striking his foot with mighty force against a large stone, till he rebounded from it, 'I refute it *thus*.'" Then follows Boswell's own observation. The incident occurred in 1763. Some editors of Boswell, Michael Kearney, for example, have, as it seems to me, mistakenly attributed the nature of Dr. Johnson's reply to the fact that he was "imperfectly acquainted with Berkeley's doctrine." It seems more likely that this was for Dr. Johnson the only way of treating the problem which would have made sense.

31. *Op. cit.*, p. 98.

32. *Principles of Moral and Political Science* (Edinburgh, 1792), I, 89 f.

## Chapter VI

1. *Essay Concerning Human Understanding*, abridged and edited by A. S. Pringle-Pattison (Oxford, 1924), p. 355.

2. *Ibid.*, p. 347.

3. *Ibid.*, p. 299.
4. III, 433 f.
5. III, 379 f.
6. III, 396.
7. III, 196.
8. I, 442.
9. I, 443.
10. I, 459. Further examples of "argument" by definition: Denizen "cannot take by inheritance: for his parent, through whom he must claim, being an alien, had no inheritable blood; and therefore could convey none to the son," I, 374; why "wrong done by the servant is looked upon as the wrong of the master himself," I, 432; "Such are held to be *nullius filii*, the sons of nobody; for the maxim of the law is, *qui ex damnato coitu nascuntur, inter liberos non computantur*. Being thus the sons of nobody, they have no blood in them, at least no inheritable blood: consequently, none of the blood of the first purchaser: and therefore, if there be no other claimant than such illegitimate children, the land shall escheat to the lord," II, 247; why bastards cannot have collateral kindred, II, 249; acquiring property in goods by marriage in consequence of unity of husband and wife, II, 433; wife's incapacity to bequeath chattels real, II, 498; women excluded from jury, because "under the word *homo*, also, though a name common to both sexes, the female is however excluded, *propter defectum sexus*," III, 362.
11. II, 150. Some of the examples of tautology concealed by the copiousness of the legal vocabulary: perfection of king, I, 246; *nullum tempus occurrit regi*, I, 247 f.; perpetuity of king, I, 249; king's ability to judge capacities of subjects for office, I, 272; king can do no wrong, III, 254 f.; no remedy for personal injury by prince to private subject, because "the law in decency supposes that it never will or can happen at all," III, 255; remedies or crown against subject allowed only where no supposition of dispossession of plaintiff necessary, III, 257; "for the law will not suppose a possibility of bias or favour in a judge, who is already sworn to administer impartial justice, and whose authority greatly depends upon that presumption and idea," III, 361; beneath "dignity" of king to receive costs, III, 400.
Rules of procedure were thus explained: executors' right of retainer based on impossibility of suing himself since "the executor cannot, without an apparent absurdity, commence a suit against himself as a representative of the deceased, to recover that which is due to him in his own private capacity. . . . The doctrine of *retainer* is therefore the necessary consequence of that other doctrine of the law, the priority of such creditor who first commences his action," III, 18 f. Idiot cannot appear by attorney, for he has no authority to appoint an attorney, III, 25 f.; trial by battle, III, 339.
The words "important" and "inferior" often concealed tautological reasoning: explanation of "the inferiority in which the law places an estate for years . . . that an estate for a thousand years is only a chattel and reckoned part of the personal estate," II, 143; Statute of Frauds explained because "some agreements . . . are deemed of so important a nature," III, 157.
12. I, 244.
13. III, 123.

14. IV, 5 f. Further examples of insistence that English law redressed all possible injuries: Apart from cases of retainer and remitter, i.e. where impossible for man to sue himself, "in all other cases it is a general and indisputable rule, that where there is a legal right, there is also a legal remedy, by suit or action at law, whenever that right is invaded," III, 23; "every possible injury that can be offered to a man's person or property is certain of meeting with redress," III, 86; "For wherever the common law gives a right or prohibits an injury, it also gives a remedy by action; and, therefore, wherever a new injury is done, a new method of remedy must be pursued," explaining the need for trespass on the case in addition to trespass, III, 123. "But depriving one of a mere matter of pleasure, as of a fine prospect by building a wall, or the like: this, as it abridges nothing really convenient or necessary, is no injury to the sufferer, and is therefore not an actionable nuisance," III, 217; remedy by suit for "every possible injury," III, 422.

15. III, 123.

16. IV, 371. Some further examples of the law remedying its own defects: Trespass on the case and the rule prohibiting wager of law by defendant were used to avoid the evils arising from wager of law itself, III, 347 f.; "Improvement" of system of attaints consisted of removing legal technicality, III, 389 f.; bigamy as counter-plea to benefit of clergy, IV, 163 n. "b."

17. *Essay Concerning Human Understanding*, p. 305.

18. I, 290.

19. II, 406.

20. II, 431.

21. II, 166.

22. I, 464 f.; IV, 21 f.

23. IV, 198 ff.

24. IV, 190.

25. III, 3 f. This kind of recognition by the law of the facts of human nature was used as evidence of the law's "humanity." See below, Chap. VII.

26. II, 389 f.

27. II, 391 f.

28. II, 392.

29. II, 39.

30. II, 395. Additional examples of the description of a legal rule as if it were merely the recognition of physical fact: "In short, as the logicians speak, corporeal hereditaments are the substance, which may be always seen, always handled: incorporeal hereditaments are but a sort of accidents, which inhere in and are supported by that substance; and may belong, or not belong to it, without any visible alteration therein. Their existence is merely in idea and abstracted contemplation; though their effects and profits may be frequently objects of our bodily senses," II, 20; "chattels are of so vague and fluctuating a nature," II, 421, cf. 398. Explanation of legal rules as to specific restitution of chattels: The "action of *replevin* . . . and the action of *detinue* . . . are almost the only actions in which the actual specific possession of the identical personal chattel is restored to the proper owner. For things personal are looked upon by the law as of a nature so transitory and perishable, that it is for the most part impossible either to ascertain their identity, or to restore them in the same con-

dition as when they came to the hands of the wrongful possessor." For *lex neminem cogit ad vana, seu impossibilia*, III, 145 f.; "But there are some things which are in their nature impartible," as a mansion house, etc., III, 189 f.; "Waste is a spoil and destruction of the estate ... by demolishing not the temporary profits only, but the very substance of the thing, thereby rendering it wild and desolate," III, 223; Forfeiture of goods and chattels has no relation backward "for personal property is of so fluctuating a nature, that it passes through many hands in a short time," IV, 387 f.

Blackstone's treatment of the law of contract clearly illustrated this method of reasoning: "Neither a court of equity nor of law can vary men's wills or agreements, or (in other words) make wills or engagements for them. Both are to understand them truly, and therefore uniformly.... Both courts will equitably construe, but neither pretends to control or change, a lawful stipulation or engagement," III, 435. Blackstone wrote here as if the question of whether or not a contract had been made was always simply a question of *fact*, and the law was powerless to affect the legal consequences of a set of facts. This sort of argument, of course, completely ignored the problem of the application of a legal rule to a particular set of facts, and assumed that in some mysterious way "the facts" provided the answer themselves. Furthermore the *Commentaries* here failed to recognize that what was meant by "the facts" was not at all clear in the absence of a purposive rule to suggest the principle on which the facts were to be selected. Only seldom did Blackstone show that such rules as those of legal capacity were the creature of the law and not of the physical world. One of the few cases but still an ambiguous one: "Natural persons are such as the God of nature formed us; artificial are such as are created and devised by human laws for the purposes of society and government, which are called corporations or bodies politic," I, 123.

31. I, 360.

32. I, 425 ff.

33. IV, 221; II, 124; III, 224.

34. II, 164 f. When Blackstone used the vocabulary of science, or of mathematics, to describe the law he was introducing an ambiguity which made it possible to identify the law with reason at the same time that he was identifying it with fact.

35. II, 235 ff.

36. III, 220.

37. III, 330.

38. III, 327. Blackstone wrote that equity, like law, was a "science" with remedies that could be defined with "precision," III, 440 f.

Another device which confused law with fact and gave the legal rule a "certainty" was the metaphor: "Dissolution is the civil death of the parliament," I, 187; king head and parliament body, I, 188; "Parliament must expire or die a natural death, at the end of every seventh year," I, 189; "As natural reason is given to the natural body for the governing it, so by-laws or statutes are a sort of political reason to govern the body politic," I, 476; "But the body politic may also itself be dissolved in several ways, which dissolution is the civil death of the corporation," I, 484; surrender of franchise by corporation to king "a kind of suicide," I, 485; In case of common because of vicinage if animals stray from one common into a neighboring one "the law winks at the trespass," II, 34; escheat from extinction of blood of tenant "by either natural or civil means," II, 72; remainders after executory devise, "though such remainders may be limited to as many persons successively as the devisor thinks proper, yet they must all be *in esse* during the life of the first devisee; for then all the candles are lighted and are consuming together, and the ultimate remainder is in reality only to that remainder-man who survives the rest," II, 174 f.

39. III, 282 f.

40. II, 51.

41. II, 362. Some additional examples of the treatment of a fiction as part of legal logic: the "use" called "this child of imagination," II, 331 f.; similar rule to oust jurisdiction of Admiralty Court in connection with fiction that a contract really made at sea was made inland, III, 107; rule that *contra fictionem non admittetur probatio* in connection with use of fiction to extend jurisdiction of King's Bench, III, 343; "feigned issue" a way of bringing facts in equity before a jury, saving time and expense, III, 452.

42. III, 42 f.

43. III, 287.

44. III, 206.

45. IV, 280.

CHAPTER VII

1. I, 245.

2. Anthony, Earl of Shaftesbury, *Characteristics of Men, Manners, Opinions, Times, etc.*, edited by John M. Robertson (London, 1900), I, 280. See also: "natural affection" of a good man the only foundation of values, *ibid.*, pp. 250, 258, 262, 265; only loss of "natural moral sense" could make man evil, *ibid.*, p. 262.

3. *The Seasons*, "Winter," lines 322 ff. in *Complete Poetical Works*, edited by J. Logie Robertson (Oxford, 1908).

4. Quoted by Frank J. Klingberg in *The Anti-Slavery Movement in England* (New Haven, 1926), at pp. 28 f.

For a discussion of humanitarianism in general, see Crane Brinton, "Humanitarianism," in *Encyclopaedia of the Social Sciences* (New York, 1937) and Hermann Kantorowicz, *The Spirit of British Policy* (New York, 1932), Chap. III. For a discussion of humanitarianism in the eighteenth century, see: Frank J. Klingberg, *op. cit.*, Chaps. II and III; E. A. Whitney, "Humanitarianism and Romanticism," *Huntington Library Quarterly*, Vol. II, No. 2 (January, 1939), pp. 159 ff.; W. E. H. Lecky, *History of England in the Eighteenth Century* (London, 1920), Vol. VII, Chap. XXI, esp. pp. 347 ff.; C. A. Moore, "Shaftesbury and the Ethical Poets in England, 1700–1760," *Publications of the Modern Language Association* (1916), XXXI, 264; Thomas Clarkson, *History of the Abolition of the African Slave Trade*, 2 vols. (Philadelphia, 1808) esp. Vol. I; *Johnson's England*, edited by A. S. Turberville (Oxford, 1933), esp. Vol. I, Chap. XI, "Poverty, Crime, Philanthropy," by J. L. and Barbara Hammond.

5. Quoted from "seventh edition" (London, 1758), I, 21.

6. *Ibid.*, II, 38.

7. *Ibid.*, I, 21. On reconsideration, Brown decided that, although the Spirit

of Liberty was natural to the English nation, the Spirit of Humanity was not natural, but was partly the effect of the Spirit of Liberty and partly the effect of the compassion which accompanied the effeminacy of the times, *ibid.*, II, 41. Still, he remained insistent that Humanity was an important and characteristic virtue of his age. He referred to the "Lenity of our Laws," *ibid.*, II, 39; and compared the Humanity of the English with the "Inhumanity of the Italians," *ibid.*, II, 41 ff.

8. IV, 10 f.

9. III, 3 f.; cf. IV, 186.

10. I, 450.

11. IV, 212 f.

12. I, 133. "Every humane legislator will be ... extremely cautious of establishing laws that inflict the penalty of death, especially for slight offences, or such as are merely positive," IV, 10. Blackstone explained homicide as that "offence of taking away that life which is the immediate gift of the great Creator; and of which therefore no man can be entitled to deprive himself or another, but in some manner either expressly commanded in, or evidently deducible from, those laws which the Creator has given us; the divine laws, I mean, of either nature or revelation," IV, 177.

In several instances the *Commentaries* suggested that punishment should not exceed the needs of public interest, and often said that penalties should not be wantonly inflicted. Since punishment is in itself an evil (IV, 7), "inflicting punishment, ought always to be proportioned to the particular purpose it is meant to serve, and by no means to exceed it," IV, 12. Moreover not all methods of punishment were permissible, for "though the end of punishment is to deter men from offending, it can never follow from thence that it is lawful to deter them at any rate and by any means; since there may be unlawful methods of enforcing obedience even to the justest laws," IV, 10.

13. Dr. Johnson's *Dictionary* defined "enormity":

1. Deviation from rule; irregularity.
2. Deviation from right; depravity; corruption.
3. Atrocious crime; flagitious villany; crimes exceeding the common measure.

Some other examples of the use of malignity as the measure of the penalty deserved by a crime: "enormity, or dangerous tendency, of the crime that alone can warrant any earthly legislature in putting him to death that commits it," IV, 9; "absurd and impolitic to apply the same punishment to crimes of different malignity," IV, 17; killing by poison "the most detestable," IV, 196; the "malignity" of burglary arises from its being done "at the dead of night," IV, 224.

14. IV, 116.

15. IV, 194.

16. IV, 216.

17. IV, 15.

18. I, 56. Blackstone seemed to find no inconsistency between this principle and the rule that in the case of treason "the bare intention will deserve the highest degree of severity." Bk. IV, Chap. VI.

Some other examples of Blackstone's use of the humanity of the law of nature as a guide or justification for English law: Rewards were not generally given by the state for good actions, "because, also, were the exercise of every virtue to be enforced by the proposal of particular rewards, it were impossible for any state to furnish stock enough for so profuse a bounty," I, 56; In the law of nations, "the custom of reprisals seems dictated by nature herself," I, 259; In deodand, "the true ground of this rule seems rather to have been, that the child, by reason of its want of discretion, is presumed incapable of actual sin," I, 300 f.; justification of husband's power of chastising his wife, I, 444; why clergy ill-fitted to judge in marriage causes, III, 92 f.; court of honour "to give satisfaction to all such as are aggrieved in that point; a point of a nature so nice and delicate, that its wrongs and injuries escape the notice of the common law," III, 104; Apparent cases of retaliation in the criminal law are "a consequence from some other principle," because it is unjust that punishment should merely equal the crime, "especially as the suffering of the innocent is past and irrevocable, that of the guilty is future, contingent, and liable to be escaped or evaded," IV, 13 f.; no implication of husband's duress on wife in case of crimes *mala in se*, IV, 29; offences against God and religion, IV, 41 ff.

Some further examples where personal feelings of victim, criminal, or witnesses of crime were made the test or justification of the punishment or of other rule of law: "*posse comitatus*" the final power "to conquer the defendant's perverseness," III, 222; relation of motive to the rightness of the verdict of a jury, and the difficulty of defining motives as reasons against attaints, III, 389; "Violence of passion or temptation, may sometimes alleviate a crime," IV, 15; The law may have as one of its purposes in restricting killing in self-defence, "to make the crime of homicide more odious," IV, 187; Stealing from ship in distress shows "inhumanity" in thief, IV, 235; Seriousness of certain thefts because of "great malice and mischief of the theft in some of these instances," IV, 239; Malicious mischief arises from "this mischievous disposition," IV, 243.

19. IV, 2 f.

20. I, 416. Blackstone explained, "It is moreover one of the glories of our English law, that the species, though not always the quantity or degree, of punishment is *ascertained* for every offence; and that it is not left in the breast of any judge, nor even of a jury, to alter that judgment, which the law has beforehand ordained, for every subject alike, without respect of persons. For, if judgments were to be the private opinions of the judge, men would then be slaves to their magistrates: and would live in society without knowing exactly the conditions and obligations which it lays them under," IV, 377 f. Every crime must be sharply defined by law, since "if the crime of high treason be indeterminate, this alone (says the president Montesquieu) is sufficient to make any government degenerate into arbitrary power," IV, 75. English law is admirable for the certainty of its definition of treason, IV, 85 f. Even outside the criminal law this clarity is to be found, for example, in the writs of entry which are so "plainly and clearly chalked out in that most ancient and highly venerable collection of legal forms, the *registrum omnium brevium*," III, 183 f. One of the chief causes of humane certainty in the law was in the fact that English law was a system of reason. The remnant of "Saxon simplicity" also explained this virtue, IV, 417.

Yet even with the aid of the law of nature, "the quantity of punishment can never be absolutely determined by any standing invariable rule; but it must be left to the arbitration of the legislature to inflict such penalties as are warranted by the laws of nature and society, and such as appear to be the best calculated to answer the end of precaution against future offences," IV, 12. Provided the fundamental principles are not violated, the criminal law "may be modified, narrowed, or enlarged, according to the local or occasional necessities of the state which it is meant to govern," IV, 2 f. Retaliation is too simple a principle because "the difference of persons, place, time, provocation, or other circumstances, may enhance or mitigate the offence," IV, 13. Beccaria's principle of proportion might at first sight seem adequate to the problem. But the complexity of human relations was such that perhaps the wise legislator could only "mark the principal divisions, and not assign penalties of the first degree to offences of an inferior rank." To make a scale of crimes with a corresponding scale of punishments from the greatest to the least may be "too romantic an idea," IV, 18.

21. IV, 353.

22. IV, 19. For a discussion of the practical workings of the criminal law in eighteenth-century England, see Jerome Hall, *Theft, Law, and Society* (Boston, 1935), Chap. III, where the mitigating practices of juries and judges are described at length. For the significance of the introduction of transportation as a punishment see George Ives, *History of Penal Methods* (London, 1914), pp. 107 ff. For some evidence against the theory that the criminal law was being much mitigated in practice, see Luke Owen Pike, *History of Crime in England* (London, 1876), Vol. II, Chaps. X and XI.

23. IV, 377.

24. IV, 166 f.

25. IV, 57.

26. IV, 198.

27. IV, 325. Another example of humane deviation from the letter of the law: wager of law only permitted where defendant bore a fair and unreproachable character, III, 347. Compare Blackstone's praise of flexibility in the law itself: equity "established for the benefit of the subject . . . to give a more specific relief, and more adapted to the circumstances of the case, than can always be obtained by the generality of the rules of the positive or common law," I, 92; Difficulty of technical terms of art arises from "the excellence of our English laws; which adapt their redress exactly to the circumstances of the injury and do not furnish one and the same action for different wrongs," III, 266; variety and complication needed in laws of "a nation of free men, a polite and commercial people and a populous extent of territory," III, 325 f. For further discussion of complexity in the law, see above, Chap. IV.

28. Jerome Hall, *op. cit.*, Chap. III.

29. III, 379 ff.

30. Jerome Hall, *op. cit.*, pp. 87 f., 93, 96, and Chap. III *passim*.

31. IV, 238.

32. IV, 387.

33. IV, 349.

34. III, 355 f.

35. Jerome Hall, *op. cit.*, pp. 87 ff. and Chap. III *passim*.

36. IV, 371.

37. IV, 396.

38. IV, 190. Blackstone explained, "In democracies, however, this power of pardon can never subsist; for there nothing higher is acknowledged than the magistrate who administers the laws: and it would be impolitic for the power of judging and pardoning to centre in one and the same person," IV, 397. Of course there was no danger of the oppressive use of the power of pardon in England since, "the king's pardon cannot be *pleaded* to any such impeachment so as to impede the inquiry, and stop the prosecution of great and notorious offenders," IV, 399.

Some additional examples of the merciful use of power of pardon: ancient Saxon practice of appealing to king or chancellor to mitigate severity of law, III, 50; excellence of English charity and royal pardon, IV, 32; King has used power of pardon to change sentences to "more merciful kinds of deaths," IV, 405.

39. IV, 18.

40. Montesquieu's statement of this theory of criminal law was found particularly in the *Persian Letters*, letter lxxxi, and in *The Spirit of Laws*, Bks. VI and XII. For a discussion of Montesquieu's influence on Beccaria see Coleman Phillipson, *Three Criminal Law Reformers* (New York, 1923), pp. 38 ff.

41. Quoted from the third edition (London, 1770), p. 4. The *Essay* had appeared first in Italian in 1764; the first English translation was published in 1767. The part of the *Commentaries* discussing crimes (Vol. IV) was first published in 1769.

42. IV, 3 f.

43. IV, 19.

44. IV, 17.

45. IV, 11, 16.

46. IV, 251.

47. IV, 16 f. Beccaria's justification from expediency of the principle of proportion in punishments is found in his *Essay*, Chaps. XLI and XLVII. Montesquieu had stated a similar position in *The Spirit of Laws*, Bk. VI, Chap. XVI.

48. III, 404; IV, 86; IV, 155. Some other examples: Where customs duties are too high, and capital penalties are prescribed for not paying them, this "destroys all proportion of punishment, and puts murderers upon an equal footing with such as are really guilty of no natural, but merely a positive, offence," I, 317; severity of penalty to be proportioned to greatness of object of crime, IV, 15; "Absurd and impolitic to apply the same punishment to crimes of different malignity," IV, 17 f.; advantage in prescribing less severe punishment for accessory than for principal in crime, in that it increased the difficulty of a person being found who would actually execute the crime, IV, 40.

Humanity seemed to conflict with expediency, however, where the legislator had to decide whether the greatness of the temptation should extenuate the crime or should justify a heavier penalty to discourage its actual commission. The former would seem to be the dictate of humanity, while the latter was clearly the requirement of expediency. See IV, 15 f.

49. Blackstone sometimes said that society had come into existence to pro-

tect the weak, I, 262. But the context of this justification nearly always showed that protection for the "weak" was considered equivalent to protecting everyone in the possession of the property he already had. See below, Chaps. VIII and IX.

## CHAPTER VIII

1. Number 161. Thursday, April 20, 1710.

2. "Imitations of Horace," Second Book of the Satires of Horace, Satire VI, lines 218 ff. The precise date of this work is unknown, but it certainly was written after 1713.

3. Dedicatory letter to the Prince of Wales.

4. Author's summary of contents of Part I.

5. "Liberty: A Poem," Part V, first published, 1736, lines 124 ff.

6. Quoted from "seventh edition" (London, 1758), I, 19. Brown later confirmed that, although the Spirit of Liberty was really natural to England (partly because of what Montesquieu described as the effect of the northern climate) the Spirit of Humanity was only the effect of it and other causes, II, 41. He also qualified his statement in the reconsiderations of the second volume where he came to the conclusion that "the Truth is, that the Spirit of Liberty subsists yet among the *middle* and some of the *lower* ranks; but is much weakened, and in many instances extinguished, among the *higher*. The Reason, I apprehend, why this Virtue abounds more in middle, than in high life, is, that the first is not yet effectually tainted by the ruling Manners and Principles of the Times. This distinction accounts for a Fact, which at first View may seem a Contradiction, that the Spirit of Liberty and Effeminacy may subsist together: They do indeed subsist together in the *same Nation*, but not in the *same Ranks*," II, 30.

7. *Ibid.*, II, 33.

8. Bk. XI, Chaps. V and VI. The quotation is from Thomas Nugent's eighteenth-century translation.

9. I, 47 ff.

10. IV, 8.

11. IV, 20 f.

12. IV, 21 f.

13. IV, 27. Other examples of the importance attached to freedom of will as a foundation of legal rules: Human law was of greatest importance on points where natural law and divine law left a man at liberty, I, 42; Declaration of war is necessary "that it may be certainly clear that the war is not undertaken by private persons, but by the will of the whole community; whose right of willing is in this case transferred to the supreme magistrate by the fundamental laws of society," I, 258; A man born deaf, dumb, and blind was looked upon by the law as the same as an idiot because he was "wanting all those senses which furnish the human mind with ideas," I, 304 (Does Blackstone mean to equate this with lack of will?); want of reason an incapacity to marry, I, 438 f.; "For our sturdy ancestors held it beneath the condition of a free man to appear, or to do any other act, at the precise time appointed. The feudal law therefore always allowed three distinct days of citation, before the defendant was adjudged contumacious for not appearing," III, 278; "Neither a court of equity nor of law

can vary men's wills or agreements, or (in other words) make wills or engagements for them. . . . Both courts will equitably construe, but neither pretends to control or change, a lawful stipulation or engagement," III, 435; In civil cases a man was bound by his own plea in bar and might not change it, "for he has made his election what plea to abide by, and it was his own folly to choose a rotten defence," IV, 338.

14. I, 6, 237.

15. I, 145. Blackstone happily accepted here Montesquieu's praise and referred here to *The Spirit of Laws*, Bk. XI, Chap. V. A few of the many references to England as a land of liberty, and the English constitution as a constitution of freedom: "zeal for liberty and the constitution," I, 34; "free constitution of England," I, 66 f.; "The idea and practice of this political or civil liberty flourish in their highest vigour in these kingdoms, where it falls little short of perfection, and can only be lost or destroyed by the folly or demerits of its owner: the legislature, and of course the laws of England, being peculiarly adapted to the preservation of this inestimable blessing even in the meanest subject," I, 126 f.; excise laws "hardly compatible with the temper of a free nation," I, 318; "In a land of liberty it is extremely dangerous to make a distinct order of the profession of arms," I, 408; dangers from military power "in a free state," I, 414; "the law, which is always ready to catch at anything in favour of liberty," II, 94; the Papists almost all "defeated or converted to better purposes by the vigour of our free constitution and the wisdom of successive parliaments," IV, 105; English law one which the Saxons "originally intended as a law of liberty," IV, 151 f. For examples of reference to English law as expressing the "genius of a free people" or having in itself the "spirit of a free constitution," see above, Chaps. I and II.

16. I, 74. Often the *Commentaries* referred to the "common law, being nothing else but custom, arising from the universal agreement of the whole community," I, 472. For instance, the executive power had been vested in a single person, "by the general consent of the people, the evidence of which general consent is long and immemorial usage," I, 90. For further references and discussion of appeal to general consent as basis of law, see above, Chap. V.

17. I, 44.

18. I, 58.

19. For Blackstone's discussion of the jury, its defects and how to cure them, see *Commentaries*, Bk. III, Chap. XXIII. He suggested that the "debasement of juries" was at least partly the result of a neglect of the property-qualification for jury-service, III, 362. He had explained elsewhere that the property-qualification (lands to the value of twenty pounds *per annum*) had been enacted by 18 Hen. VI, c. 11, because, contrary to earlier statutes, "men of small substance had crept into the commission, whose poverty made them both covetous and contemptible," I, 352. Blackstone explained the advantage of requiring the sheriff (who returned jurors) to be "a man of some fortune and consequence," that "so he may be not only the less tempted to commit wilful errors, but likewise be responsible for the faults of either himself or his officers," III, 355.

20. I, 154 f.

21. I, 125.

22. I, 158.

23. I, 171. Blackstone went on to explain that the English constitution had a great advantage over the Roman, because in England the property-qualification did not entirely displace the consideration of numbers. He insisted, "Only such are entirely excluded as can have no will of their own: there is hardly a free agent to be found who is not entitled to a vote in some place or other in the kingdom," I, 172.

Montesquieu several times had expressed this idea. For example: "All the inhabitants of the several districts ought to have a right of voting at the election of a representative, except such as are in so mean a situation as to be deemed to have no will of their own," *The Spirit of Laws*, Bk. XI, Chap. VI. Voltaire explained, "You are free at all times, and in all places, when you can do what you wish to do," art. "Liberty," *Philosophical Dictionary* (Second edition, London, 1824), IV, 349. Compare with these views, Aristotle's statement that "he who is by nature not his own but another's and yet a man, is by nature a slave," *Politics*, translated by Benjamin Jowett (Oxford, 1905), ii, 6.

24. For a general discussion of the revolutionary and individualistic uses of the doctrine of natural rights, see A. B. Ritchie, *Natural Rights* (London, 1894), and Otto Gierke, *Natural Law and the Theory of Society*, translated by Ernest Barker (Cambridge, England; 1934).

25. I, 251.

26. I, 125.

27. I, 127. Blackstone later explained that "all these rights and liberties it is our birthright to enjoy entire; unless where the laws of our country have laid them under necessary restraints: restraints in themselves so gentle and moderate, as will appear, upon further inquiry, that no man of sense or probity would wish to see them slackened," I, 144.

For a suggestive attempt to discover the ambiguities in the legal concepts of "rights," "liberties," "duties," etc., see Wesley Newcomb Hohfeld, *Fundamental Legal Conceptions* (New Haven, 1920). Hohfeld's work is analytically of great value. Yet it is doubtful whether the words can by any process of analysis be divested of their eulogistic or dyslogistic connotations. To avoid these connotations, it would be necessary to use entirely new symbols which have no traditional overtones. Even if such symbols could be found or made they would, in the course of time, surely acquire such overtones. To believe that such a result could be avoided, would be to assert that one could escape from history.

28. III, 2.

29. This is an example of the importance of using something besides the process of logical analysis to discover the "meaning" of such a term as "right" to Blackstone, or, for that matter, to anyone else. See n. 27 above.

30. I, 123.

31. I, 124.

32. I, 124 f. Further evidence of the primary place of rights in Blackstone's scheme: general discussion in Bk. I, Chap. I, "Of the Absolute Rights of Individuals"; priority of rights in discussion of private wrongs in Bk. III, Chap. I; Even the criminal law was to be founded on principles "conformable to the dictates of truth and justice, the feelings of humanity, and the indelible rights of mankind," IV, 2 f.; priority of rights in discussion of public wrongs in Bk. IV, Chap. I.

33. I, 129 ff.
34. I, 129.
35. IV, 176.
36. IV, 6.
37. This was Bk. III, Chap. VIII. Chapter VII of the same book did, however, deal in part with such remedies. Blackstone discussed protection of the "habitations of individuals" apparently as an aspect of the protection of their bodily security. See Bk. IV, Chap. XVI.
38. I, 134.
39. I, 135 f.
40. Yet Blackstone was eloquent in his insistence on the importance of such devices: "Of great importance to the public is the preservation of this personal liberty; for if once it were left in the power of any, the highest, magistrate to imprison arbitrarily whomever he or his officers thought proper, (as in France it is daily practised by the crown,) there would soon be an end of all other rights and immunities. . . . To bereave a man of life, or by violence to confiscate his estate, without accusation or trial, would be so gross and notorious an act of despotism, as must at once convey the alarm of tyranny throughout the whole kingdom; but confinement of the person, by secretly hurrying him to a gaol, where his sufferings are unknown or forgotten, is a less public, a less striking, and therefore a more dangerous engine of arbitrary government," I, 135 f. He was lavish in his praise of *habeas corpus*: I, 134 f.; III, 134 ff.; IV, 438.
41. IV, 151 ff.
42. III, 23.

## CHAPTER IX

1. For a discussion of the use of Locke in this period, see Paschal Larkin, *Property in the Eighteenth Century with Special Reference to England and Locke* (New York, 1930). This author, however, hardly mentions the ambivalence in Locke's theory. See also, Walton H. Hamilton, "Property — According to Locke," *Yale Law Journal*, Vol. XLI (1931–32), 864–880.
2. II, 2 f.
3. II, 4 f.
4. II, 14. For discussion of the natural limits of property: in light, air, and water, II, 39, 395, 402; in wild animals, II, 389 f., 392.
5. I, 139.
6. I, 140.
7. I, 448.
8. III, 138.
9. II, 2.
10. IV, 8 f.
11. II, 2.
12. Blackstone preferred to explain that, when the total property rights of the individual were considered, they had not in any way been diminished by entering society. Even the requirements of taxes were explained as "a portion which each subject contributes of his property in order to secure the remainder," I, 281.
13. II, 14 f.

14. II, 412.

15. II, 393 f.

16. II, 405 f.

17. I, 139.

18. I, 140.

19. IV, 382. Another description of alienation of property as a provision of the positive law: acquiring property in goods by marriage a consequence of the legal unity of husband and wife, II, 433. See also, II, 293 f., 498.

20. II, 10 f. Some further examples of the conception of positive law enlarging or creating property: Exclusion of the half-blood from inheritance was no injustice "since even the succession of the whole blood was originally a beneficial indulgence, rather than the strict right of collaterals," II, 230; "For this purpose therefore of continuing the possession, the municipal law has established *descents* and alienations," II, 294; Right of testament and particular provisions were matter of positive law, II, 409 f.

Even the law of inheritance, however, according to the *Commentaries*, seemed to accord with the natural right of occupancy, since the right to make a will was originally founded on the fact that "a man's children or nearest relations are usually about him on his death-bed, and are the earliest witnesses of his decease. They become therefore generally the next immediate occupants, till at length in the process of time this frequent usage ripened into general law," II, 11 f.

The role of the state in creating property was made to seem still greater by the frequent discussion of the "gradations" or "stages" toward perfection of title, which seemed to be the creations of positive law. Some examples: "the inferiority in which the law places an estate for years, when compared with an estate for life," II, 143; The "several stages or degrees requisite to form a complete title to lands and tenements. We will consider them in a progressive order," II, 195 ff.; As to remedies, "next follow another class, which are in use where the title of the tenant or occupier is advanced one step nearer to perfection," III, 179.

21. I, 299. Some passages suggesting that all property was founded in civil law: "By the law of nature every man from the prince to the peasant, has an equal right of pursuing, and taking to his own use, all such creatures as are *ferae naturae*, and therefore the property of nobody, but liable to be seized by the first occupant. . . . But it follows from the very end and constitution of society, that this natural right, as well as many others belonging to a man as an individual, may be restrained by positive laws enacted for reasons of state, or for the supposed benefit of the community," II, 411; Certain crimes were merely "an infringement of that right of property, which, as we have formerly seen, owes its origin not to the law of nature, but merely to civil society," IV, 9; larceny impossible until the time "in social communities, when property is established," IV, 229 f.

For a discussion of the conflict in eighteenth-century theories between the notion that property was anterior to society and the notion that it was created by society, see Gaetano Salvemini, "The Concepts of Democracy and Liberty in the Eighteenth Century," in *The Constitution Reconsidered*, edited by Conyers Read (New York, 1938), pp. 114 ff.

22. III, 243.

23. II, 384.

24. I, 326 f.

25. IV, 399.

26. II, 400. Some other examples of the close connection between property and peace: dangers of the fight for occupancy, II, 10 f.; why the common law abhorred vacancy of possession, II, 11; The abatement of a freehold would be somewhat similar to "an immediate occupancy in a state of nature. . . . But this, however agreeable to natural justice, considering man merely as an individual, is diametrically opposite to the law of society, and particularly the law of England: which, for the preservation of public peace, hath prohibited, as far as possible all acquisitions by mere occupancy," III, 168; Blackstone's careful and often-repeated distinction between possession and property, as, for instance at III, 167 ff., 180.

27. III, 145.

28. II, 2.

29. III, 142; cf. I, 429.

30. III, 142 f.

31. Some forms of this statement in the *Commentaries*: The king can do no wrong "since it would be a great weakness and absurdity in any system of positive law, to define any possible wrong, without any possible redress," I, 244; "All possible injuries whatsoever, that do not fall within the exclusive cognizance of either the ecclesiastical, military, or maritime tribunals, are for that very reason within the cognizance of the common law courts of justice. For it is a settled and invariable principle in the laws of England, that every right when withheld must have a remedy, and every injury its proper redress," III, 109; "For wherever the common law gives a right or prohibits an injury, it also gives a remedy by action; and, therefore, wherever a new injury is done, a new method of remedy must be pursued," III, 123; remedy by suit given for "every possible injury," III, 422. For further discussion of this method of proving the completeness of English law, see above, Chap. VI.

32. For Blackstone the system of checks and balances in the English constitution was more than a device for preventing any one branch of the government from securing the ascendancy. It was also a device for preventing any one kind of property-interest in the community from overbearing the others. Thus, "the two houses [of parliament] naturally drawing in two directions of opposite interest, and the prerogative in another still different from them both, they mutually keep each other from exceeding their proper limits," I, 154 f. He called attention to how the method of choosing representatives for parliament served this purpose: "The counties are therefore represented by knights, elected by the proprietors of lands; the citizens and boroughs are represented by citizens and burgesses, chosen by the mercantile part, or supposed trading interest of the nation," I, 159; Members for the universities represented "those students who, though useful members of the community, were neither concerned in the landed nor the trading interest; and to protect in the legislature the rights of the republic of letters," I, 174; Qualifications for election to parliament resulted in "obliging the trading interest to make choice of landed men," I, 176. The English method of trial also seemed to contain in it the balance of different interests, the judges representing the interests of "the few" and juries representing the interests of "the many," III, 379 f.

33. IV, 105.

34. Blackstone explained, "A body of nobility is also more peculiarly necessary in our mixed and compounded constitution, in order to support the rights of both the crown and the people, by forming a barrier to withstand the encroachments of both. It creates and preserves that gradual scale of dignity, which proceeds from the peasant to the prince; rising like a pyramid from a broad foundation and diminishing to a point as it rises. It is this ascending and contracting proportion that adds stability to any government; for when the departure is sudden from one extreme to the other, we may pronounce that state to be precarious," I, 158.

All property ultimately depended on the decision of the House of Lords, III, 56. "Yet, vast as this trust is, it can nowhere be so properly reposed as in the noble hands where our excellent constitution has placed it; and therefore placed it, because, from the independence of their fortune and the dignity of their station, they are presumed to employ that leisure, which is the consequence of both, in attaining a more extensive knowledge of the laws than persons of inferior rank, and because the founders of our polity relied upon that delicacy of sentiment so peculiar to noble birth; which, as on the one hand it will prevent either interest or affection from interfering in questions of right, so, on the other, it will bind a peer in honour . . . to be master of those points upon which it is his birthright to decide," I, 12.

This distinction of rank, besides producing a class well fitted to govern, excited ambitious ardour and generous emulation in others. "Such a spirit, when nationally diffused, gives life and vigour to the community; it sets all the wheels of government in motion, which, under a wise regulator, may be directed to any beneficial purpose; and thereby every individual may be made subservient to the public good, while he principally means to promote his own particular views, I, 157 f. See also, I, 271 f.

Some other examples of the connection of property and power: men of property the "most useful as well as considerable body of men in the nation," I, 7 ff.; subordination the guarantee of property under feudalism, II, 46; History of Church of Rome showed that "(among the bulk of mankind) power cannot be maintained without property," IV, 106.

35. I, 349.

36. II, 14 f.

37. III, 211.

38. IV, 241 f., 31 f. Blackstone's justification of the rule concerning stealing to keep oneself alive seemed to make irrelevant all the arguments of the students of natural law: "In this country, especially, there would be a peculiar impropriety in admitting so dubious an excuse: for by our laws such sufficient provision is made for the poor by the power of the civil magistrate, that it is impossible that the most needy stranger should ever be reduced to the necessity of thieving to support nature. The case of a stranger is, by the way, the strongest instance put by Baron Puffendorf, and whereon he builds his principal arguments: which, however they may hold upon the continent, where the parsimonious industry of the natives orders every one to work or starve, yet must lose all their weight and efficacy in England, where charity is reduced to a system, and interwoven in our very constitution. Therefore, our laws ought by no means to be taxed with being unmerciful for denying this privilege to the necessitous; especially

when we consider, that the king, on the representation of his ministers of justice, hath a power to soften the law, and to extend mercy in cases of peculiar hardship. ... But the founders of our constitution thought it better to vest in the crown the power of pardoning particular objects of compassion, than to countenance and establish theft by one general undistinguishing law," IV, 32.

39. Blackstone wrote, "But when mankind increased in number, craft, and ambition, it became necessary to entertain conceptions of more permanent dominion; and to appropriate to individuals not the immediate *use* only, but the very *substance* of the thing to be used. Otherwise innumerable tumults must have arisen, and the good order of the world been continually broken and disturbed, while a variety of persons were striving who should get the first occupation of the same thing, or disputing which of them had actually gained it. As human life also grew more and more refined, abundance of conveniences were devised to render it more easy, commodious, and agreeable; as, habitations for shelter and safety, and raiment for warmth and decency. But no man would be at the trouble to provide either, so long as he had only an usufructuary property in them, which was to cease the instant that he quitted possession; if, as soon as he walked out of his tent, or pulled off his garment, the next stranger who came by would have a right to inhabit the one, and to wear the other," II, 4.

40. For a short discussion of the economic significance of the Glorious Revolution, see Paul Mantoux, *The Industrial Revolution in the Eighteenth Century* (London, 1928), Pt. I, Chap. II. Although the economic significance of the events of 1688 has not yet been clearly settled, even our present knowledge seems to justify the statements in this paragraph.

41. Number 69. Saturday, May 19, 1711.

42. Quoted from a reprint of the first edition (Oxford, 1927), p. 7.

43. IV, 387.

44. II, 384 f. Some evidence of Blackstone's consciousness of the commercial character of the England of his day: "The English know better than any other people upon earth, how to value at the same time these three great advantages, religion, liberty, and commerce," I, 261; "a trading people," I, 328; "a commercial country," II, 442; "trading nations," II, 457; "this commercial age," III, 437; the English a "great commercial people," IV, 431; character of a great commercial people assumed by English beginning with the time of Henry VIII, IV, 431.

Some references to the change in the nature of property and to the growth of commerce: "Thus in the dark ages of monkish superstition and civil tyranny, when interest was laid under a total interdict, commerce was also at its lowest ebb, and fell entirely into the hand of the Jews and Lombards: but when men's minds began to be more enlarged, when true religion and real liberty revived, commerce grew again into credit: and again introduced with itself its inseparable companion, the doctrine of loans upon interest," II, 454 f.; "the great change in property by the extension of trade and the abolition of military tenures," III, 55; "our improvements in trade and opulence," IV, 240. For a discussion of idea of progress in the *Commentaries*, see above, Chap. III.

45. II, 442.

46. II, 288.

47. III, 329. Some additional examples of arguments in favour of the free transferability of property: justification of absence of restriction on spendthrifts in English law, I, 305 f.; objections to excessive customs-duties, I, 317; objections to perpetuities, II, 174; excellent means used to "get the better of that stubborn statute *de donis*," II, 360; objections to future property in chattels, II, 398.

48. II, 174, 398.

49. IV, 382. Blackstone often explained how competition served the public interest: Sometimes the wool trade was identified with the general interest as in the case of a statute of Charles II which "encourages the staple trade on which in great measure depends the universal good of the nation," I, 126; Distinctions of rank and honour gave rise to competition "which, under a wise regulator, may be directed to any beneficial purpose; and thereby every individual may be made subservient to the public good, while he principally means to promote his own particular views," I, 157 f. For a discussion of Blackstone's concept of the natural identity of interests, see above, Chap. II.

50. III, 219.

51. II, 449.

52. I, 418.

53. I, 427 f.

54. IV, 159. Blackstone did, however, complain of some of the complications of conveyancing, and actually suggested a system of registration of title, III, 439. But he did not attack the delays of chancery despite the fact that examinations by a master in chancery "frequently last for years," III, 453.

55. III, 226.

56. IV, 169.

57. I, 449.

58. II, 215.

59. I, 365. Some other examples of remarks on the importance of industriousness in the community: industriousness good in lower ranks, II, 411 f.; Laws preserving Sabbath are useful for keeping up spirits of the "industrious worker," IV, 63; Men should be "decent, industrious, and inoffensive in their respective stations," IV, 162. But, contrast the statement that poverty is considered by moralists the best medicine "*pro salute animae*," IV, 217 f.

60. Art. "Property," *Philosophical Dictionary* (2d ed., London, 1824), V, 326. Voltaire, too, connected progress with the development of commerce, *ibid.*, V, 326 ff. For a discussion of eighteenth-century political theory as the theory of a business civilization, see Gaetano Salvemini, "The Concepts of Democracy and Liberty in the Eighteenth Century," in *The Constitution Reconsidered*, edited by Conyers Read (New York, 1928), at pp. 116 ff. Blackstone favoured moderate fortunes and opposed too great accumulations of wealth in "a commercial country whose welfare depends on the number of moderate fortunes engaged in the extension of trade," II, 374.

# A LAYMAN'S GLOSSARY

The following is a list of the principal legal terms contained in the quotations from the *Commentaries*. No attempt has been made to provide a technically precise definition but rather, as concisely as possible, to aid the layman in understanding the general significance of the illustrations.

ACTION: a suit at law.

ACTION OF DEBT: an action at law for a specific sum.

ALIENATION: a transfer of property.

AMENDMENTS TO PLEADING: corrections by a party to a suit of errors in the written documents in which he had set forth to the court the reasons for his action or his defences.

ANIMALS *ferae naturae:* wild animals.

ASSIZE: a court held semi-annually in each county.

ATTAINT: in old English practice, a writ to inquire whether a jury had given a false verdict.

AULNAGER: an inspector of English woolen cloth.

*Autrefoits attaint:* a plea by a criminal that he had been convicted of another felony and sentenced to death, so that he was legally dead, and hence not subject to trial.

BENEFICE: a right of a clergyman to enjoy certain ecclesiastical revenues.

BENEFIT OF CLERGY: a right of exemption from punishment, originally available only to the clergy, but later extended generally.

BOROUGH-ENGLISH: a custom in certain parts of England by which land descended to the youngest son or youngest brother instead of by primogeniture.

CANON LAW: the law of the church.

CANONS OF DESCENT: rules of inheritance.

*Capias:* an order to a sheriff to arrest a person.

CHANCERY: a court of equity, originally supplementary to courts of law, and having its beginning in the chancellor protecting the king's conscience by preventing the rigorous application of the common law; finally, itself, developing a system of fixed rules.

CHATTELS: moveable goods and all other property except freeholds (*q.v.*).

CHATTELS REAL: a non-freehold interest in real estate.

CIVIL INJURY: a wrong which is occasion for civil redress or compensation to the individual injured, as distinguished from a crime, which is an occasion for punishment by the state.

COMMON RECOVERY: a method of utilizing certain legal fictions to remove the limitations of an estate tail (*q.v.*).

**CONDITIONAL FEUD:** a feudal interest in land which would end on the happening of a certain event.

**CONSTRUCTIVE TREASON:** an extension of the definition of treason to include many types of conspiracy against the king, even though not specifically intended to cause his death.

**CONTEMPT:** disobedience of a court's orders or disturbance of its proceedings.

**CONTINGENT REMAINDER:** a future interest in land the owner of which is not yet ascertained or cannot claim the property until a certain event has occurred.

**CONTRACT:** an agreement, breach of which will entitle the injured party to damages.

**CORODY:** a feudal right to receive sustenance.

**CORSNED:** in old English law, a piece of bread over which a priest uttered certain imprecations. A person accused of crime was then made to eat the bread, and, if it stuck in his throat, he was believed to be guilty.

**COURT OF CHIVALRY:** an old English military court.

**CRIMINAL CAPACITY:** the quality of possessing sufficient age and intelligence to be held guilty of a crime.

**"CRIME AGAINST NATURE":** sodomy.

**DEED:** a document transferring property rights.

**DEFENCE:** a denial by a defendant in a lawsuit of the truth or sufficiency of the plaintiff's complaint.

**DEFENDANT:** the person against whom any type of legal proceedings is brought.

**DESCENT:** the feudal principle of transmission of estates, downwards from parent to child, and never in the opposite direction.

**DISTRESS:** the taking of personal property to enforce the payment of rent or other duties from the owner.

**EJECTMENT:** a method of securing possession of land and determining the title by an action at law involving the use of certain legal fictions.

**EMINENT DOMAIN:** the power to take private property for public use.

**ENGROSSING:** the act of buying a large quantity of any commodity for the purpose of selling it at an unreasonable price.

**ENTRY:** the taking possession of land.

**EQUITY:** the system of rules administered in a court of equity or chancery (*q.v.*).

**ESTATE:** interest in real property.

**ESTATE AT WILL:** a right to possess property subject to the will of another.

**ESTATE FOR LIFE:** a right to hold property until the death of a specified person or persons.

**ESTATE TAIL:** an interest in land that can descend to bodily heirs only.

**ESTRAY:** an animal that has escaped from its owner.

**FELONY:** a crime sufficiently serious to occasion, at common law, the forfeiture of lands or goods, and, with few exceptions, involving capital punishment.

FIRST ESTATE: the present interest in property as distinguished from succeeding interests.

FOREST COURT: a court for administering the king's forest and punishing killers of the king's deer.

FORFEITURE: punishment by confiscation of goods.

FORMS OF ACTION: the comprehensive term for the kinds of remedies at common law.

FREE FISHERY: the exclusive right of fishing in a public river.

FREEHOLD: any inheritable or life interest in real property, but not a term for years.

FULL DISCOVERY BY BANKRUPT: the complete revealing of his financial status by one who claims to be unable to meet his liabilities.

FUTURE PROPERTY: an interest in property which is recognized by the law as existing before its owner actually possesses the property and even though he may never actually possess the property.

GOODS: inanimate moveable things.

GRAND LARCENY: the crime of stealing property worth more than one shilling.

GUARDIANSHIP IN SOCAGE: the guardianship of a feudal lord over a minor who held land in return for fixed services.

HEARTH-MONEY: a tax, dating from the time of Charles II, of two shillings on every hearth or stove in England and Wales.

HEIRLOOM: a moveable thing which, by special custom, on the death of the owner passed to the person entitled to take the real estate of the deceased, instead of to the person entitled to take the deceased's personal estate.

HEIRS: the persons designated by the law to succeed to freehold interests in real property.

HOMICIDE: the killing of one human being by another, whatever the circumstances.

HUNDRED COURT: an inferior court, long obsolete, the jurisdiction of which was confined to a subdivision of a county, called a hundred.

IMPLIED CONTRACT: an agreement the existence of which the law assumes from the presence of certain facts, or to prevent an unjust enrichment.

IMPRESSING SEAMEN: the practice of seizing men and forcing them into the navy.

INDICTMENT: a written accusation by a grand jury, charging one or more persons with having committed a crime or misdemeanor.

INFORMER: a person who accuses another of a crime, especially one who accuses in order to secure a reward provided by law.

INHERITANCE: an interest in real property which will descend to the owner's heir.

JUDGMENT DEBT: a debt that can be proved by the records of a court.

*Laches*: neglect, carelessness, or delay; especially failure to make a claim or to take other legal steps within a reasonable time.

**LEASE AT WILL:** a lease revocable at the will of either landlord or tenant.

**LIMITATION IN REMAINDER:** a provision setting forth in a document the future ownership of property after the present ownership has been determined.

**MANSLAUGHTER:** the unlawful killing of another under circumstances not amounting to murder.

**MARKET OVERT:** a place in which a sale of goods passes a valid title regardless of the seller's lack of title or authority to sell.

**MISDEMEANOR:** a minor offense.

**MUNICIPAL LAW:** the legal system governing a particular community, as distinguished from international law.

**NUISANCE:** the unwarranted doing of an act that interferes with another's enjoyment of property.

**OCCUPANCY:** the taking possession of a thing that has no owner.

**OUSTER:** the wrongful exclusion from real property of the party entitled to its possession.

**PARTICULAR ESTATE:** the present interest in property, as distinguished from the remainder (*q.v.*), or future interest.

**PATENT:** a grant by the state of certain privileges, for example, of exploiting an invention or of using a title of nobility.

*Peine forte et dure:* the torture of pressing to death inflicted on a person charged with felony who refused to answer to the charge.

**PERPETUITY:** an attempted arrangement of property interests which the law prohibits because the arrangement would prevent the transfer of the property for a longer period than public policy will allow.

**PERSONAL ESTATE, PERSONAL PROPERTY:** all property rights less than a freehold (*q.v.*).

**PETIT LARCENY:** the stealing of property worth not more than a shilling.

**PLAINTIFF:** a person who brings a civil action against another.

**PLEA:** the defendant's answer to the plaintiff's statement of the cause of action.

**PLEA IN BAR:** a plea that sets up a positive bar of a rule of law to the plaintiff's recovery; as, for example, the Statute of Limitations, or a decree in another court.

**PLEA OF** *autrefoits acquit:* a plea, made by a defendant who is charged with committing a crime or misdemeanor, that he has already been tried for the offence, and has been acquitted.

**PLEADING:** the process of determining the point at dispute between the parties by their successive written statements.

**POPULAR OR PENAL STATUTE:** a statute which, to punish an act, provides for a penalty to be paid by the wrongdoer to anyone who will sue for it.

**POSITIVE LAW:** law specifically set up by the state for the government of society.

*Praemunire:* the name of any of several offenses against the king and his government not subject to capital punishment and originally connected with ecclesiastical affairs.

PRECEDENTS: previous judicial decisions to be followed in courts of justice.

PRIMOGENITURE: the system of inheritance by which the deceased's real property passed to his eldest son.

PRIVATE WRONGS: injuries redressable in court by a lawsuit to which the state is not a party.

PURGATION: the clearing oneself of an offence by denying the guilt on oath or suffering an ordeal.

QUEEN-GOLD: a revenue belonging to queens of England from the demesne lands of the crown.

REAL ACTION: an action for the recovery of the ownership of real property, as distinguished from an action merely for possession.

REBUTTER: the defendant's third statement in the common law system of pleading (q.v.).

REJOINDER: the defendant's second statement in the common law system of pleading (q.v.).

REMAINDER: an interest in property, the owner of which will not be entitled to possession of the property until the expiration of a present estate created by the same document.

REMAINDER FOR LIFE: a remainder (q.v.) that ceases to exist upon the death of a named person or persons.

REMAINDER IN FEE: a remainder (q.v.) which is inheritable.

REPLEVIN: a proceeding for the recovery of specific goods.

REPLICATION: the plaintiff's second statement in the common law system of pleading (q.v.).

REPRESENTATIVE: a person who has succeeded to the rights of a deceased person; an executor, administrator, or heir.

RETURN OF THE SHERIFF: a short written account by the sheriff or similar officer to whom a writ had been directed, which account told how he had obeyed the command contained in the writ.

RETURNING DAY: the day on which a writ must be returned to the court that issued it.

SEAL: any thing, but usually a wax wafer, affixed to a document in place of a signature, or in addition to a signature for its legal effect.

SPECIAL PLEA: a plea (q.v.) that by denying part of a plaintiff's allegation destroyed the ground of his claim.

SPECIAL PLEA IN BAR: a plea (q.v.) that set forth new matter upon which the defendant relied for his defense.

STATUTE OF LIMITATIONS: a statute that limited the time within which a claim could be asserted or a crime prosecuted.

SUR-REBUTTER: the plaintiff's fourth statement in the common law system of pleading (q.v.).

SUR-REJOINDER: the plaintiff's third statement in the common law system of pleading (q.v.).

TAKING IN EXECUTION: the act of a sheriff or similar officer in seizing goods at the order of a court.

TENANT AT SUFFERANCE: one who wrongfully refrained from surrendering the possession of real property, after his right to possession had terminated.

TENANT IN TAIL AFTER POSSIBILITY OF ISSUE EXTINCT: a tenant who held lands which could not descend to his heirs unless these heirs were also descended from a specific named person, but where, due to that named person's death without children, heirs possessing the required qualifications could never exist.

TENURE: the mode of holding a feudal estate in land.

THINGS PERSONAL: goods (q.v.), money, and all other moveables, and the rights relating to them.

THINGS REAL: immoveable corporeal things and the rights relating to them.

TIME OF LIMITATION: the length of time, the passing of which was sufficient to bar a legal proceeding.

TRESPASS: an unlawful touching of the person or property of another.

TRUST: a property right held for the benefit of another involving active duties by the trustee, and enforceable only in courts of equity.

USE: a property right held for the benefit of another, involving no active duties, and enforceable only in courts of equity.

VALUABLE CONSIDERATION: a consideration regarded by the law as sufficient to make a grant or agreement enforceable.

WAGER OF LAW: a sworn statement by a defendant, supported by the oaths of eleven other persons, that he did not owe the sum or the thing claimed by the plaintiff.

WASTE: destruction of real property by a person in possession, to the damage of persons entitled to take possession at a later time.

WITHERNAM: A "capias in withernam," is a writ issuing where goods taken in distress (q.v.) have been carried away or concealed by the landlord, so that the sheriff cannot find them; it commands the sheriff to take other goods of the person who has levied the distress by way of reprisal for the distress and as a punishment for withholding it. The dispute is then adjudicated.

WRECK: anything thrown up on the land by the sea.

WRIT: a written order by a judicial authority directing a person to do something.

WRIT OF ESTREPEMENT FOR WASTE: a common law writ to prevent waste (q.v.).

# INDEX

**Daniel J. Boorstin**, The Librarian of Congress Emeritus, began his career as a lawyer and legal historian. After graduating from Harvard, he was a Rhodes scholar at Oxford University, where he received two degrees in law, and was called as a barrister of the Inner Temple in London. He has taught at universities throughout the world, including Harvard University, the Sorbonne, the University of Rome, Kyoto University, and the University of Chicago, where he was professor of American history for twenty-five years. His many books include *The Lost World of Thomas Jefferson*, *The Genius of American Politics*, *The Image*, the trilogy *The Americans*, which was awarded the Bancroft, the Parkman, and the Pulitzer Prizes, *The Discoverers*, and *The Creators*. He has received the National Book Award for Distinguished Contribution to American Letters.